The Role of Affect in
Motivation, Development, and Adaptation

Ethel Spector Person, M.D., Series Editor

Rage, Power, and Aggression

EDITED BY

Robert A. Glick, M.D.
& Steven P. Roose, M.D.

Yale University Press   New Haven and London

"Women in the Maze of Power and Rage" was originally published in *Retelling a Life: Narration and Dialogue in Psychoanalysis*, by Roy Schafer, 1992, published by Basic Books, a division of HarperCollins Publishers. Reprinted by permission. "The Psychopathology of Hatred" was originally published in the *Journal of the American Psychoanalytic Association*.

Designed by James J. Johnson and
set in Ehrhart Roman by
The Composing Room of Michigan, Inc., Grand Rapids, Michigan.
Printed in the United States of America by
BookCrafters, Chelsea, Michigan.

Library of Congress Cataloging-in-Publication Data

Rage, power, and aggression / edited by Robert A. Glick and Steven P. Roose.
    p.   cm. — (The Role of affect in motivation, development, and adaptation ; v. 2)
    Includes bibliographical references and index.
    ISBN 0-300-05271-5 (alk. paper)
    1. Aggressiveness (Psychology)—Congresses.   2. Anger—Congresses.   3. Control
(Psychology)—Congresses.   I. Glick, Robert A., 1941–   . II. Roose, Steven P.,
1948–   . III. Series.
    [DNLM: 1. Aggression—congresses.   2. Power (Psychology)—congresses.   3. Rage—
congresses.   BF 575.A5 R141]
RC569.5.A53R34   1993
152.4'7—dc20
DNLM/DLC
for Library of Congress   92-49297
                                                                                              CIP

A catalogue record for this book is available
from the British Library.

10   9   8   7   6   5   4   3   2   1

To Aaron Karush

Contents

III. Origins and Sources

IV. Historical and Political Expressions

Acknowledgments

As the editors of this second volume of the series on affects, we wish to thank Dr. Ethel Spector Person, the series editor, for her inspiration and guidance in the creation of this collection. Bernard C. Mendik receives our deepest appreciation for his generous financial support of the series of symposia on the theory of affects honoring Dr. Aaron Karush, director of the Columbia University Center for Psychoanalytic Training and Research from 1971 to 1976. Dr. Karush's intellectual legacy endures both in this series and in the Center's scientific and educational activities. We are grateful to Irwin Freeman of the Education Fund of the Upjohn Corporation for his support.

We thank the symposium committee—Doctors Stanley Bone, Sheri Katz-Bearnot, Deborah Hamm, David Lindy, Elena Lister, Philip Lister, and Lisa Sinsheimer, for the enormous time and attention given to the details necessary to successfully offer the program that was the basis of this collection.

The dedication and steadiness-under-pressure of the administrative staff of the Columbia Center—Joan Jackson (administrator), Lutricia Perry, Judith Kronenberg, and Martha Garvey—were essential to the completion of this volume.

We are grateful to Gladys Topkis, our senior editor at Yale University Press, whose vision and sensitivity encouraged the best from us throughout the project.

Finally, we thank our families for their patience and support.

Robert A. Glick, M.D.
Steven P. Roose, M.D.

Introduction

ETHEL SPECTOR PERSON, M.D.

Affects, emotions, and feelings, although always central to clinical work, have been undertheorized, being largely regarded as instinctual derivatives. Some of the reasons for this deemphasis of emotion in theoretical writings may go back to the origins of psychoanalysis. Freud, in attempting to achieve a science of mind, focused on forces rather than on feelings as the catalysts of behavior. He tried to establish psychoanalysis as a reputable science by presenting his theories in the guise of "objective" science so as to render them acceptable and palatable. This meant that he focused on instincts as something quantifiable— hence (at least implicitly) tamable or controllable. As Kathleen Woodward has described the result, "in Freud's writing hands and in those of most of his descendants, psychoanalysis is an oddly clinical discourse which speaks coolly and generally in terms of 'affect,' of 'instincts,' and 'drives,' and *specifically* of affects as a kind of 'elementary entity' of energy . . . that can be quantified. Freud gave us a kind of straightforward 'particle physics of the emotions.' . . . And in Freud's work, emotion—*affect*—is figured primarily as dangerous, as something to be repressed, or as something one hopes—or rather, Freud wishes—will subside" (1990/91, 8).

In relegating emotion to a peripheral role in motivation, psychoanalysis was following a contemporaneous trend in nearly all intellectual disciplines. There are two main reasons for the virtual absence of discourse on affective life: the positivist project of replacing passion with reason, and the enormous prestige accorded science—attitudes that ultimately have proved problematic. These very same biases have banished the "mind" from psychology and made behaviorism its dominant voice for over fifty years. In psychoanalysis, the propensities to devalue passion and to shy away from studying anything not amenable to testing, quantification, verification, and replication have not

1

been absolute but have, unfortunately, led to the assumption that the role of emotions in motivation is marginal. (Moreover, since psychoanalytic theory has only recently been enlarged to emphasize adaptational and developmental perspectives, the role of affect in adaptation and development is still relatively uncharted territory, with a few exceptions, for example, Melanie Klein's elevation of the depressive position to a pivotal role in development.)

A countermotion, however, is developing in current intellectual life, including in psychoanalysis—a return to a major interest in and investigation of the central role of affect. The volumes in this series on affects are part of this movement, the agenda being to spur the integration of affect theory into contemporary psychoanalysis.

"Pleasure beyond the pleasure principle" was chosen as the topic of the first volume because of the core position of concepts of pleasure and pain in psychoanalytic theory. In the present volume, we turn to a different group of affects, sometimes referred to as "the darker passions." This choice is a good complement to the book on pleasure, particularly given Freud's emphasis on key dialectical pairs: love and hate, Eros and Thanatos, libido and aggression. But the darker passions should not be viewed, as they too often are, merely as derivatives of an underlying aggressive instinct. The decision to address rage, power, and aggression (and anger and hostility as well) in one volume is intended to convey the complex sources of and relationships among these distinct but sometimes overlapping entities. Let me begin with some broad definitions: rage and anger are feelings that may or may not mobilize destructive behavior; hostility and aggression by definition imply action in the form of some destructive behavior directed toward an object, which may or may not be prompted by immediate emotion; power involves a psychological relationship that implies a more or less stable interaction with the object.

The frequent conflation between rage and anger, on the one hand, and aggression, on the other, probably has to do with the fact that in nonhuman animals rage almost always results in some aggressive discharge; conversely, aggression is almost always rooted in emotion (rage or fear). (I leave aside the problem of how we know what the animal "feels," as opposed to the physiological and behavioral reactions that we observe.) In lower animals, then, there appears to be something that can be called a rage reflex.

As has been described by the physiologist Walter Cannon and the psychoanalyst Sandor Radó, both rage and fear are preprogrammed, involuntary responses almost universally present in lower animals—alternative responses to a perceived threat. Such responses comprise feelings (or what we interpret as feelings), which lead to physiologic reactions that in turn are preparatory to action—either fight or flight—or, when neither is possible, to freezing. The medley of bodily changes invoked by rage, for example, includes increased adrenal secretions, elevated blood sugar, an accelerated heart rate, altered breathing, changes in electrical skin resistance, goose pimples (which make body hair stand on end so that the animal appears larger to its adversaries), increased muscle tension, pupil dilation, and the list goes on. Rage thereby serves the emergency purpose of putting the animal into a state of alert toward, or in readiness for, an anticipated threat. Most of the observable changes are brought about by a mobilization of the sympathetic division of the autonomic nervous system and the arousal of hormonal secretion. In the lower animals, then, no great distance exists between apparent feeling, on the one hand, and arousal and discharge into aggressive behavior, on the other.

The human animal, however, presents a different case. Although there may well be a rage reflex in the human, anger does not invariably give rise to the physiologic reactions just described, nor does anger necessarily (or even generally) trigger direct aggression. It may be that we should limit the usage of the term *rage* to episodes of extreme, angry passion that are associated with aggression and that we need to distinguish such apparently primal reactions from anger.

Anger, which is all too often appraised as no more than a weak form of rage, is radically different from the preprogrammed rage reflex in several significant ways. Both the developmental sources of anger and the insults that prompt it are more diverse and the ways of expressing it more various. According to Seneca (quoted by Tavris, 1982), "Wild beasts . . . are not subject to anger, for while it is the foe of reason, it [anger] is nevertheless born only where reason dwells" (p. 35). I take this to mean that anger in humans enters consciousness as a specific response to a specific provocation and that it has an intellectually elaborated (and, I would add, symbolic) valence.

Humans feel anger not only in response to frustration or threats to survival or security but also in response to injuries to various forms of self-esteem— pride, status, position, and dignity. Such insults, which can involve being ridiculed, humiliated, overlooked, ignored, made to feel inconsequential or superfluous, or merely denied pride of first place, are often called narcissistic injuries (Terman, 1975). Other reasons for anger may simply have to do with a low tolerance for frustration, causing some people to be more irritable than others and particularly vulnerable to explosive reactions. Anger in humans may also be evoked in response not just to a current event or situation but to something remembered from the past or anticipated in the future.

The manifestations of anger in humans are as diverse as its catalysts. Anger may be expressed directly, in which case it serves a clear-cut communicative function. In fact, communication may be the primary adaptive function of anger. Ideally, rather than discharge anger in destructive behavior, the angry individual uses verbal confrontation or assertion to resolve the provocation to anger. Such expression informs the object of anger of the protagonist's feelings and grievances; in healthy interactions, some mechanism for conflict resolution is achieved. The expression of anger may also be ego enhancing, insofar as it represents the victory of assertion over intimidation, strength over fear. (Consequently, anger probably cannot be fully understood within the purview of a one-person psychology alone—that is, from an intrapsychic view only; also required are an object relations psychology and an interpersonal psychology that focus on emotional attunement or its lack and on the regulation of interactions among individuals. Even when it is directly expressed, anger may appear hot or cool, verbal only or physically threatening as well. (The importance of the communicative function of anger is readily apparent in the phenomenon of discerning when someone else is angry even when he or she claims to be unaware of that emotion.)

Sometimes, out of fear or some other kind of reticence, anger is expressed or enacted only indirectly. Indirect expressions and enactments include the utterance of subtle or not so subtle belittling or demeaning remarks, sarcasm, or passive-aggressive behavior. Anger may lead to a pervasive preoccupation with revenge, and plotting revenge may become a kind of life's work. Displaced, sublimated, or transmuted anger plays a role in humor, teasing, and "dishing," in masochistic and sadistic interactions, in distorted communications, in failures of sexuality, in perversions, and in transference distortions. Anger may be displaced from the offending object onto a less threatening object (as when a husband belittled by his wife at breakfast becomes an extremely aggressive driver on his way to work). Just as important as the direct or indirect expression of anger is its inhibition, not only the inability to express anger but also the not infrequent inability to be aware of it—in either oneself or others. The denial of one's own anger may eventuate in depression, apathy, or low self-esteem; the denial of another's anger, in ruptured relationships, since one cannot address or redress what goes unnoticed.

In humans, anger is even more complex because it leaves a residue. Unlike the nonhuman experience, in which anger is a reflex that has only to be discharged for the animal to be returned to the status quo, humans are not restored to ground zero after cathartic discharge. They are changed. Insofar as prior experiences of anxiety and anger are encoded and symbolically elaborated, these affectively laden memory complexes may come to exert a continuing influence on an individual's subsequent perceptions of frustration and threat, sometimes predisposing him or her to low thresholds for the precipitation of extreme anxiety or anger. Such predispositions may be so constant and predictable that they essentially become part of character. As Gaylin (1984) cogently remarks, the problem is not the release of anger but "the unwarranted generation of anger" (p. 93). We all know people we regard as chronically angry or indiscriminately hostile. Some thin-skinned individuals, easily hurt, quickly cover over their feelings with explosive anger; the therapeutic task is to put them in touch with the initial provocation, which is so often out of awareness.

As a more complicated example of how strong affect comes to color subsequent experience, behavior, and character, consider paranoia, in which anger projected onto an object is then experienced as emanating from that object and directed toward oneself. Or take Otto Kernberg's (1976) exegesis of the development of narcissistic pathology, which he sees as clearly related to chronic childhood deprivation and reactive anger. In his view, the child of cold, neglectful, and even rejecting parents defensively withdraws from others and fails to learn to trust anyone, coming to rely on himself or herself alone. The resulting narcissistic pathology in adulthood prevents the individual from giving what was experienced earlier as denied to him or her, and thus, even in such relationships as he or she establishes, the narcissist remains essentially ungiving, selfish, and isolated. Such an apparently self-contained, even superior attitude, is a defense against an intense inner anger and resentment that covers over a fragile sense of self. Though the narcissist, unlike the paranoid, may not appear to be overtly hostile and may in fact be superficially charming, those who come too close may be shocked when they discover the exploitation to which they have been subjected.

In sum, then, anger can be seen as a necessary regulator of some kinds of social interaction or as a defense to maintain self-esteem and even the integrity of the self. Too often, though, anger has been considered merely as destructive and dangerous, as problematic and maladaptive. Consequently, our theoretical models have emphasized its control, attenuation, and taming in the service of socialization and development—the point Woodward makes when she says that *affect* is figured primarily as dangerous, as something Freud wishes would subside. Certainly our knowledge of psychopathology attests to the potential maladaptive effects of suppressed or excessive anger; this is the everyday stuff of a clinical practice. But there is another side. Anger in response to a threat or frustration is often highly adaptive, and, in fact, assertion, which is so closely related, is a necessary component of the development of autonomy and as such is prerequisite to a full sense of an integrated self. It is only when there is no hope for redressing a wrong, no way to salvage communication or to restore a relationship, that anger most often gives way to hostile behavior, aggression, and even violence.

Aggression, too, is a confusing term; our field is beset by the history of the term in psychoanalytic theory. Part of the confusion is because the term has been used to describe both a drive and the destructive behavior believed to issue from that drive. (For some analysts, the aggressive drive is the ultimate source of anger as well as all other negatively tinged emotions.) Thus aggression has many different meanings in the psychoanalytic literature. As I am using the term, aggression implies action. Whereas anger is not generally destructive, not even necessarily expressed in action, aggression always is. Aggression suggests the purposeful infliction of harm—ranging from hurt and humiliation to pain and even death—on an object. Whereas anger may be directed toward particular aspects or characteristics of the object, generally in an effort to get the object to change, aggression is more global, directed toward the whole object.

Paradoxically, though, aggression, unlike anger, need not involve strong emotion. Sometimes the emotion that precipitates aggression is fear rather than rage—for example, when one kills in self-defense. Aggression may sometimes be red-hot and tied to extreme anger, but it also may be affectively neutral, exercised primarily in the service of survival or of a religious, political, or professional mission. The hit man kills his target, surely an act of aggression but most often an impersonal one; he probably does not even know his victim. The bomber drops his payload from a feeling of duty or of patriotism, though the act may subsequently be elaborated at the symbolic level, both consciously and unconsciously, often leading to profound guilt. The human is clearly capable of aggression without the act deriving from any putative aggressive drive. (I would regard hostility, like aggression, as linked to a destructive urge; but hostility, unlike aggression, invariably implies an angry or resentful affective component. Hostile behavior might best be regarded as the discharge of anger that either was unexpressed or, having been expressed, failed to effect a change.)

Leo Stone (1971), in his outstanding article on aggression, argues: "Unlike sex, in itself a primary and motivating force, aggression is, with rare pathological exceptions, usually clearly and extrinsically motivated" (p. 238). As already suggested, the question of the status of aggression within psychoanalysis relates to the fact that it is variously regarded as a drive that fuels all or some aggressive behavior, as a response to provocation, or as a strategy to assert power and dominance. Some analysts, especially Kleinians and some classical Freudians, firmly believe in the existence of an aggressive drive and assume that aggressive behavior is de facto a derivative of that drive, which is viewed as being on a par with libido. (I leave aside the even more complex question of the arguments for and against the existence of a death instinct.) Nonetheless, despite their conviction, deciding whether aggression derives from an aggressive *drive* rather than from the release of an innate pattern of response triggered by some external or internal stimulus proves to be a complex question, much debated not only among psychoanalytic theorists of different persuasions but among child observers, ethologists, social psychologists, and anthropologists as well.

Even if an aggressive drive in humans were demonstrated, it would be erroneous to attribute to it all of the various manifestations of aggression, rage, and anger—just as when we talk about sex, it would be extremely naive to attribute all manifestations of sexuality to the sex drive. Just as we know that many sex acts are motivated more by a need for closeness and security than by sexual desire and that some sex acts appear to be fueled more by anger or the will-to-power than by lust, so too we know that many acts of aggression are motivated more by the need for security and rational and cognitive motives than by anger. Or they may be fueled by the wish for revenge, extreme anger, or jealousy, none of which is necessarily related to drive. Whatever the status of the aggressive drive, then, we need to use frames of reference other than instinct theory to account for the diverse acts of aggression, hatred, sadism, and cruelty that we observe.

The alternative to postulating an aggressive drive is certainly not to assume that human nature is innately good. There are too many destructive elements all around us to hold to such an assumption. But it is possible to interpret them as being the product of political necessity, unchecked anger, chronic anger generated in response to cumulative childhood trauma, the attempt to counter pervasive anxiety, competition, greed, or a thwarted will-to-power rather than derivative from instinct.

The relationship of aggression (actual or potential) to the will-to-power may prove more central to psychoanalytic theory than has as yet been theorized. Aggression, or the threat of aggression, may be mobilized to retain or gain power. Within psychoanalysis, it is power more than either rage or aggression that has been inadequately conceptualized. Such neglect may well be the result of psychoanalysts' historical disaffection with Alfred Adler's attempt to elevate the "will-to-power" to *the* central place in the psyche. Although Freud, in his 1924 paper on masochism, speaks of "the destructive instinct, the instinct for mastery, or the 'will to power'" (p. 163), these terms are not identical. Some motive other than aggression (which, as previously discussed, implies destruction) is required to account for the wish to dominate or the will-to-power. (The analogue to the will-to-power in nonhuman animals is jostling for a spot in the pecking order.)

If anger is about changing an interaction with an object while aggression is about the destruction of an object, then power is about the structuring of an ongoing relationship with an object. One of the best definitions of power is that provided by political theorist Hans Morgenthau: "Power is a psychological relation between those who exercise it and those over whom it is exercised. It gives the former control over certain actions of the latter through the impact which the former exerts on the latter's mind. This impact derives from three causes: the expectation of benefits, the fear of disadvantages, the respect or love for men or institutions" (quoted in Russell, 1990, 120). In this passage, Morgenthau describes the reasons why one succumbs or surrenders to the power of another. What psychoanalytic theory contributes is an understanding of why power is sought: power confirms one's omnipotence. Not only does the exercise of power guarantee access to the object and the gratification the object can supply, it is also intimately connected to one's sense of self. Power is a major mode by which the individual secures gratification, preserves his or her security, and wrests recognition. Among other sources of the power motive is its potential to serve as a kind of pseudo-omnipotence, which acts as a denial of or a counter to the existential anxiety of death and finiteness: the individual sometimes seeks to deny weaknesses and to gain control through domination. This analysis suggests that the will-to-power originates as an ego motive, as a major regulator of narcissistic well-being and self-esteem. Alternatively, the individual can transcend personal weakness and loneliness not through dominance but through surrender to what is conceived of as a greater power, someone or something with whom to identify. The submergence of self into the Godhead is, in part, an identification through surrender with a greater power and thus a roundabout fulfillment of omnipotent gratification.

Given that power is about relating, power is almost by definition intrinsic to our personal relationships. Because of the child's dependent attachment to its caregivers, love is born in the context of a marked power differential, with the inevitable consequence that love and sex always carry the symbolic resonance of a power differential. But power is even more pervasive in our lives. Whenever there is a question of priority—and there always is in every human relationship—some balance of power is established or a struggle for power ensues. Power relationships are the ground of human experience. Power may be role-related, as with teacher and student, employer and employee; age-related, the power gradient operating against both the very young and the very old; it may be affected by social, sexual, physical, or financial factors; or it may be related only to force of personality or character predilection. A power balance is always delicate and can be easily disrupted by small intrapsychic or interpersonal changes. Even when an equilibrium appears to be secure, it can be disrupted and give way to a power struggle. Power, like anger, is the stuff of everyday life.

Just as psychoanalysis inadequately theorizes anger and rage as merely maladaptive, so too the will-to-power is sometimes viewed as nothing more than an unfortunate contaminant. But power should not be theorized only in its maladaptive mode. Like anger and even aggression, it has many constructive, adaptive dimensions; for example, the legitimate disposition of power is as essential to family structure as to the body politic. The pursuit of power, whether rational or irrational, is inevitable. As Morgenthau makes clear, a viable political goal cannot be to eliminate power politics, which are part of the fabric of social life, but only their destructive effects. A stable social and political organization, based on a legitimate disposition of power, is necessary to provide acceptable channels for gratification of the individual's wishes and to set limits to his or her aggression. Similarly, a stable family organization, likewise dependent on some adjudication of power, is prerequisite for optimal psychological development, while the precise disposition of power in a given family will inevitably shape a child's emerging personality.

Anger, aggression, and the will-to-power are adaptive modes (sometimes corrupted into psychopathology) that both assuage anxiety and provide some remedy to a perceived threat. For example, anger, appropriately expressed, may be the best safeguard against being dominated, controlled, or exploited. Anger, rage, aggression, and power are clearly not only, or even primarily, destructive; they are also dispositions requisite to individual growth and development and to the maintenance of a viable social structure. Nonetheless, it appears to be part of our tragic nature that violence, hatred, and destruction—however we construe their causes—are endemic to the human condition.

As in the preceding volume, an interdisciplinary approach appears indispensable to comprehending affective life; thus the current topic is scrutinized not only from the psychoanalytic perspective but from the perspectives of the brain sciences, ethology, political science, religion, and gender studies. The editors, Drs. Robert Glick and Steven Roose, have been both persevering and ingenious in conceptualizing and organizing an important diversity of telling viewpoints about the constructive and destructive aspects of anger, rage, aggression, and power.

REFERENCES

Freud, Sigmund. 1924. *The economic problem of masochism. S.E.* 19:157–170.

Gaylin, Willard. 1984. *The rage within: Anger in modern life.* New York: Simon and Schuster.

Kernberg, Otto. 1976. *Object relations theory and clinical psychoanalysis.* New York: Jason Aronson.

Rado, Sandor. 1956. Emergency behavior with an introduction to the dynamics of conscience, in *Psychoanalysis of behavior: The collected papers of Sandor Rado.* New York: Grune and Stratton.

Russell, Greg. 1990. *Hans J. Morgenthau and the ethics of American statecraft.* Baton Rouge: Louisiana State University Press.

Stone, Leo. 1971. Reflections on the psychoanalytic concept of aggression. *Psychoanal. Q.* 40:195–243.

Tavris, Carol. 1982. *Anger: The misunderstood emotion.* New York: Simon and Schuster.

Terman, David. 1975. Aggression and narcissistic rage: A clinical elaboration. *The Annual of Psychoanalysis.* Chicago Institute of Psychoanalysis (vol. 3), 239–255.

Woodward, Kathleen, ed. 1990/91. *Discourse: Journal for theoretical studies in media and culture* 13(1) (Fall–Winter).

I

Clinical and
Theoretical
Perspectives

In *Clinical and Theoretical Perspectives*, we begin with the clinical psychoanalytic process as our basis for assessing theoretical models of rage, power, and aggression. The emotions, both experienced and inferred, guide us in the clinical situation, and we interpret their meanings from within the framework of models of the mind that include wishes, fears, drives, needs, structures, functions, and representations as organizing principles. Ultimately, psychoanalytic theories have always had to prove their utility and robustness by enriching and advancing clinical understanding. In this section, the authors draw upon their clinical experience to both illuminate and challenge aspects of our theories of rage, power, and aggression.

In "Women in the Maze of Power and Rage," Roy Schafer examines the meanings of victimization, power, and dangerousness as dimensions of both the internal and the external world. Focusing on important themes in the psychoanalytic treatment of women, he describes powerful and successful women who nevertheless present themselves as victims trapped in rageful relations with narcissistic, power-hungry, hurtful men. Their conscious frustration and anger at the male-dominated world in which they feel imprisoned reflect unconscious rage against their powerful emotional bonds to an intrusive mother and an absent father. This dilemma leads these powerful women to collude unconsciously with their persecutors. Among the potential obstacles to the effective analysis of such patients are the insufficient appreciation of the reality of sexism in political and social life and the undue indictment of the world for victimizing the patients. In his exploration of this clinical problem, Schafer seeks to understand the maze of rage and power in terms of a language of experience, eschewing metapsychological mechanisms and causes such as an aggressive drive.

In "Male Sexuality and Power," Ethel Person continues the exploration of the meanings of power relations in the minds of men and women, this time from the male point of view. Through an examination of male fantasies of sexual dominance, she describes the role of power as a defense against various narcissistic injuries developmentally experienced by men. Incorporating regressive exaggerations of appropriate gender roles, the patients Person describes use sexuality in the service of fantasies of power and aggression to modulate turbulent internal affect states and to control problems of identity. Here we confront questions of the interaction of gender-role socialization, developmental trauma, and the organizing influence of sexual motivation.

Helen Meyers, in "Two Successful Characterologic Adaptations to Aggression," reviews the major psychoanalytic theories of aggression, particularly within the ego-psychological and object relations paradigms, and sees both clinical and theoretical merit in separating assertion and aggression. True destructive aggression and concomitant affective expressions of rage result from threat and frustration. By examining two intriguing representatives of effective aggressive adaptation, she critically considers hostile aggressive motivation and the way healthy character structure organizes reactions to frustration and threat from without. She suggests that an essential element of what we consider power reflects this successful adaptation to aggression.

Moving from clinical observation to the development theories that inform it, Otto Kernberg, in "The Psychopathology of Hatred," applies his views on the integration of primitive internal object relations and the organization of drives to the question of the nature of rage and aggression. For Kernberg, rage is mobilized in the child by the mother, who frustrates as well as nurtures; the child's object-related rage seeks to change the mother and is part of a normal repertoire of time-limited affects. But what happens when the frustration, for whatever reasons, cannot be abated or extinguished? This frustration, for Kernberg, is the origin of hatred. When normal anger and rage, engendered by frustration and threats to internal security, are transformed into hatred, conditions of pathological self and object representations and relations result, with powerful consequences for further affect regulation and intrapsychic structuralization. Clinically, it follows that these pathological affect and representational structures create severe character disorders that rely on primitive defenses and potential explosive action.

Classical psychoanalytic theories of female psychology include assumptions about the developmental vicissitudes of rage, power, and aggression. Lucy LaFarge, in "The Early Determinants of Penis Envy," explores these issues as they pertain to gender difference, gender identifications, and early object relations. Though all girls must face the issue of penis envy, according to LaFarge its persistence and organizing importance in ongoing development reflect crucial, non-gender-specific, archaic struggles over the establishment of integrated, internalized object representations. Penis envy in women, in her view, has a role in defensive structuralization parallel to that of castration anxiety in men. Clinical illustrations are offered to demonstrate the utility of this concept.

As self psychology has parted company with traditional psychoanalytic drive concepts, it too has had to struggle to explain aggressive motivation and its relation to rage and anger. Paul Ornstein and Anna Ornstein, in "Assertiveness, Anger, Rage, and Destructive Aggression," emphasize that a metapsychology that assumes a primary aggressive drive can negatively affect the clinical situation. A therapist's search for the patient's "hidden rage" can lead to a specious "finding" that is neither experienced nor confirmed by the patient. A circular process can develop. The interpretation of the supposed rage may actually elicit an angry response from the patient, which is then erroneously seen as confirmation of the original intervention and the theory itself. The Ornsteins believe that it is clinically truer and more useful to see rage as a reflection of the failure of the normal organization of self structures. Narcissistic rage, a central feature in this schema, is then the pathological consequence of a failure to meet the needs of the self. The enfeebled and threatened self is always struggling to ward off the threat of fragmentation. Effective treatment can modulate and facilitate the redirection of narcissistic rage toward the integration of normal healthy and aggressive self structures.

1

Women in the Maze
of Power and Rage

ROY SCHAFER

Themes of aggression and power pervade the accounts one hears in one's daily work as an analyst. Sometimes the stated or implied emotional violence is cold, as in the cruelty of prolonged withdrawal into silence; sometimes it is hot, as in burning rage and envy. Commonly, the analysand is presented in these narratives as the sufferer, perhaps reactively angry, perhaps passively resigned, but in any case victimized and in pain. Commonly, the exploration of these accounts of emotional violence seems to find its destination in the complex dramas of the analysand's family of origin. It is inappropriate for the analyst automatically to regard these painful accounts as altogether unreliable, for up to a point they are likely to enrich the treatment with useful information.

In order to work analytically, however, the analyst must also anticipate—and go on to establish—that much more is involved in the analysand's suffering than having been victimized by her or his family's unmistakably cruel or otherwise disturbing exercises of power. What is that "more"? It is likely to include the analysand's having become, over the course of development, either a seducer of sadism or, through identification, a ruthless wielder of power and a cruel victimizer of others, often in the most subtle way—or, as is true in many cases, both at once. Once the treatment is under way, the analyst is included among those others who are to be seduced into cruelty or victimized themselves or both. Those analysts who can moderate the resulting countertransferences will not fail to note the ways in which these analysands feel frightened and penitent about resorting to masochistic and sadistic strategies. That is to say, these analysands may be understood to be pursuing this course of action unbeknown to themselves and in an acutely conflicted manner. Implied in this conflicted course of action are hidden loving kindness, desperate self-protection, and adaptedness to a history of family relations that has

17

required violent and perverse orientations to the self and others, these orientations having been prerequisite to feeling that one belonged and was not an outsider furtively looking in or an object of derision.

Further, the analyst who is not afraid of Melanie Klein will recognize in each analysand's productions the activity of cruel internal objects. These are imagined internal objects or introjects that have been created chiefly in two ways: first, by the projective identifications perpetrated on, and accepted by, children whenever parents use them in an attempt to rid themselves of their unwanted bad parts or characteristics and, second, by the sequence of the child's projecting his or her own cruel fantasies about others onto them and then incorporating the bad figures that result from these unhappy creative efforts. In these fantasies, these incorporated cruel internal objects will finally fill so much of the "inner world" and so far establish an atmosphere of hostile surveillance and persecutory retaliation, much like an army of occupation, that in part they will stimulate continuous efforts at expulsion into or onto others (on an anal model, usually). Those who later enter analysis as adults repetitively replay the painful interactions of their early lives and early fantasies; this they do in direct or inverted form, both with the analyst and with others in their current lives.

I present here a psychoanalytic summary of my work with one such group of analysands. In the present instance, "psychoanalytic" refers to work organized chiefly around Freudian analytic descriptions and interpretations of the analysand's past and present lives, lives now being repeated in interpretable form in transferences and evoked countertransferences.

The Analysands

The locale of my presentation is my analytic work with a series of successful career women. Although these women seemed to be different from each other in many ways, the ones with whom I am here concerned shared a proclivity to enter into painful relationships with narcissistic and sadistic men. The manifest content of these relationships showed them to be simply and extremely masochistic: these women seemed to lose the high level of cognitive, administrative, and social skills and the resourcefulness and poise that they typically manifested in their work; instead they became helpless, blindly repetitive, self-accusatory, and emotionally labile, seemingly addicted to their victimization, very often unaware of the rage they felt at the way they were being treated, deficient or at least erratic and ineffective in their self-assertiveness, and greatly restricted in allocating responsibility for their interpersonal difficulties to anyone but themselves. All power seemed to have passed from their hands.

Typically, these women worked long hours in institutional settings, and it was mainly there that they developed their love relationships and other significant social relationships. Not rarely, the love relationships were with older men, married men, or both; if not, they were either with men on the rebound from broken marriages or disturbed love affairs or with men who, it seemed on reflection, could well have been married long ago but somehow were not, a fact that could have served as a warning but was ignored.

As a rule, these men were portrayed as hard-driving and highly successful, capable of being charming and of serving as helpful mentors; however, they were also ruthlessly critical, exploitative, and unfeeling. Even as colleagues, they were said to act like members of a club that excluded women from membership, men who made a point of looking supercritically at the work contributions of any women, no matter how outstanding or profitable, to delay rewarding them with recognition or advancement in the institutional hierarchy, and to subject them to the harassment of sexist attitudes, language, and other provocations.

When they became the lovers of these women, they rarely accepted responsibility for misunderstandings or hurts. Instead, they expected the women to accommodate them and to be available on short notice, even while they showered their victims with criticism for self-interest, unresponsiveness, and similar "sins." After the relationships ended, sometimes more so after they ended, they found ways to harass and further torment their victims. It seemed then that they were determined to undermine the self-confidence and reality testing of these women and, beyond that, to undermine their sense of having an ethical or moral center. Sometimes in these narratives, it seemed as though they were engaged in brainwashing of the sort carried on by O'Brien, the torturer and soul-murderer of Winston Smith in George Orwell's novel *1984*. Moreover, the women went on clinging to their ex-lover tormentors, rationalizing their behavior as motivated by hopefulness or loneliness or as still trying to settle the score, perhaps aggressively but perhaps only reparatively.

Although I have presented no more than a composite picture of these entanglements, I believe each of these women eventually gave a variation of its details convincingly, even if in an obviously one-sided manner. Yet, with respect to this apparent abuse and exploitation, consciously they characterized themselves primarily as failures rather than as enraged victims and as buffeted about by unkind, arbitrary fate rather than as driven uncomprehendingly to repetitions of insult and injury. These women were in a maze from which they could not find their way out.

One could not fail to be impressed by the decline in the level of functioning that was evident in the repetitive, self-abasing, and hopeless relations these women maintained with one man or with a series of men, in the painful confrontations they insisted on reexperiencing, and in the prevalence of depression over rage or even enlightened self-assertion in response to patent cruelty. Clearly, there was far more to the matter there than met the eye and the ear.

On this understanding and after an appropriately careful initial screening, psychoanalysis was recommended as the treatment of choice. Apparently accustomed to the long hard grind of achievement, these women seemed ready to accept that recommendation and agreed to the analytic procedure as the necessary, disciplined approach to resolving their basic problems. Once the work was under way, however, and for some time, they seemed mainly to want and often demand from the analyst comfort and counsel rather than self-understanding. As befit their varied circumstances, they wanted direction in gratifying their desires for love, marriage, family, personal dignity, and a career with recognition, for in their own eyes they were good-hearted women in dire straits, eager to be shown their mistakes, ready to go on learning how to perform well—hardly making even the most superficial distinctions between work and analysis. From this shift of emphasis alone, one could infer that preoccupation with the trials and tribulations of the current relationships served as a flight from the inner world of conflicted longings and also as a clinging to an implied self-concept of the helpless infant or good little girl in need of guidance.

On Writing on the Therapy of Women

I believe that those who write on the psychological therapy of women are obliged to give some account of how they view the historical-cultural conditions that affect the development of girls and women in family life, school, love, and work. Because these writings touch on the general psychology of women, they must somehow convey perspectives on the place of women in the world, and inevitably those perspectives will have political and ideological implications and consequences, some of them of great social significance. It follows that these writings must also include some discussion of expectable countertransferential issues in the therapy of women because the author's social viewpoint is bound to contribute both to shaping the phenomena being reported and to the meanings and significance attributed to them. Like any other countertransferences, those in question here will, if understood and mastered, be potentially useful in the therapeutic interaction and in the reader's understanding. If, however, they are screened out by defensive measures, they will limit and may even damage treatment and the proper understanding of its text. Certainly, the astute reader may not agree that the author's account of his or her work conforms closely to the stated intentions; nevertheless, these intentions are bound to affect significantly the treatments being reported, so that there is something to gain by the author's stating his position frankly.

Any discussion of countertransference may be overwrought or imbalanced to the point that it enacts unresolved or uncontained countertransference issues. It does not, however, follow that calling attention to the play of historical-cultural factors in countertransference is itself a sign of countertransference. Indeed, it is not only defensive but politically reactionary to argue that this kind of attention necessarily manifests countertransference, as though it were possible to elude completely the issues of culturally rooted countertransferences. Accordingly, I shall first summarize my perspective on the place of women in today's world, including appropriate psychoanalytic insights.

I seek to break with the now discredited convention of writing as though it were possible, in areas of weighty social controversy, to be an utterly disinterested, value-free psychoanalytic observer of mental and behavioral phenomena. One may no longer claim that these phenomena are "out-there-in-Nature"—phenomena with a fixed essence waiting to be discovered and univocally described once and for all by an objective investigator.

Much of our social order has been arranged and is controlled by men whose attitudes toward women are discriminatory, demeaning, and exploitative. Many high-achieving men may be characterized accurately as seductively manipulative, self-centered, and at least implicitly hard and cruel in their social relationships. Consequently, the women under study here work and live against great odds in occupational and social settings that too often neglect and even oppose their interests. These settings are continuations of those in which they grew up, gifted girls whose giftedness encountered at best highly ambivalent welcomes. In this respect, I see the reality testing of these women to have been seriously compromised in their families and their surroundings, in that they had finally organized much of their perception and feeling along the lines of depressive self-blame and low self-esteem.

Nevertheless, one would have to ignore too much about these women's considerable assets and achievements to settle quickly for the correct but limited social-psychological perspective within which they appear to be merely disadvantaged members of a sexist society. Although I agree that they are that, I would also emphasize that, in the sense most immediately relevant to psychoanalytic *therapy*, the maze in which they were lost was made up of the twists and turns and dead ends of their unconscious mental processes; for these were the winding, entangled paths along which the women could distribute all the sadomasochism and dreams of omnipotence that flourished in their growing up in disturbed and biased family settings and social environments. It seemed to be part of their lostness and also part of their unconsciously devised strategy to collaborate with their persecutors. That this was so became evident once these women began to benefit from insights developed during analysis, when they found that they could often renounce some habitual self-destructive course of action, take previously inconceivable corrective or protective action, and go on to enjoy more assertive and happier kinds of relationships and subjective experiences. They also found that they could elicit more respectful and warmer attitudes and actions—"bring out the best"—in parents, siblings, and all those with whom they shared their lives. It is not easy to apportion weight to the factors involved in these changes: decreased distortion, decreased provocation, and increased social poise and adroitness, together with efforts to "please" the analyst in the transference. Individual personal changes of any of these sorts, however, cannot significantly or promptly reduce the general male chauvinism that continues to surround women in our society.

In these cases, although it would have been confusing and counterproductive to focus the analyses *exclusively* on the origins and dynamics of their unconscious, self-injurious collaboration, it was helpful to have elucidated as far as possible the complex part they had played and were now playing in their own *manifest* victimization. I focus on the results of this work of elucidation in spite of recognizing that to some of those concerned with these social-psychological issues it will seem politically naive or offensive to take this tack. To them such a view may still smack of blaming the victim. My view, however, I take to be the usual psychoanalytic view, whereby treatment does not apportion blame. Rather, it seeks to clarify the complex structure of tragic human situations so as to facilitate the personal changes that could lead to the alleviation of neurotic suffering. In neurotic suffering, the social pathology of sexism plays its part mainly in the most indirect and elusive ways. Victimizers, too, must be understood, both analytically and social-psychologically, as themselves victims of countless generations of every form of rage and power. Of more immediate consequence, however, is the recognition that—generally, tragically—chronic victims begin to participate in and even to long for further victimization and to become themselves victimizers as well.

The Mothers

The principal clues leading to understanding the vulnerabilities and conflicts of each of the gifted women were established in the course of analyzing her relationship with her mother. By "her mother," I refer not to the mother as she "really" was, for as modern historians acknowledge, one can never re-create the one and only "real" version of a piece of history. Rather, I refer to the mother of psychic reality, that is, the figure the daughter constructed and experienced in an inevitable mix of fantasy, misunderstanding, and consensually verifiable fact and memory. Many negative aspects of this psychically real mother were repressed, and those that were not repressed were denied or suppressed in the mother's physical presence. In the analysis, however, many negative aspects were readily described in the course of the analysand's complaining of always being victimized by this woman, even in her physical absence. Significantly, these complaints were regularly accompanied or followed by guilty reactions, although often these reactions would be repressed or projected.

Interpretively, it was helpful to accept for some time the analysand's stated or implied experience that the internal object was operating with a force of its own, that is, as an introject or what would be better named an imagined presence of shifting or uncertain location. It was only later in the analysis that it became both possible and desirable to interpret the patient's reviving this imagined figure in stressful situations, investing power in it through fantasy, putting it into operation, and then submitting to it—which is to say that ultimately it had to be analyzed as one of those quasi-delusional symptoms that are by no means restricted to the seriously ill or so-called borderline cases.[1]

I shall concentrate on two themes in the daughter-mother relationships I am describing, which seem to be two sides of the same coin—at least they stood out as allied themes in my work with these women. The themes are damaged self-esteem-regulation and unconscious ambivalent identification with the dominating and intrusive mother.

The mothers of the women tended to be extraordinarily intrusive, controlling, and critical. They were so ruled by shame that keeping up appearances was for them a fanatical preoccupation. At times their preoccupation seemed to be barely in touch with reality, riddled with contradictions, and inevitably fragmenting in its approach to people and situations. Always on the lookout for flaws, these mothers would constantly and tactlessly raise questions not only about clothes, boyfriends, and physical appearance but also about intellectual and cultural interests, the need for solitude and privacy, and countless other matters. In their controlling, they set up powerful barriers to any overt engagement with the father, thereby limiting the daughter so far as possible to the daughter-mother relationship. They used this one-on-one, or dyadic, strategy in the family to the point where they disrupted alliances even among the children, if there were other children, or between the child and friends. It emerged that these mothers had themselves usually been victims of mothers even more mentally disturbed or disturbing than they were. Their own self-esteem was in ruins, and in their conduct they seemed to show much identification with their persecutory mothers. Persecutors in one perspective, they were victims in another, and links in a chain in a third.

On the face of it, these mothers so occupied the minds of their daughters, my analysands, that it seemed at first that the daughters had been blocked from setting up their own ego ideals or ideal selves—blocked, that is, from what would traditionally be called structure-building and direction-setting internalizations. When in love, the analysands presented themselves manifestly in just that way, so dependent on the affirmation of their lovers that they had no source of self-esteem. Often, their fathers had been side-lined in the family, blocked from showing the interest and appreciation, the normal fatherly seductiveness, and the power and ideals that might have partly compensated for the mother's deprivations and depredations. The daughters brought forth these growth-blocking experiences to account for how crushed they were by the callousness and abuse of their lovers and by the ultimate collapse of their love relationships. Without the love of their lovers, they claimed, they felt they were nothing, even though they said they knew that, objectively, it was not so. Primarily at fault for this was the invasive, overoccupying mother and only secondarily, the sidelined father. It seemed that their development into a full-

---

1. See in this regard my *Aspects of Internalization*, chap. 4 (New York: International Universities Press, 1968).

fledged positive oedipal phase had been severely limited; in the positive transference, after some initial pseudo-oedipal moves, the patients approached the entire realm of intimacy with a man with much guilt and anxiety and a great readiness to regress. Freely felt love for a man seemed to add a new dimension to their lives that was simultaneously thrilling and threatening.

Further Complications

The allegations and implications seemed to be true as far as they went, but they did not go nearly far enough; a host of other factors was defined as analysis proceeded. First, the constant love and appreciation of others were needed not simply for love's sake alone or for generalized intimacy or consolation but also and mainly to drown out, refute, or show up the persecutory mother-presence. Second, there were complex, unconscious phallic fantasies at play, for in one respect, in her psychic reality the high-achieving, good-girl daughter served as the compensatory phallus for a castrated mother, an arrangement that seemed designed to take care simultaneously of the castration fantasies of both of them. In this aspect, then, the daughter no longer seemed to be merely a passive tabula rasa completely covered with the mother's derogatory inscriptions.

In yet another and related respect, the daughter as upwardly mobile star proved to be arrogant and disdainful in relation to both parents and to men. In her psychic reality, she was the proud embodiment of an upwardly mobile penis, that is, an erection, someone who or something that would omnipotently subdue others—if necessary even through guilt-provoking tears and protestations of misery—and who would be furious and vengeful if turned back or away, though perhaps at first only feeling misunderstood and doubly betrayed. This is to say that much of so-called inner structure could be ascribed to her: specifically, a grandiose self-image that involves identificatory participation in both the overwhelming force and the defectiveness of her apparently despotic mother-presence.

In every respect, therefore, each of the women was not so lost in the maze as she seemed on first telling. Indeed, it became absolutely clear and understandable that in her transferences to the male analyst, the very idea of truly yielding to a man, that is, yielding at or close to what she felt to be her inner emotional core, was anathema to her. In this, bound as she was to her mother, she seemed to take a stance toward men modeled on her mother's stance toward the father.

Her being a high achiever in occupational worlds that are traditionally subject to male authority and privilege was also, and not surprisingly, based in part on the phallic fantasy that she was in fact "one of the boys." Thus, when she encountered professional barriers, her outrage and grief were based as much on her unconsciously imagining that she, along with her mother, was being castrated as on, (1) those situational elements that repeated her disappointment in her father's relative inadequacy and unresponsiveness, (2) those that repeated the ultimate inaccessibility of her mother, for whom her occupational superiors, male or female, were stand-ins, and (3) those that stemmed from powerful social traditions inimical to the well-being of women in love and work. Each of the women was "up against it" both in her inner world and in her manifest daily life, the two realms being, as always, inseparable.

Three more factors are significant aspects of these daughters and these mothers. The first factor is the evidence that these analysands seemed to maintain loving, intimate, and enduring relations with at least one other woman. Although these relationships were usually in full flower before analysis commenced, they began to be used defensively in relation to the transference. They diluted the transference, for often the friend was the first to hear about significant emotional experiences and the first consultant on meanings and conceivable courses of action, while I was made to feel that I was merely one consultant among others and, at that, at a disadvantage, being neither an old and intimate friend nor a woman. I was put in my place by being displaced, as the father had been. This defensive use of friends might also be seen as acting out by living out that part of the ambivalence felt toward the mother that was loving and dependent, while directing the split-off aggression toward the minimized analyst. This enactment also protected the patient from the dangers of attack and engulfment by the mother that would, it was felt, surely result should both sides of the ambivalence be shown directly to her.

The second factor is the deadening effect on emotional experience that could be traced largely to the mother's critical and possessive invasiveness. These mothers and mother-presences were experienced as constantly pulling the rug out from under the spontaneous enthusiasms of their developing daughters. The enthusiasms ranged from girlfriends, boyfriends, teachers, clothes, and make-up to intellectual interests and creative endeavors. They were unresponsive when they were not directly inflicting shame, guilt, or anxiety on their daughters, and otherwise made them doubt their spontaneous feelings. As they developed, the daughters came to inflict this affect-destruction on themselves. In this, they were identified with their aggressor-mothers. The identification served to lessen the shock of facing attack in the external world unprepared and then impulsively reacting to an intolerant mother or mother-surrogate and facing the consequences. The defensive strategy was peace at any price.

More than defense, however, the identification helped to preserve the exclusive tie to the mother that overwise would be felt with terror to be totally severed and that, emotionally, was subtly severed every time the mother failed to respond positively to her daughter's signs of growth and separate identity. As I mentioned, the mother's influence had limited the range and depth of her daughter's investment in other relationships that might have provided a more developed context for a definite and affirmed identity; hence, the mother's withdrawal into nonresponsiveness had great power.

In treatment, these analysands backed off from excitement and the possibility of somehow getting excited. They were careful to maintain their own rigid controllingness. But they sensed the resulting deadness, and that lowered their self-esteem further, even though they also valued deadness as a barrier against the transference relationship. In one way the analyst was put in the role of the persecutory mother; in another, that of the weak father; in a third, however, the analysands, disclaiming their own aliveness, seemed to want to put the analyst in the role of the one who argued for life, liberty, and the pursuit of happiness while they clung to their controls and defenses and thereby to their invasive mothers and their identification with them. Obviously, the analyst had to try to maintain the fine balance between, on the one side, blindly accepting this projective identification laden with anxiety and guilt and, on the other, lapsing into a subdued, hands-off countertransference.

Reparation is the third and last factor to be mentioned at this point. In being the phallic completion of the crippled mother—the mother wounded into cruelty by her own mother as well as by men—the daughter was healing her. She was making her mother whole, realizing her mother's dreams through being a good-girl high-achiever. In that reparative role, it could not be acceptable to enter knowingly into a deep love relationship with a man experienced. For the daughter to do so would be to abandon her own mother, cripple her once again, "empty her out," and depress her beyond what the daughter could bear. Here, love and guilt joined forces with rage, grandiosity, and humiliation to make of these analysands victims who were simultaneously powerful forces in their own right. However much each one suffered in love and however abjectly she conducted herself outwardly in her heterosexual affairs and even in the workplace, she carried power and rage with her in the maze that was her life.

Countertransference

The maze in which these women seemed to stay lost is the maze of human tragedy, so much of which is necessarily beyond independent, conscious reckoning. Consequently, progress in analysis is slow and painful, the work is arduous for the analyst as well as the patient, not every patient gets deeply into treatment or continues it, and not every one of them emerges with the same types or amounts of gain. In my experience, however, traditional Freudian analysis, particularly of the complex, androgynous, multivalent merger with mother as it takes place in a sexist world, is often able to make a significant difference. For the analyst, the work requires eliciting and dealing with much rage on many levels of functioning, with much manipulative and vengeful exercise of power, often enacted in the subtlest ways and with much maternal transference that sometimes is hostile and grandiose and sometimes blissful and seemingly purely heterosexual.

This work requires much analysis of the countertransferences peculiar to working with acutely suffering, abused but powerful, successful, and by all indications, exceptionally well-endowed women. For example, there is the countertransference response of letting oneself be sidelined emotionally, as the father had been all along, while at the same time being the recipient of furtive and somewhat erotic positive oedipal gestures and responses. Another example is the countertransference response of wanting to assert one's own force against the formidable latent power and control of these women, that is, not to feel that one is the analytical equivalent of a "castrated wimp" and to resort then to more emphasis or more interpretation when, on further reflection, it would be in order to work with greater precision, depth, or restraint of interpretation. Another countertransference features the analyst's wanting to prove, by shows of respect, support, warmth, and so on, that he is not the narcissistic persecutory mother or a sexist male stand-in for her; also, that he is there to bind up wounds rather than inflict them or suffer them. This countertransference may touch the central reason why one has become an analyst in the first place, and it is all the easier to rationalize if one shares the outlook on sexism in the world that I presented earlier.

Countertransference may induce declarations of support for the patient's angry view of men and our society. But this move will only make it harder to analyze the distortions and provocations that the patient has come to rely on defensively—specifically, it will obscure the play of these factors in the transference. Consequently, the disturbances of reality testing and of self-enhancing adaptation will be left in place, and crucial, unconsciously maintained conflicts will continue to limit the patient's development.

As always, every other kind of countertransference may be at play in these cases. I mention here only a few, each of which narrows interpretive focus. One may remain at only one psychosexual level, such as the oedipal or preoedipal level or the anal level. One may stress only the positive (heterosexual) oedipal at the expense of the negative (homosexual) oedipal; one may focus too much on negative transference, in these cases on the woman's destructive, envious, castrating desires, thereby minimizing or dismissing her struggle against loving, admiring, idealizing, and submissive tendencies. Also, it is possible to disembody or desomatize the psychosexual factors and refer only to dependency, trust, control, empathy, and the like, meanwhile playing down concretely oral, anal, and genital feelings and fantasies. I do not attempt here a complete coverage of the analyses carried out; anyone familiar with psychosexual theory can easily fill in the bodily referents of many of the major developments reported.

How They Love

Returning now to these women in love—or more usually, desolate among the ruins of love affairs—it seemed that their lovers, like most of the other men they worked with, combined features of their mothers, fathers, and the masculinized selves or body parts that they had projected onto their lovers. Their desolation and excruciating pain combined oedipal and preoedipal features. It was *oedipal:* (1) in its repetition of failure with father and confirmation of castrated status, high achievement to the contrary notwithstanding; (2) in its providing a stunted version of positive oedipal gratification in playing the seductive but aim-inhibited role of the wonderful little girl; and (3) in its providing negative oedipal gratification in the sexualized union with mother. It was *preoedipal* in the centrality of the primitive merger with mother that was unconsciously played out in heterosexual relationships; with the undoing of that merger went the loss of the mother's love on the other grounds, such as a failure of reparation and consequently the collapse of their joint grandiosity; and further, much of their clinging to these men, much of their tolerance of criticism, demand, and abuse, involved the repetition of the early projective-introjective relationship with their mothers, the seductively cruel, pregenital love relationship of early infancy. Thus, their way of being in love with men could be viewed as helping them to keep in check overt expressions of their multileveled omnipotence, rage, and envy, and at the same time obscure their relatively retarded individuation and engenderedness. Their painful and costly victimization in this sexist world was therefore not without its rewards in defensive security and unconscious pleasure.

Although I believe my account of descriptive features and developmental and dynamic factors to be the valid outcome of helpful work with one subset of analysands, I do not claim to have laid out the necessary and sufficient conditions for a well-circumscribed disorder of living. Many of the factors I have mentioned turned up in the course of clinical work with women who presented themselves as the crushed, ineffectual victims of powerful, vain, and persecutory mothers. Some high-achieving women seem to attach themselves not to the sadistic-narcissistic type of man described above but rather to men they experience as passive and crippled on the surface—rather like the weak father and the handicapped mother—even though not lacking sadistic and narcissistic tedencies of their own. These women may have experienced less criticism and more idealization during their development. Further, the kind of pairing I have described may be encountered in relationships between men, between women, and in reverse form between men and women. Finally, the intimate relationships of high-achieving women need not be deeply troubled at all. I have written here only about those who have come for therapy and seemed to show one of a number of possible patterns of disturbance.

Whatever the limits may be on making generalizations from my findings, they will be useful to clinicians in following the twists and turns of the unconsciously maintained mazes of power and rage in which women can lose themselves as they try to make their way effectively in a sexist environment. Psychoanalytic work on this kind of tragic situation is of particular moment in our modern era of critical reexamination of relations between the sexes. It seems to increase the possibilities for a liberated and fulfilling existence in the inner word and in society.

2

Male Sexuality and Power

ETHEL SPECTOR PERSON, M.D.

Male psychology is beginning to attract the kind of attention paid to its female counterpart over the past fifteen years. However, while the assumption that female sexual masochism is primary, universal, and defining has been challenged, the popular belief that male sexuality is innately aggressive and sadistic has persisted with minimal questioning.

The cultural stereotype of male sexuality is of a kind of phallic omnipotence and supremacy. At the very least, this view depicts a large, powerful, untiring phallus invested with the power of mastery and attached to a very cool male, long on self-control, experienced, competent, and knowledgeable enough to make women crazy with desire. As Bernie Zilbergeld has said, "It's two feet long, hard as steel, and can go all night" (1978, 23). In the shared cultural fantasy, even the normally reticent female is perceived to be utterly powerless and receptive when confronted by pure macho sexuality.

But phallic power is also viewed as easily corrupted into sexual domination and violence. This is clear in the common depiction of male sexuality in pornography, movies, television, sexual humor, and in much of the major fiction of our time.

Although Kate Millett's *Sexual Politics* (1970) is certainly one of the seminal books in the feminist movement, it is essentially a study of male psychology and a condemnation of the power motive perceived in male sexuality. Millett analyzes the work of four male authors whose descriptions of male sexuality center on ideas of ascendancy and power: Henry Miller, D. H. Lawrence, Norman Mailer, and Jean Genet. According to Millett, "As one recalls both

This chapter was originally published in *Psychoanalytic Inquiry* (1986), vol. 6(1), pp. 3–25. It is reprinted by permission of the publisher and has been very slightly edited for inclusion in this volume.

the euphemism and the idealism of descriptions of coitus in the Romantic Poets (Keats's 'Eve of Saint Agnes') or the Victorian novelists (Hardy, for example) and contrasts it with Miller or William Burroughs, one has an idea of how contemporary literature has absorbed not only the truthful explicitness of pornography, but its anti-social character as well. Since this tendency to hurt or insult has been given free expression, it has become far easier to assess sexual antagonism in the male" (1970, 46). Zilbergeld quotes Harold Robbins, Mickey Spillane, James Baldwin, and others as well as Henry Miller and Norman Mailer to make the same points about the ways in which our culture sees male sexuality as domineering and even violent.

There is currently a genre of popular fiction in which the common thread is heroic, macho, adventurous, and virile. The male preoccupation with this type of literature is comparable to that of women with the romance novel. These female novels are so popular that the word "harlequin," as in the name of the publishing house that issues much of this material, has become a descriptive noun for such books. I would suggest that the equivalent term for the male novel might be "herotica."

A passage from Eric van Lustbader's *The Miko* captures the way in which male sexuality is typically portrayed. The plot hinges on the idea that Akiko, a woman trained in the arcane mystic and martial arts, has sworn to avenge a loved one by killing the hero, Nicholas. She is portrayed as a master assassin in perfect control of her feelings, but her response to Nicholas compels her to have a sexual encounter with him:

> For the first time in her life, Akiko was open to the universe. Nothing in her long, arduous training had caused this ignition inside of her.
>
> She was so dizzy that she was doubly grateful for his strong arms about her. All breath had left her as he had uttered her name, how she ached for him! Her thighs were like water, unable to support her. She felt a kind of ecstacy at his touch she thought only possible in orgasm.
>
> What was happening to her? Swept away, still a dark part of her mind yammered to be heard. What strange force had invaded her mind? What turned her plans of vengeance inside out? What made her feel this way about a hated enemy? (p. 277)

In one remarkable example of "herotica," the hero is so well schooled in the erotic arts that if he hates a woman and wishes to destroy her forever, he makes love to her so skillfully that she knows she will never be satisfied by any other man.

Observers from diverse disciplines have suggested either that macho sexuality is sanctioned—glorified really—as the cultural ideal or, conversely, that it is an accurate portrayal of male sexuality. Rollo May says that in addition to the cultural directive for males to be assertive in general, "the popular prescription for male sexuality is also heavily invested with assertion and activity. The man is supposed to be constantly on the move and on the make. The image of the tireless seducer differs only in style and degree from that of the rapist" (1980, 131). The only question is whether the male attracts and seduces the female or overpowers and forces her. May's view echoes Susan Brownmiller's in *Against Our Will: Men, Women, and Rape* (1976). Brownmiller declares: "Throughout history no theme grips the masculine imagination with greater constancy and less honor than the myth of the heroic rapist. As man conquered the world, so too he conquers the female. Down through the ages, imperial conquest, exploits of valor and expressions of love have gone hand in hand with violence to women in thought and deed" (p. 320).

As already noted, there is an assumption, particularly in some of the feminist literature, that the pervasive macho image accurately reflects the individual male's preoccupation with sexual domination and violence. Sexual violence, including wife abuse, marital rape, and rape, is regarded as the tip of the iceberg, an indicator of the innate male propensity to sexual sadism. This position postulates a continuum between male sexual violence and normal male sexuality.

Yet there has been no systematic attempt to assess the pervasiveness of the macho stereotype as an ego ideal in individual men or the extent to which it dominates the interior fantasy life of men. The larger question is whether the domination and sadism fantasies and impulses one does see are primary. Is male sexuality inherently aggressive, or are the aggressive feelings a reaction to life experiences or compensation for feelings of inadequacy?

In this chapter, I challenge the popular cultural notion that male sexuality is by nature aggressive. To some extent, males' conscious sexual fantasies, as revealed in both clinical work and nonclinical survey studies, do resemble the cultural stereotype. But there are significant differences. First, sexual violence and aggression are not primary fantasy themes for many males; some men do not have fantasies of sexual domination. Furthermore, it would be naive to restrict one's conclusions about male sexuality to conscious wishful fantasies alone. Fearful fantasies must also be taken into account. Wishful fantasies are often about domination and aggression, but they are also about size, hardness, endurance, skill, and willing females. Fears are partly the negative reflections of the wishful fantasies; as such, they focus on inadequate penis size, impotence, lack of skill, fear of female rejection, female damage to the male (vagina dentata fantasies), and homosexual dread. (While unconscious fears do not appear to be fantasies, at least not to those who experience them, they are clearly fantasies or fantasy derivatives.) Most important, data from analyses reveal the unconscious fantasies of patients that underlie conscious wishful and fearful fantasies and suggest the correspondence of these fantasies to developmental events.

The dominant and aggressive theme of male sexual fantasies, and of the macho image in general, may represent a shared cultural ideal to some degree, but it is ego-syntonic or an actual personal ego ideal for only a minority of men. Those men for whom sexual domination is a primary concern generally reveal particular conflicts in their sexual development. The nature and origin of their unconscious conflicts as revealed in psychoanalyses, however, point to the universal "faultlines" in more typical ("normal") male development.

Drawing on conscious male wishful and fearful fantasies and some clinical material that reveals their interplay, I am here attempting to place power and domination concerns in perspective by proposing that control over the penis and the sexual object is a central concern in male sexuality, more fundamental than aggression and intimately intertwined with the genesis of castration anxiety. The emphasis on the power of the phallus and power remedies vis-à-vis the female (or male) partner are, at least in part, compensatory responses to anxieties engendered in the male developmental experience. These anxieties must be understood as an amalgam of castration anxiety, fear and envy of both sexes, and the fear (or experience) of loss of the object and loss of love.

My focus is on some of the sources of the central anxieties concerning control that have been less extensively explored than castration anxiety. The case material I present suggests one set of developmental factors that predisposes men, on the one hand, to unusually intense sexual anxiety and fear of loss of the object and, on the other hand, to sexual dominance and macho sexuality as compensatory mechanisms. Male sexual aggression may be almost universal, but it is a transitory and generally inconsequential stage in childhood unless it is reevoked and consolidated in a series of power strategies as a defense against sexual anxieties. In this respect, male sexual aggression may be viewed as analogous to primary and secondary female sexual masochism.

Conscious Fantasies

Fantasy life is extremely varied, and sexual fantasies are no exception. Among men, the wide range (even within our culture alone) is well documented in popular books and professional journals. Despite this variability, there are fundamental differences between males and females in fantasy life.

Men, like women, have sexual fantasies that may be diffusively romantic, but males also produce more fantasies that are explicitly sexual and often impersonal; autonomy, mastery, and physical prowess are central concerns (May, 1980). Male fantasies frequently portray domination, as the widespread rape, control, and transgression themes would indicate, but they may also be passive, submissive, or masochistic in content (Person et al., 1989). In fact, Freud first described "feminine" masochism as it occurred in men (1924).

There are other male fantasies that are at least as common and possibly more so. Two of the most prevalent are fantasies of "the omniavailable woman" and "lesbian" sex. The omniavailable woman is totally accessible. She is often fantasized as lying on a couch awaiting the arrival of her lover, forever lubricated, forever ready, forever desiring. Both from my patients' reports and from the popular and scientific literature, it seems evident to me that for men, the woman's availability, ready sexuality, and unqualified approval constitute a major common thread. It is her availability and enthusiasm that bolster his virility.

Andrew Barclay (1973), in a study on the sexual fantasies of college men and women, noted that "male fantasies sounded like features of *Playboy* magazine or pornographic books, and included elaborate descriptions of the imagined sexual partner. They were stereotyped . . . without personal involvement. Women are always seductive and straightforward, ready to have intercourse at any given [moment]. . . . [The] major emphasis [is] on visual imagery" (p. 205). In men's fantasies, women are viewed as desirable but dispensable. In contrast, as Edward Thorne (1971) points out, women see themselves as both desirable and indispensable. Young boys, prepubescent and pubescent, commonly have fantasies about naked girls available to them in such powerless positions as being bound to a bed (Thorne, 1971). These fantasies often but not always contain elements of sadism (Lukianowicz, 1960). A young boy's sexual fantasies are mainly involved with the exploration and discovery of female anatomy. They are colored by a literal preoccupation with girls. Boys seem generally to fantasize about the sexual compliance of girls or about sexual advances from them. In these fantasies, girls do not complain about the way they are treated but gratefully accept the status of sexual toys.

The same themes continue to be found in young men, although some of the overt force may be reduced. It is the developmental significance of the change in male fantasies as boys grow older—the partial replacement of physical dominance as a theme by the presence of a bevy of willing females—that suggests these fantasies are on a continuum. The common feature is the sexual availability of the female. The fantasy is that girls are really panting for sex; in extreme cases, this accounts for the common defense in rape trials: "She was really asking for it."

Forcing a partner is one way of ensuring her presence. The fantasy of domination in its intent seems to be on a continuum with the fantasied presence of a woman in a perpetual state of sexual readiness, with no other aim than to await the man's sexual advances. Nancy Friday, in her study of write-in fantasies (1980), found that the largest single fantasy category for men was that of sadomasochistic sex. She noted, however, that the intent was not usually to hurt the woman. Control of the woman, even in domination fantasies, is most often in the service of phallic narcissism. It may also protect against the potential threat of castration from the woman. Only rarely is the point to harm the woman for the sake of sadism and violence per se.

The Fantasy Project at the Columbia Psychoanalytic Center for Training and Research (Person et al., 1989), designed to study sexual fantasies and behaviors, has analyzed data from 193 students who responded to a questionnaire. The somewhat striking results suggest a greater predilection for dominance among males as compared to females; 44 percent of the men reported fantasies of forcing a partner to submit to sexual acts, including 11 percent who reported fantasies of torturing a sexual partner and 20 percent of whipping or beating a sexual partner. The comparable figures for women are 10 percent, 1 percent, and 0 percent.

As striking as the sex difference is the number of men who do not report any conscious fantasies of domination: 56 percent. Furthermore, far fewer men report fantasies of actual violence or torture than report domination fantasies. We have not tested the results of an older population, but I would guess that there are progressively fewer fantasies of overt force with increasing age.

A prominent feature of the erotic fantasy life of heterosexual men (though not of homosexual men) is its preoccupation with lesbian themes. Although both male and female heterosexuals fantasize having homosexual sex, essentially it is primarily heterosexual men who also fantasize about observing homosexual encounters involving the opposite sex. Male fantasies that focus on lesbian sex have two major variants. In the first, the sexual encounter is exclusively between the women; in the second, the women are joined by either a male onlooker or a male participant. These fantasies appear to be on a continuum; the transitional fantasy between lesbian sex and threesome sex is the fantasy in which the male is initially an onlooker, then joins in the sex-play. A scene depicting lesbian sex is so much a part of pornographic films intended for heterosexual men that it is almost a convention. The visual depiction of lesbian sex seems to arouse even men who do not have the fantasy independently. In part, the fantasy of two women making love suggests an overabundance of women whose primary interest and sole function are sexual, ensuring that the man will never be humiliated by the absence of a sexual object. At this level, the fantasy is one variant of the fantasy of the omniavailable woman. Like fantasies of women happily making love with animals that have gigantic penises or women masturbating with dildoes, fantasies of lesbian sex portray lusty women. They cannot accuse men of being animals or dirty; they are female versions of the man's own sexual self-image. In part, though, the fantasy reveals an unconscious feminine identification, which is personified in the image of one or the other of the women (Person, 1986).

Conscious Fears: Their Interplay with Cultural "Macho Sexuality"

As already noted, sexual fears are almost mirror images of wishes. A very large number of men feel that their penises are inadequate in either length or girth. This concern appears to be more widespread than female self-doubts about breast size, perhaps more closely approximating female concerns about being fat. Both heterosexuals and homosexuals agonize not just about their physical endowment but about their performance as well, with one significant difference: heterosexuals feel much more threatened by the appearance of another man's erect penis.

As to performance, men worry about getting it up, keeping it up, and satisfying their partners. That they frequently ask the partner, "Did you come?" is testimony to this. It also betrays a basic imbalance in sex: the fact that man's sexual excitement is visible. There is no hiding the failure to achieve an erection, but no certain way to gauge the woman's sexual arousal or orgasm. It is difficult for a man to really know whether he is a good lover, and men are often unable to accept a compliment or reassurance. The fear surfaces in some men's obsessions about their partner's past lovers: "Was he better?" "Did you have more orgasms with him?" "Better orgasms?" and so forth. Of those men confident in their performance, some are so intent on controlling the female that their own participation lacks spontaneity. Some men feel comfortable pursuing their own pleasure only after they have brought the woman to orgasm; and some attain full erection only when the woman is sated.

The most striking feature of the male's sense of inadequacy is his belief that other men are truly in possession of macho sexuality. Such a man feels that macho sexuality is unobtainable for him personally but not that it is a myth. In light of this belief, his own endowment and skills appear even more meager. Many men suffer because of their idealization of the male adolescent experience, the only time perpetual readiness appears to be the rule. But overestimation of other males' sexuality appears to have its deepest roots in the oedipal boy's awe of his father's superior sexual endowment.

To compensate for the sense of genital inferiority, performance anxiety, and fears of female rejection or infidelity, men resort to power remedies in fantasy. Through denial and reversal, the penis emerges as all powerful, performance as extraordinary, and sexual partners as plentiful. Thus, dominance and aggression are reparative themes that betray quite another state of affairs—a fear of sexual powerlessness, female unavailability, and rejection. When I say that the male resorts to power remedies, I use the term "power" not in the sense of a set of impulses to defeat competitors but in the sense of imbuing the penis with mastery and ensuring a source of gratification by supplying a fantasized plethora of lusty women over whom the man is lord.

On one level, macho sexual fantasies are adaptive and counteract underlying fears; at the same time, they aggravate an already pervasive sexual anxiety. Since the man literally believes that other men are doing better, his uncertainty about his sexuality appears to be much more basic than its reputed aggressive content. This is not to deny the aggressive element but to suggest that it is neither universal nor primary.

Living the Life: Clinical Examples of Macho Sexuality

The following clinical vignettes are of patients who lived and idealized some version of macho sexuality entailing multiple partners, lesbian sex, or phallic narcissism. These patients all shared certain conflicts that lie hidden behind the macho defense. While these conflicts are not synonymous with Everyman's erotic sensibility, they are suggestive of faultlines in male development. All these patients were periodically beset with fears about sexual adequacy.

The first two vignettes are extremely brief, simply examples of the different forms macho fantasies may take. The second two are rendered somewhat more fully. All these patients were "lovers" of women, though their need to dominate and their hostility toward women were not far from the surface. None of the patients showed extreme hostility or violence to women. However, I have never had in analysis any man who fell at the violent end of the sexual spectrum. I do not think this is accidental. Such individuals are not likely to present themselves voluntarily for analytic treatment, particularly to a female therapist.

R. M. R. M. fantasied about having sex with two women simultaneously and about lesbian sex, but he did not enact this. What he did instead was to set up his primary mistress and an ancillary mistress in apartments within walking distance of each other and of the apartment he shared with his wife. He essentially established a harem, though the women were unaware of this. He was particularly proud of the fact that he could see his own apartment from those of his mistresses. Despite his sexual bravado, he was not infrequently impotent, an occurrence he generally attributed either to a wish to be elsewhere or to guilt. When either his wife or his primary mistress threatened to leave him, he fell completely to pieces, even going so far as to threaten suicide.

B. D. B. D. always maintained at least two sexual relationships, both of which he considered significant. He never asked the women to have a simultaneous sexual encounter, but be did apprise each of his sexual activities with the other. He was apparently one of those extremely proficient lovers utterly devoted to the sexual fulfillment of his partner during any sexual encounter. His sexual withholding was enacted by his ostentatious alternation of weekends between the women and his refusal to see them during the week.

M. D. M. D., a middle-aged writer of considerable reputation and affluence, sought treatment at the insistence of his wife of fifteen years. She felt it was a sign of his emotional disability that he insisted on an open marriage, which she refused. Their relationship gradually deteriorated, and their time together was spent in petty power struggles with mutual withholding of sex.

In adolescence and early manhood, M. D. had a retarded sexual life, having come out of a repressive religious background, and he was monogamous in his first marriage. It was only when his first wife left him that he embarked on a totally different kind of sexual career. He moved out of a sheltered conservative suburb into a more artistic and bohemian milieu, never again pursued a monogamous path, and always had at least two female friends nearby. It was with some trepidation that he married for the second time, now with the conviction that he would not be faithful. He saw his passion for multiple sexual relationships not as neurotic but as an interest in variety, a sincere appreciation of many different women. He had begun to lie to his wife to avoid conflict but very much resented the fact that he was lying and ultimately felt that it was a bourgeois compromise.

During the treatment he became emotionally involved with another woman. Despite his many dissatisfactions and his new lover's willingness to share him with other women, he maintained that he could not "make it" with either his wife or his mistress. When his wife was out of town he became frightened at being alone with his mistress and arranged to see other women as well. One of his worst fears was that he might suddenly lose all the women with whom he was involved. Being with no one seemed to him the worst fate of all.

He periodically experienced sharp pain in his penis and lived in fear of the time when his sexual powers might fail. He had a glimmer of awareness that his inability to leave his wife or attempt to ameliorate the situation betrayed a conflictual attachment.

S. M.   S. M., a professionally successful man, came into treatment because of recurrent depression. He was extremely proud of his beautiful, well-preserved wife and obviously pleased at her voracious sexual appetite. Although he was morbidly jealous about lovers she had had prior to their marriage, he had initiated threesome sex, primarily with one other woman but occasionally with another man. He enjoyed talking about how much his wife liked these sexual encounters. He was proud of her rapture but also of the fact that she was so clearly at his disposal. Despite her willingness to oblige, he had a number of ancillary lovers, though he in no way regarded this as unfaithfulness.

During his depressions, usually triggered by business reversals, he became impotent. His impotency was invariably followed by obsessive preoccupation with his wife's former relationships, pathological jealousy, and the suspicion that she was currently unfaithful. He would then reject her and accuse her of being a dog in heat.

He had a series of paired dreams with slight variations. In one dream of the pair, his wife was all-powerful and drove a chariot, while he clung to her feet and she fertilized the land with great streams of water. In the other dream, he controlled the chariot, now pulled by two giant stallions, and dragged his wife along behind him. These oscillations in his perception became rapid, revealing his perception of his wife and himself as locked in a bitter struggle for power, yet yoked together.

To varying degrees, the men I have described perceived themselves as living the macho life. They played out different facets of two prominent macho fantasies: the omnisexual woman and the fascination with lesbian sex. None of these four men initially viewed himself as having ongoing sexual fears or concerns. In fact, their sexual behavior was not only ego-syntonic but idealized, viewed as the emblem of true manhood. Periodically, however, each was subject to intermittent fears about the health and intactness of his penis, impotence, and the loss of a sexual partner. All described themselves, and were described by their partners, as being unusually proficient lovers. This proficiency, particularly in the case of B. D., was seen as an important instrument in maintaining control over their women, despite the women's objection to some of the arrangements. All had experienced in their adolescence or young adulthood what they bitterly regarded as rejection by women. These experiences had not dampened their enthusiasm for women but had made them wary of investing all their emotions in only one.

All hid their dependency needs and narcissistic vulnerability behind a fairly primitive phallic chauvinism; they symbolically controlled their women through phallic mastery and supremacy. The underlying dependence was revealed only in symptomatic outbreaks (anxiety, depression, impotence) when the relationships were on the verge of rupture.

All relied on their wives' (or girlfriends') accounts when reporting their problems to the analyst. There was an explicit belief that the wife was a better observer and reporter. Their faithful repetition of the women's complaints, however, delivered in the most rational way imaginable, gave only lip service to their powers of perception; the emotional significance of the accusations of their female partners was given the lie behind their cool, rational, sincere facade of fair-mindedness.

None of these men had intimate friendships with other men; the emotional reference points of their lives were women. In fact, they had not only excluded "fathers" from their emotional lives but "brothers" as well.

In treatment there was an attempt to establish the same covertly needy, manifestly dismissive or controlling relationship they maintained with their wives. These patients had relatively strong needs to negotiate and switch appointment times, to stop and restart analysis, and to retaliate for the analyst's vacations. Simultaneously, they regarded the (female) analyst as powerful and phallic, though not sexual. All four analyses were distinguished by the marked absence of any well-developed erotic transference (Person, 1985).

Developmental Sources of Feelings of Sexual Inadequacy and Fears of Female Unavailability

What is the source of the male's sense of sexual deficiency and potential "starvation"? Theories of male sexuality are somewhat skewed, focusing almost exclusively on the resolution of the positive oedipal complex. In this standard formulation, the boy avoids the threat of castration from the father by renouncing his mother; he chooses the narcissistic cathexis of his penis over the libidinal cathexis of his mother, thereby preserving and strengthening his phallic narcissism. The fundamental sexual problem for boys is viewed as the struggle to achieve phallic strength and power vis-à-vis other men. Indeed, oedipal themes and fears are explicit in male fantasy life; they are copiously revealed in conscious fantasies, dreams, and analytic associations, leaving little doubt as to their centrality in the male experience.

This formulation is accurate as far as it goes, but by focusing predominantly on the father-son struggle, the threat of castration at the hands of the father and resolution through a powerful paternal identification, the importance of the developmental components of male sexuality is minimized.

Castration anxiety is itself obviously affected by factors other than fear of the father. It is difficult to accept a direct and exclusive link between castration anxiety (at the hands of the father) and fears of female rejection and genital inferiority. There are clearly other sources that accentuate and contribute to these anxious preoccupations.

What is missing from traditional formulations is the impact of the mother-son relationship on sexuality at different developmental stages and the nature of the male's sexual realities at different points in the life cycle. Too often, the female is portrayed more as a prize than a protagonist in the boy's sexual development. There are important contributions to the psychoanalytic literature that focus on the effects of the mother-son relationship (Horney, 1932, for example), but these studies and the effects on male sexuality they detail tend to be relegated to footnotes (the exception being studies on perversion, in which some focus on preoedipal issues is inescapable). Even so, the ample evidence of everyday life emphasizes their importance. Another variable is related to the ambiguous masculine identification seen in some men and the degree of feminine identification that may be present.

Freud (1920), Karen Horney (1932), and more recently some French theorists (McDougall, 1980; Chasseguet-Smirgel, 1984) have suggested that the first blow to a boy's sexual narcissism is his inability to secure his mother's sexual love. In other words, the boy's fear of his father and the threat of castration at the hands of his father are not the only factors in the boy's renunciation of his mother. As Freud (1920) suggests, the boy also withdraws his libidinal investment from his mother because he feels he does not have the genital endowment to compete with his father. His sense is that his mother rejects him in favor of his father because his penis is too small. Charles Brenner (1979) makes a similar point, stressing both the narcissistic injury and the depressive affect that may be generated in the phallic-oedipal period and their connection to castration anxiety. Many men never recover from this literal sense of genital inadequacy. It appears that many men are therefore destined to suffer lifelong penis envy.

It was Horney who most fully elaborated this formulation of male sexuality:

The anatomical differences between the sexes lead to a totally different situation in girls and in boys, and really to understand both their anxiety and the diversity of their anxiety we must take into account first of all the children's real situation in the period of their early sexuality. The girl's nature as biologically conditioned gives her the desire to receive, to take into herself; she feels or knows that her genital is too small for her father's penis and this makes her react to her own genital wishes with direct anxiety: she dreads that if her wishes were fulfilled, she herself or her genital would be destroyed.

The boy, on the other hand, feels or instinctively judges that his penis is much too small for his mother's genital and reacts with the dread of his own inadequacy, of being rejected and derided. Thus he experiences anxiety which is located in quite a different quarter from a girl's; his original dread of women is not castration-anxiety at all, but a reaction to the menace of his self-respect. (1932, 355–356)

As Horney notes, the boy suffers a blow to his sense of genital adequacy and consequently to his masculine self-regard. At the same time, he is reminded of earlier frustrations (oral, anal) at the hands of that same mother. Consequently, in accordance with the talion principle, "his phallic impulses to penetrate merge with his anger at frustration, and the impulses take on a sadistic tinge" (p. 356). This might be regarded as nearly universal but essentially transient. If the anger and sadism are great, the female genital (again by virtue of the talion principle) will itself become the source of castration anxiety, and the mother, along with the father, will be seen as a potential castrator.

Horney observed, however, that sexual sadism and fear of the female as castrator were not invariable among her male patients, whereas the anxiety connected to masculine self-regard was almost universal. As she puts it: "According to my experience the dread of being rejected and derided is a typical ingredient in the analysis of every man, no matter what his mentality or the structure of his neurosis" (p. 357).

Horney quotes Freud to the effect that the boy "behaves as if he had a dim idea that his member might be and should be larger" (p. 358). She points to the continuity between the narcissistic blow to the oedipal boy and the adult man's ongoing anxiety about the size and potency of his penis. This mental set has several components: fear that his genitals are inadequate, the corollary fear of female rejection, and a sense of the superior endowment of his rivals.

In addition to the castration anxiety engendered by paternal rivalry, men suffer from a sense of inadequacy in relation to the mother and from fear of her as well. The male's fear of the female, of his inability to please her (and his anger at her), stem from different developmental levels: fear of the preoedipal mother who abandons/engulfs; of the anal mother who intrudes/indulges; of the phallic-narcissistic-level mother who falsely seduces/denigrates masculinity; of the oedipal mother who cannot be fulfilled, rejects, falsely seduces. Out of the amalgam of potential fears arises the male propensity to compensate through sexual fantasies of power and control and through denial of his dependence on female sexual acceptance and participation.

I believe that this formulation delineates an important developmental strand in male sexuality. Yet it remains difficult to substantiate the continuity between hypothetical childhood events and adult fears. We do know, though, that the conjectured events are recapitulated in adolescence by virtue of the male and female adolescents' real situation and again in adulthood by the adult's real situation.

The boy's narcissistic wound—his inability to secure the object of his childhood sexual desire—is recapitulated in adolescence by the hypersexuality of the adolescent male compared to his female counterpart. The typical male adolescent experience is one of perpetual arousal with masturbation as his primary outlet. His arousal and desire come at a time when he is not equipped to maintain a secure sexual relationship easily. This discrepancy reinforces his fears about securing a sexual object and his own genital adequacy. Yet he resents the unavailability of a female partner. Since he assumes that other males are doing better (a derivative of his oedipal defeat), his feelings of inferiority in relation to other men are intensified.

Furthermore, the ambivalence about his control over his genital equipment and sexuality can be traced to physical aspects of the adolescent induction into genitality. In adolescence, the male is overcome by a sexual arousal over which he feels he has little control. While spontaneous erection and ejaculation are best understood as release phenomena, the subjective experience is an ambivalent one. The boy's anxiety arises out of a contradiction: pride in the pleasure and power of the phallus but the simultaneous sense that it is not really under his control.

The idea that the penis has a separate life is reflected in the tendency of young men to personify it by bestowing pet names upon it. Adolescent boys feel dread and shame at inopportune erections. One middle-aged man still described himself as being led around by his "joint." The young man's tragedy has been described as having a gun and ammunition but no control. By the time control is achieved, the ammunition has been taken away. Wet dreams betray the boy's sexuality to his parents, particularly to his mother. He feels he has no privacy.

Partly because self-control is crucial to mastery and partly from gender training, control over his penis—and, through it, over the outside world—has high priority for the boy. Sexuality becomes imbued with issues of control and dominance. Yet the adolescent's sense of lack of control over the penis is never completely resolved. It becomes a locus for symbolic elaboration, predisposing men to fears of impotence or premature ejaculation, the subjective evidence that they are not fully in charge of their members.

How do men cope with these anxieties about performance and female rejection? Collectively and individually, they submerge their fears in an overestimation of male sexuality. Horney speculates, and I concur, that the boy's remedy for the narcissistic mortification implicit in the renunciation of his mother is a defensive phallic narcissism. Identification with the phallic father and his power, and subsequent identification with male sexual strength and independence, form the psychological core of the collective male ideal of male sexuality—macho sexuality. The boy's phallic narcissism, intensified by his adolescent pride in the erectile power of the penis, coalesces with the magical sexual properties with which he has endowed his father and other rivals. Out of this emerges the individual and collective male pride in some version of macho sexuality. (This solution is no doubt reinforced by male gender socialization, or "male bonding.")

Men attempt to assuage their sexual self-doubts through active sexuality (or fantasies of it), in which control over the penis is sought through sexual mastery and control over the sexual object. In his wishful fantasies, the male reverses his self-doubts and anxieties by endowing his penis with supernatural powers, those he once attributed to his all-powerful father.

The fear of female unavailability and rejection leads to compensatory fantasies featuring a cornucopia of sexually available women. We too often take fantasies of the omniavailable woman and their enactments at face value, requiring no further understanding. The male interest in multiple or simultaneous partners is accepted as part of his sexual voraciousness (rapaciousness?). These sexual enthusiasms enter into the collective male ego as part of an idealized macho sexuality. Yet there is something haunting in the fantasies: a denial and reversal of the realities of female sexuality, a magically exaggerated picture of male sexual prowess, and a wistful desire for a different sexual world. In fact, the male appears to project his own sexual desires onto his fantasy females. It is they who are forever randy, perpetually aroused, and ready. Most important, they are always available and never reject him.

Fantasies of the omniavailable woman reveal not only the pressing desire for female availability but the simultaneous desire to erase any one woman's individuality or importance. This obliteration provides reassurance about virility, the "on-call" availability of the sexual object, and the inherent importance of the man vis-à-vis a woman. While the fantasies may sometimes be contaminated by the need to discharge aggression, they are not fueled by it. These are not domination fantasies per se; they are more subtle, revealing the widespread need to bolster the male's subjective sense of control and command. They counter the dread of personal inadequacy, male subordination, and female rejection. The assumption is that women are automatically satisfied and require no special stimulation; they take their pleasure from the male's pleasure. But the fact that the omniavailable female (even in fantasy) is often viewed with condescension, contempt, or even sadism is evidence of the resentment caused by the experience of frustration at the hands of the rejecting mother (and subsequent female objects).

Consequently, men may be internally driven to conquer women, to possess them, and to do so repeatedly. They may also split their sexual desires between several women, usually those seen to be in an inferior position and therefore easily dominated. Men can thereby control the source of sexual gratification and ensure the availability of one sexual object if another vanishes. In fantasy, it will be the woman, not the man, who is humiliated. It is she who will serve him, admire his penis, and submit.

Control of the sexual object serves as a compensatory device for the male child's sense of inadequacy and inferiority vis-à-vis both parents and the humiliation of the unavailability of a sexual object at different points in his life. Out of revenge, the man reverses the humiliation implicit in both his infantile and his adolescent experience: he stands ready to demand sexual availability and fidelity of women while disavowing it for himself.

Normal Resolution Versus Power Resolution

I have suggested a series of developmental issues in understanding male sexuality that are intended not as alternatives to the importance of castration anxiety but as factors that may modify its intensity and interfere with its resolution. Intense and persistent castration anxiety can be the end result of a number of contingent factors. One important factor, beyond the scope of this chapter, is the strong female identification seen in some men, usually as a result of early separation anxiety (see, e.g., Ovesey and Person, 1973). Once it has developed, it may serve as an inhibitory force (one sees here the various forms of sexual inhibitions) or as a stimulus to a variety of reactive solutions, among them the development of a macho sexuality.

By and large, in normal development, castration anxiety, envy and fear of both parents, and fear of female rejection will be largely resolved. In "normal" male sexuality, however, there will remain some latent or moderately active interest in multiple partners and lesbian sex (Person, 1986). In those instances in which there is failure of an adequate father identification or intense pre-oedipal rage (particularly directed against the mother), the (heterosexual) male has a propensity to develop a sexuality imbued with power concerns and preoccupations. These may easily revolve around sadomasochistic inter-actions and in extreme cases may find expression in sexual sadism, either fantasied or enacted. Consequently, it is probably accurate to say that the male tendency to sexual aggression has preoedipal roots related to the fact or the fear of loss of the object or loss of love. But sadism should not be consid-ered the norm among men any more than masochism is the norm among women.

At the same time, there do appear to be specific problems inherent in male development that predispose the majority of men to a central concern with control and power. The impulse to solve these problems through sexual domination grows out of the conviction that only possession and domination will guarantee fulfillment and give surcease to the endless wheel of desire. Ultimately, the power of sexual domination is (mistakenly) utilized to preserve a precarious sense of self. This option is most readily invoked in a cultural milieu that glorifies such domination, takes its apparent strength at face value, and minimizes its compensatory functions.

REFERENCES

Barclay, A. M. 1973. Sexual fantasies in men and women. *Medical aspects of human sexuality* 7:5, 205–216.

Brenner, C. 1979. Depressive affect, anxiety, and psychic conflict in the phallic-oedipal phase. *Psychoanal. Q.* 48:177–197.

Brownmiller, S. 1976. *Against our will: Men, women, and rape.* New York: Bantam.

Chasseguet-Smirgel, J. 1984. *Creativity and perversion.* New York: Norton.

Freud, S. 1920. Beyond the pleasure principle. *S.E.* 18:7–64.

———. 1924. The economic problem in masochism. *S.E.* 19:157–170.

Friday, N. 1980. *Men in love: Male sexual fantasies: The triumph of love over rage.* New York: Delacorte.

Horney, K. 1932. The dread of women: Observations on a specific difference in the dread felt by men and women respectively for the opposite sex. *Int. J. Psycho-Anal.* 13:348–360.

Kinsey, A. C., Pomeroy, W. B., Martin, C. E., and Gebhard, P. H. 1948. *Sexual behavior in the human male.* Phila.: Saunders.

———. 1953. *Sexual behavior in the human female.* Phila.: Saunders.

Lukianowicz, N. 1960. Imaginary sexual partners and visual masturbatory fantasies. *Arch. Gen. Psychiat.* 3:429–449.

May, R. 1980. *Sex and fantasy: Patterns of male and female development.* New York: Norton.

McDougall, J. 1980. *Plea for a measure of abnormality.* New York: International Universities Press.

Millett, Kate. 1970. *Sexual politics.* Garden City, N.Y.: Doubleday.

Ovesey, L., and Person, E. S. 1973. Gender identity and sexual psychopathology in men: A psychodynamic analysis of homosexuality, transsexualism, and transvestitism. *J. Amer. Acad. Psychoanal.* 1:53–72.

Person, E. S. 1985. The erotic transference in women and in men: Differences and consequences. *J. Amer. Acad. Psychoanal.* 13(1): 159–180.

———. 1986. The omni-available woman and lesbian sex: Two fantasy themes and their relationship to male developmental experience, in *The psychology of men: New psychoanalytic perspectives,* ed. G. Fogel, F. M. Lane, and R. S. Liebert. New York: Basic Books, 236–259.

Person, E. S., Terestman, N., Myers, W., Goldberg, E., Salvatore, C. 1989. Gender differences in sexual behaviors and sexual fantasies in a college population. *J. Sex Marital Therapy* 15(3): 187–198.

Thorne, E. 1971. *Your erotic fantasies.* New York: Ballantine.

van Lustbader, E. 1984. *The Miko.* New York: Villard Books.

Zilbergeld, B. 1978. *Male sexuality.* New York: Bantam.

3

Two Successful Characterologic Adaptations to Aggression

HELEN C. MEYERS, M.D.

Aggression, hatred, and violence are rampant today, as they have always been, and trying to understand them is very much on our minds: the violence in our city streets; serial murders; the viciousness of power struggles in politics and other institutions; the bloody wars between neighboring countries and between competing factions within countries; the Holocaust—a topic we have been able to think about only many years after its actual horrifying occurrence. Much has been written and many questions have been asked about why man seems to be the only one of earth's creatures with the urge to hate. Explanations have been offered: an inborn destructive drive; repair for and reaction to personal, economic, and political impotence, helplessness, and frustration; identification with the aggressor—that is, someone else's aggression; the joining of a group because of a charismatic leader, with the superego taken over by the group to permit a socially acceptable outlet for the individual's own aggression; even apocalyptic fantasies of world destruction in order to build a whole new, better world. None is fully satisfactory. Nor do we seem to understand fully the opposite: why some individuals and countries (like Denmark during World War II) do not seem to feel or need to participate in this hatred, violence, and aggression—beyond negative explanations of superego inhibition and fear of punishment, on the one hand, and generalizations of temporarily inspired leadership or unbiased educational systems (as in Denmark), on the other.

It is my hope that we will get closer to some understanding of aggression if we narrow our focus away from large issues to the individual, from the extreme to the more ordinary. In this chapter, then, I address not extreme aggression, violence, and hatred but issues in the characterologic handling of ordinary aggression, in others and in ourselves in everyday life.

Definition of Aggression

The term *aggression* comes from the Latin *ad gradi*, "to go forward in steps"; the original meaning was based on the battle tactic of the Roman legion to attack *ad gradi*—that is, in a solid line stepping forward. According to the *Oxford English Dictionary*, *to aggress* means "to approach" or "to make attack on," but *aggression* is defined solely as an "unprovoked attack, an assault." According to the *Psychoanalytic Glossary* (Moore and Fine), it refers to "a hostile action or behavior"; but for Lionel Trilling (1973), it is more benign; it is "the expression of the will which is directed outward upon resistant or challenging objects or situations." These definitions, although leaning toward the destructive aspects of the word, include nondestructive concepts as well and certainly include adaptive functions. This dual significance, then, addresses one of the confusions about aggression: is it always destructive? or does it include nondestructive aspects, such as mastery or assertiveness? Is it maladaptive or adaptive?

Eli Marcovitz (1973), for instance, considers aggression an umbrella term, referring to a seven-step hierarchy of behavior in relation to objects, summarized as:

1. Curiosity, alertness, and exploration, thus the motor for all activity
2. Self-assertion
3. Assertion of dominance
4. Exploitation, which may be destructive but is not necessarily
5. Hostility, with the intention to *destroy* or hurt the object only as a *secondary* aim, the primary purpose being different, that is:
   a. to accomplish a goal, like killing for food (instrumental hostility)
   b. to overcome that which frustrates
   c. in reaction to a threat of trauma (defensive hostility for survival)
   d. in response to a challenge when any of the above are challenged (reactive hostility)
6. Hatred (violence), with injury or *destruction* of the object as the *primary* aim for a number of reasons:
   a. betrayal of love or trust: love turned to hatred
   b. being shamed or humiliated: narcissistic injury
   c. envy or jealousy: a feeling of righteousness at being deprived
   d. the bad self projected onto the other: repudiated, unacceptable, unconscious impulses put onto the other, now-hated object
7. Sadism: *pleasure* in hurting and *destruction*

Henri Parens (1980), as discussed elsewhere in this volume, has described four currents in aggression in the push from symbiosis through separation individuation.

1. *Nonaffective destructiveness*, where there is neither pleasure nor anger, but destruction in the service of self-preservation

2. *Nondestructive* current, which includes the exploratory and motor-muscular activity of the one-year-old, with the aim to assert oneself, to control and master oneself and the environment
3. *Hostile destructive* current, which involves the unpleasure-related discharge of destructiveness and rage reaction
4. *Sadism:* pleasure-related destructiveness

Rollo May has described an ascending hierarchy in reaction to increasing frustration and obstacles: from assertion to aggression to hostility to violence.

Most writers point out the essential need for human aggression in both its nondestructive and destructive forms. Without the nondestructive type of aggression there would be no curiosity or exploration, no impetus or drive toward learning and development, no energy or power for mastery and self-assertion and sense of self. Destructive aggression, however, also has its adaptive uses. What Marcovitz (1973) calls "hostility," for example, is essential in the service of self-preservation—such as in the forceful removal of obstacles, frustration or the threat of trauma, and killing for food—as well as being necessary for certain aspects of infantile development. While we may deplore violence, even hostile destructive aggression has its uses in the psychic balance in the discharge of rage outward, preventing or relieving inward-directed aggression, which could lead to depression, suicide, or other masochistic disorders.

Origin of Aggression

The second major controversy on theories of aggression concerns its origin. Freud originally conceived of aggression as the active, assertive, power component of the erotic drive (1915). By 1920 *(Beyond the Pleasure Principle)*, however, as a result of his puzzlement over war and man's destructiveness, he had ideated aggression as being a separate instinct of destruction—the "death instinct," functioning by way of the repetition compulsion to push for a return to the inorganic state, according to the Nirvana principle. Later analysts—except Melanie Klein (1952) and her followers—discarded the concept of a death instinct but accepted the idea of an inborn aggressive drive (Hartman, Kris, and Loewenstein, 1949). One group of analysts, however, conceptualizes this as a drive with its own maturational vicissitudes, while another group sees it as an inborn potential only that requires frustration or attack to develop into true aggression—defining aggression as the reaction to obstacles to be overcome (Rizzuto et al., 1991). Developmentalists would, I believe, come down on the side of aggression as a potential to be developed. Or, as John McDevitt (1983) has put it: biologic urges and wishes, if frustrated, turn into anger and hostility, that is, the affects and behavior of aggression.

My own preference is to use the term *assertion* for what has been described as nondestructive or nonhostile aggression and reserve *aggression* for anything tinged with destructiveness or hostility. As I see it, we are born with a drive toward assertion, important for curiosity, growth, and general "push" and mastery. Only when frustrated, threatened, or attacked does this assertion become destructive or hostile aggression in reaction. This aggression, then, manifests itself in the need for dominance, anger, rage, hate, destructiveness, violence, and sadism (pleasure in hurting and destroying), in ascending order of intensity. Of course, frustration being inevitable in our growing up, reactive aggression is inevitable and ubiquitous, and thus the argument of inborn versus reactive (nature versus nurture) exists in theory only. In this chapter, then, I address the everyday characterologic handling of what I call aggression that is essentially of the hostile or destructive variety, although it may also involve aggression in the service of self-definition (nondestructive or self-assertion), as well as self-preservation (instrumental aggression or nonaffective destruction) in the borderline patient.

Two Types of Characterologic Adaptation to Aggression

For some time now I have been interested in observing two particular, very common and successful but very different characterologic constellations dealing with everyday aggression. Though very different, they have some things in common: they both apparently deal with aggression from the *outside* but, of course, are based on how internal aggression is dealt with; they are both behaviors frequently seen in very *successful* people, though, of course, not exclusively so; they both involve manipulation of the object, predominantly unconsciously, resulting in a subtle, or not so subtle, *power* over others.

Type 1

A, a woman highly successful in many areas, came for analysis for reasons consciously not related to the issues under discussion, although clearly unconsciously they were not unrelated. At times extraordinarily charming, at other times cool and distant, she was highly intelligent, the head of a prestigous law firm, and a concert-quality pianist. However, she had not succeeded in an earlier musical career, had married relatively late, and had sexual and gender difficulties. I will not discuss either her exact initial complaints nor the analysis as such. I will bring up only a few selected aspects of the case that are relevant to the issue of handling aggression.

The patient, though firmly established and respected, would repeatedly experience a threat or attack from a colleague, subordinate, or rival attorney. She would then counterattack with devastating, steely fury and intimidation and would demolish the opponent. Then she would extend a warm hand, literally and emotionally, to the beaten opponent and invite him or her into her inner circle, so to speak, to which the other again and again would respond with pleasure and gratitude and pride. The former opponent, let us call him B, would then become a loyal, admiring, even idealizing supporter of A. This is different from fearful and angry submission in the recipient (B) but instead involved pleasure and increased self-respect in B and genuine admiration for A from the new supporter (B).

I am sure everyone has seen such a constellation in their own clinical and social experience. It is a common constellation, observable in some successful politicians (even Hitler seemed to fit this description in relation to his inner circle), heads of boards in industry and successful administrators, sometimes applicable to a child-abusing parent, recorded in television dramas (such as "L.A. Law"), and even used by some well-known therapists as a treatment technique. I am thinking of a particular, very successful family therapist who would confront—I might say attack—a patient harshly and then symbolically put a protective, loving arm around him or her. His patients usually responded with admiration, respect, and genuine affection.

These people, like my patient A and other similar cases of mine, are ever watchful of significant people around them, paranoidly safeguarding against a constant expectation of danger, which is projected rage from an ever-available supply of inner rage in the first place. What apparently is involved dynamically, then, is that there is an upsurge of internal aggression, an unacceptable bad self representation, which needs to be eliminated by externalization, that is, split off and projected outward, for self-preservation, to the other, while the good inner self is retained. This is a kind of projective identification, as the silver thread of control of the object is maintained and the aggression is utilized by the self. The "bad" outer object is then demolished; that is, the bad object, which is the projected former bad self, is defeated by the good, and the threat of aggression from inside and outside is temporarily eliminated. This now permits the good internal self to relate in a loving way to the object, which is no longer experienced as bad. Another conceptualization is that some of the built-up rage and aggression is abreacted and the internal aggressive intensity lessened, which now permits a nonthreatened and nonthreatening libidinal attachment. This, then, is a genuine, positive outreach by A, not just a manipulation, although there is unconscious manipulation of the self by the externalization, and of the bad external object by attack and seduction. Added to this, the maneuver permits narcissistic repair for the vulnerable, threatened self of A by way of a new sense of mastery and power, by victory and control over the now diminished, weak, and humiliated object: The now aggrandized self-image, with increased self-esteem, permits the self to be more generous, offering kindness and support to the other. Once the other is then included in the loving or narcissistic bond, any further aggression (in A) needing to be eliminated may then be projected onto a third party, and the process may or may not be repeated.

One might, to be neat, be tempted to liken to first step in this process to "identification with the aggressor" (A. Freud, 1936) and the second to "seduction of the aggressor" (Loewenstein, 1957). It is, however, not as simple as it might seem. While patient A may, by projection, *perceive* the other as the aggressor and then defend herself by assimilating the other's (B's) aggression and respond by a reversal of roles, the aggression is really predominantly from inside A. Often, however, there is in the background an identification with a primary parental object perceived as exercising power and control, which constitutes one form of identification with the aggressor. The importance of such identification with a parent aggressor in the children of aggressive parents, leading to an intense need for power and domination over others, was stressed in relation to the Nazi phenomenon in cases presented at the International Psychoanalytical Association Congress in Hamburg some years ago (Eckstaedt, 1986), and in our case was related to an identification with a dominant, controlling father.

As for seduction of the aggressor, at the point where patient A reaches out lovingly, the other (B) is actually no longer experienced as the aggressor needing to be seduced but as a good object, at least for the moment. At most, we could think of the maneuver as containing an element of preventive seduction of a potential future aggressor. One might, on the other hand, liken the whole sequence to Rudolph Loewenstein's (1957) description of the infantile sequence of provocative teasing and smiling in playful aggression and seduction of the aggressor parent, which he postulates to be a form of protomasochism. Our case, however, is hardly playful, and the whole interpersonal sequence seems closer to a sadomasochistic interaction, with patient A as the sadistic partner experiencing some excitement in the aggression, and partner B perhaps experiencing some masochistic excitement in submission, buying love with pain and humiliation; and, of course, there would be mutual identification. However, while no doubt there are sadistic and masochistic elements involved, it seems to me that the character structures of the people who respond positively to these maneuvers on A's part are too variable to consider this mechanism of masochism as the complete explanation. Of course, not everybody responds positively to A's maneuvers—although it is amazing how many do—which may be owing to an intuitive, careful selection by A as to who she tries this on. In the rare situation where I have seen it not to work, A turns away from B quickly and angrily, without hesitation, regret, or further attempts at reconciliation. The former object of attack and embrace (B) now either ceases to exist for A or becomes the permanent object of paranoid, destructive denigration.

Now let us consider what these particular coping mechanisms may be related to genetically. First let us look at the one who initiates the sequence (A). My general conclusions, of course, must be speculative; but specifically, in my particular patient A, there was the early loss of a significant object: her father. We know that such a loss will be processed intrapsychically by the patient, not only as the traumatic event in itself, but more importantly as determined by what went on before and after in terms of the quality and content of significant object relations with the lost object himself as well as with other available objects. In my patient, there was a mixture: there were other deprivations in inadequate object-relation experiences related to a cool, contained mother, as well as some gratifying experiences with other family members. This combination resulted in a mixture of helpless and self-deprecatory self-images as well as compensatory grandiose self-images, periodic all-good and all-bad object images together with some more solid self and object representations. In other words, there were narcissistic and borderline features together with some good ego strength. The patient (A) seemed to have processed the object loss, incomplete mourning, and related experiences with intense *rage*, outrage, and a sense of deprivation with a strong hunger for objects to replace the loss, as well as with some *hope* for the establishment of a solid attachment. This combination appeared to have its derivatives in her current, easily mobilized rage and aggression and view of the world as depriving and attacking—as well as her successful reaching out for reestablishment of attachment with genuine longing and warm feelings.

Of course, the process is not as simple as the direct transposition of the early experience. The intensity of need for power and control, for example, also related to the incomplete mourning and identification with the lost father—who was perceived as powerful, harsh, and controlling—as well as to her need to reverse the process and angrily undo and control all losses. (This early loss and identification also contributed to some of her sexual and gender difficulties.) Furthermore, the timing and nature of her early deprivations and trauma led not only to the narcissistic and borderline features referred to earlier but also involved the development of anal defensive features of need for control of herself and power and domination over others. Guilt over her sadistic aggression, however, though it contributed somewhat to her at times low self-image, seemed to play a relatively minor role.

This particular successful combination of dealing with aggression on A's part—of attack followed by embrace, resulting in idealization and attachment from the other (B)—is clearly different, as noted earlier, from pure aggression, which would more likely result in only fearful, angry submission from the other. The successful combination described seems to involve some warmth in A from an early object—a good, internalized object, in addition to the described object loss and deprivation, a warmth to which others can respond.

Intriguingly, this sequence seems to me not unrelated to Margaret Mahler's (1975) concept of normal infantile ambitendency in the rapprochement phase: anger mixed with affection, with its alternating behavior of angry pushing away and loving reattachment. This theoretical connection might be meaningful in relation to my patient (A) in terms of possible interference with the normal passing of ambitendency in the resolution of the rapprochement phase in A because of the object loss and related developmental interferences experienced by A at the time of rapprochement. This would also be conceptually compatible with the narcissistic and borderline features observed in the patient.

I am not suggesting that all people using this one–two step of dealing with aggression have had early object loss, nor that all people with early object loss develop this mechanism. Although my material is suggestive and I have seen a number of such cases that did involve early or even later object loss, I am at this point only describing and theorizing about aspects relevant to this particular case. In other people, other issues, such as identification, anal issues, or even entirely different issues may be more important, partially or exclusively.

Now to B, the partner and object or recipient of this attack-embrace. Here, too, my data and conclusions come from my own and supervisory patients who seem to have responded positively to such maneuvers in their lives and from observations of everyday life—as well as from the characters in A's story. While my interest in these pairs was primarily in A's impressively successful handling of aggression—and thus the recipients of A's maneuvers are less clearly sculpted out, primarily because they vary so in their character structures—they, too, deserve attention here. As mentioned earlier, surely there are masochistic elements involved in B: the buying of love with pain, the paying a price of humiliation for ultimate pleasure, even some erotization of the process. As also mentioned above, however, the character structures of these responders (B) are too varied, in my experience—the same response too common in different people—for me to consider masochism as the total explanation. I think the answers are more universal and at the same time more specific: What I have observed is at first a response of fear of the aggressor, a sense of helplessness, then reactive rage and guilt. B feels helplessly demolished but also guilty for his reactive rage and often experiences some sense of acceptance of a primary responsibility for the attack by A, based on his own general sense of guilt as well as a reaction to the projective identification, that is, he feels as though he has become the bad object. When A then holds out her hand, B feels relieved of his fear of further attack but also relieved of his guilt because he has been forgiven—that is, the bad object has been withdrawn from within him; he has paid his price and now is reestablished in someone's powerful good graces. His superego is temporarily handed over to the aggressor, who can punish but also forgive. In some cases the aggressor becomes the permanent *ego ideal* for the recipient. B feels forgiven, loved by his ideal, and protected by this strong aggressive figure, as well as basking in his new participation in the narcissistic orbit of the powerful aggressor, A. This constitutes a new alliance with the aggressor, raising his self-esteem and feeling of well-being. Having been enabled to overcome former guilt and reactive rage and feeling loved now by the former aggressor, A, because of A's genuine reaching out for attachment, B responds with freed libidinal attachment, resulting in loving admiration as well as idealization of A. Raised from the depths of humiliation, B is now more ready and available to respond positively, to appreciate, admire, adore. This is the opposite of Racine's famous quote in *Le Cid:* "De la place élevée d'où tombe mon honneur," loosely translated as: The bigger they are the harder they fall. Here the truism reads: The smaller or the lower they are the higher they can be lifted.

The important point, however, is that this reaction seems almost universal in the recipient of the attack-embrace approach and not limited to any one particular character structure in B. I think it has universality because we all have some masochism or vulnerability to guilt, some narcissistic needs or interest in power and the restitution of primary omnipotence (by being included in A's narcissistic orbit), and have a remnant of wanting to be loved and protected by a powerful "mommy" or a wish for reestablishment of a connection—or even reunion—with the omnipotent mother of the practicing or rapprochement phase.

This entire sequence and interaction seems to be one very successful way of using and dealing with aggression.

Type 2

I now turn to a very different behavior of dealing with external aggression, something I call *defusion* or *detoxification* of aggression. My original term was unsatisfactory since it seemed to imply submission to or seduction of the aggressor, which is not what I have in mind here. This behavior does not involve submission, surrender, or masochistic self-damage or depreciation. These type 2 people handle other people's aggression easily, without combative, hostile response; they tend to put others at ease and are experienced by others as nonthreatening. Yet they are successful and respected by others, by both aggressive and passive people. This seems to involve an inner security in the person.

I'll call this type 2 person E. E seems to have an ability *not* to feel destroyed by another's attack as well as to have empathy for the other (let us call him F). F's hostile aggression, thus, while acknowledged, is seen by E in the context of the larger picture, which includes the other person's (F's) needs and fears as well as positive qualities. This conceptualization seems somewhat related to Jacob Arlow's (1973) concept of "compassionate identification," which includes empathy and sympathy for the other—that is, the ability to feel how others would feel and feel bad with them and for them—as an essential part of a solid, mature superego. E is thus able spontaneously to respond emotionally to F's vulnerabilities and assets—with support and encouragement, or just nonjudgmentally—thus engaging the aggressor, F, on a level that raises self-esteem and security in F, enabling F in turn to respond more positively. It thus may deflect, lessen, or defuse the need for hostile aggression on F's part. As the saying goes, it takes two to tango or to fight. While this may constitute a manipulation of the other (F) and may even give E some power over F, this is unconscious and E's reactions are genuine. The fact is, people like E react more comfortably to and elicit less aggression toward them from others.

I think we all have met such people, in our patients, our friends, in literature or film, but we do not quite believe them to be real. "They look good," we say, "but it is only on the surface"—the result, perhaps, of reaction formation; of unconscious fear of aggression and castration; of inhibition due to a strict superego that does not permit aggression; of guilty repression of hostile wishes; of masochistic redirection of rage against the self in the form of depression; or displacement of aggression of which we are unaware. This may, of course, be so. In fact, these dynamics are probably frequently involved. Or it may involve a quite different set of dynamics, a matter of narcissistic grandiosity in these people where the real world, as is, is meaningless, unimportant, or to be ignored: other people and their vagaries, including their aggression, are too insignificant to count or be responded to. Indeed, others often go along with such a grandiose narcissistic attitude, where they themselves and their aggression are grandly ignored, that is, they respond favorably with less aggression. As we know, grandiosity and narcissism are appealing to the unsatisfied narcissism in all of us.

However, I think there are also other important factors. I am suggesting that the people I am discussing (like E) actually have less aggression within themselves, that is, aggression of the destructive kind, though not less assertion of the adaptive or constructive kind, the latter enabling them to be successful and respected as well. This would be due, I think, to particularly good early object relation experiences that permitted these people to form abundant good internal self and object representations, to establish more than ordinary solid self and object constancy, and thus to create a workable, harmonious inner world and an external world image as a reflection thereof—the expectation of a good world according to E. This expectation would then be responded to favorably by others since the hope for a good world has not yet become extinct in any of us. All of which would lessen the need in the people I am discussing (like E) to attack or counterattack and enhance their ability to be giving, from a fund of good feeling.

Particularly important seems to be an identification with a successful, nondestructively assertive parent. My patient E, a successful physician, for example, had very good early interactions with both his parents and with the rest of his family, who provided adequate limits as well as appropriate loving-libidinal and self-esteem-narcissistic gratification, reflecting back to him their pride, acceptance, and approval of him. This led, by way of identification, internalization, or reaction, to very positive internal self and object representations and good intrapsychic object relations. The patient particularly identified with his successful and strong, gentle but not passive, caring father. The "goodness" of his father may, of course, have been the result of all kinds of compromises in the father's inner world, such as repression of rage and guilt owing to a harsh superego, but the patient's identification with his father, despite some oedipal issues, was mostly unambivalent, both in his ego ideal and in his real self-image as part of his character identity.

An interesting question is what happens to the reactive hostile aggressive urges, the rage that does get stirred up temporarily, even in these easy people (like E) as the result of inevitable frustrations or attacks. The aggression may be expressed hostilely directly, but more often it seems to just disappear. It may, of course, simply be repressed, displaced, or held in check in a more or less stable compromise formation by means of any of the other familiar defense mechanisms. It may, however, also be conceptualized as being eliminated or inactivated in becoming permanently fused with or balanced by a preponderance of available libido, in accord with Freud's (1924) concept of the variously balanced fusion of libido and aggressive drive. Another, and to me more congenial, way of putting this would be that the new bad, aggressively invested self or object images would be balanced and bound, and thus permanently immobilized, by the preponderance of internal good or libidinally invested self and object images.

Yet I would like to go a step further. It has been postulated that the individual must have had some good early experience—let us say with mother—some internalized good object representation to call on, to recall, to attach to, in order to be able to experience trust in the present, to experience the good object in the present. Similarly, it seems to me, current "bad" experiences, "bad" objects and self-images invested with hostile aggression, will also need to call on earlier, aggressively invested images for support and substance. I would like to suggest, then, the possibility that such current reactive hostile aggression, or aggressively invested self and object images, gets destroyed or "dispersed" and actually disappears in these people (like E), where there are not sufficient bad internal images to attach to, and the preponderance of good internal self and object representations overwhelm and thus eliminate the new negative ones—a conceptualization similar to the concept proposed by Klein (1952) that the aggressively invested internal object could destroy the good, only in reverse. In less theoretical language, this would mean that all past and ongoing positive experiences and images of the self and the other would emotionally and rationally so outbalance the temporary, new, current bad experience, that the temporarily aroused anger and aggression cannot find a foothold and disappear as quickly and completely as they came. I am aware that this theoretical formulation is a rather fanciful concept, since even the well-known notion of the bad inner object destroying the good object is only a construct of a fantasy, a fantasy of fear and internal battle, in patients with lower-level pathology (borderline or narcissistic personality disorders), and not a reality. But the reactive anger or hostile aggression in the particular group of people (like E) I have been discussing does seem to evaporate totally, requiring no apparent energy to keep it away, nor does it appear to remain stored away, available for reemergence, as it would in the "return of the repressed." Rather it is like the aggression spreading itself upon the wind until it no longer exists.

This formulation is not to suggest that E has no problems. He will have his share of adaptive and deviant compromise solutions, with any number of content distortions in his self and object images and object relations. His problems, however, do not particularly lie in the area of aggression, which is the only part I am addressing here. If we think of aggression as primarily the result of frustration or the building up of bad frustrating and frustrated internal objects and self-images, then the metapsychological formulation suggested above of the elimination of the negative in the well-nourished ego, having been filled with good early objects that fortify, to a degree, against the influence of aggression, seems to have some usefulness. In contrast to A, described earlier, E would differ exactly in this amount of good early inner objects and self-images built up through good early object relations, need gratification or minimal optimal frustration and identification with good internalized, originally external objects. Whereas A developed much aggression and distrust and bad inner objects and self representations due to early frustration and bad object relation experiences and identifications, which then lead to easy rearousal of these images and of aggression. However, it needs to be stressed that A, too, has her share of genuine good internal objects and good internal object relations, which enable her to proceed to the second step in handling aggression, as described.

Further Defenses and Early Defensive Behavior in Coping with Aggression

I have singled out for in-depth discussion two particular, successful characterologic ways of handling aggression of everyday life that have been of special clinical and theoretical interest to me. There are, of course, many other well-known and much discussed adult ways of coping with, reacting to, and defending against aggression from within and without.

McDevitt (1983) has pointed out that already in the practicing and rapprochement phase of separation-individuation the toddler has coping mechanisms for dealing with internal aggression; he describes certain modifications of angry behavior as *defensive behaviors*. These modifications include inhibition, displacement or deflection, turning on the self, fusion with libido, and ambitendency. These certainly look like precursors of later adult defenses in coping with aggression, after formation of the superego, which is one of the main motivational agencies in dealing with aggression. These adult defenses include repression, reaction formation, displacement, projection, fusion with libido in the id, and self-punishment or masochism. We are all familiar with these coping devices in adults and certainly with their manifestations in the treatment situation: take, as a simplified example, a patient who clearly is furious at the analyst but cannot get in touch with his anger—this is repression. Instead the patient may expound on his loving, admiring feelings for the therapist, which is reaction formation, but then goes home and picks a fight with his wife, which constitutes displacement, or has a car accident on the way home from the session, that is, punishes himself, or is sure the therapist is angry at him when he arrives at the next session, which equals projection. Or consider the patient who is unable to let himself succeed or enjoy success outside therapy, besides not permitting himself to get better or feel good, despite getting better, in treatment; this is the negative therapeutic reaction. This negative therapeutic reaction, in addition to other meanings and functions, such as maintenance of object relations and need for self-definition, usually involves angry refusal to accept something good from the therapist (narcissistic defense) and almost always serves superego self-punishment for anger (masochism). Then, of course, there is the patient who does permit himself direct, subtle (or not so subtle) expressions of hostility toward the analyst, such as provocative behavior in the session, repeated demands and questions, discussing the therapist unflatteringly, though humorously, outside the treatment, or has occasional temper outbursts in the session. I do not need to describe the well-known superego role in the unconscious regulation of internal aggression in character pathology in general, particularly in depression where aggression is turned inward, in obsessive-compulsive character disorders where there is inhibition of aggression, in passive-aggressive character disorders where we find alternating inhibition and expression of aggression, or in masochistic character disorders, which involve self-punishment.

As for my two types of successful handling of everyday aggression, some of the defense mechanisms described above clearly are at work. Repression, displacement, projection, and direct expressions of hostility play their part in type 1, while reaction-formation and fusion of aggression and libido may be implicated in type 2, and sadomasochism may be operative in both types. So much for internal aggression, aggression from *within*.

There are several well-known mechanisms for dealing with external aggression, aggression from *without*, in particular two mechanisms that I have already referred to in my discussion here, but that would benefit from further clarification: Anna Freud's "identification with the aggressor" and Loewenstein's (1957) "seduction of the aggressor," both originally described as normal infantile mechanisms on the way to adult superego formation or potential pathologic masochism, but both also applicable to adult defensive functioning in relation to external aggression.

Identification with the Aggressor

Anna Freud conceptualized this as an infantile way of handling aggression from the outside, from the powerful adult world, by defensively taking over or assimilating the aggressor and aggression. This concept was a fairly extended one, much more inclusive than commonly thought and encompassing a variety of manifestations:

1. Making magical gestures, consciously or unconsciously, in imitation of the dreaded *aggressors* in order to join them and become one of them
2. Identifying with the *aggression* itself, that is, doing something aggressive in order to feel in control of aggression
3. Identifying with the *strength* of the aggressor, such as wearing the insignia of masculine strength

4. *Reversal* of roles: Becoming the attacker, in reaction to anticipating criticism or attack from the other and therefore attacking the potential attacker first; or, by displacement, attacking someone else, usually someone weaker, as if they were the powerful potential attacker.

It has only been in more recent discussions between Anna Freud and Joseph Sandler (1985), that it has been acknowledged that some of this "external" aggression may really be a projection of inner "badness" to the outside. This is not unrelated to the concept of *projective identification*, wherein, by an internal split and projection, the person retains and becomes the good self who can pronounce judgment on and attack the split-off bad other, the projected bad self, while keeping control of and connection with the split-off bad self. While having the appearance of being moral, according to Anna Freud and Sandler (1985), this projection of responsibility or guilt does not constitute true morality. True morality—namely, a mature superego—would require acknowledging one's responsibility and blame, as well as being able to criticize one's own negative thought or feeling. Like Roy Schafer (1989), they stress the importance of acknowledgment of self-agency and self-responsibility.

As noted earlier, although this mechanism of identification with the aggressor was conceptualized as an infantile way station in superego formation, it is also a defense against aggression used by adults. Indeed, the adult use of this defense is legion and rather obvious in everyday life. For example, let us think of the student who unconsciously adopts the accent of his feared, powerful teacher (imitation of the aggressor); the man whose car was just hit by another, storming around at home, slamming papers (identification with aggression); the wife yelling at her husband whom she expects to be critical of her (reversal of role); the employee chastised by his superior, chastising the next in line below (reversal of role and displacement). On a more dramatic scale, the role of identification with the aggressor (together with "submission to the aggressor") has been implicated in the behavior of concentration camp victims who attacked or betrayed their fellow inmates (Eckstaedt, 1986) or in the attitude of some hostages who begin to identify with the cause of their captors.

Of course, the identification mechanism is never as neat as dealing with aggression from outside only. Some of the aggression experienced as coming from the other may be one's own aggression projected onto the other. In a related issue in analysis, in *projective counteridentification*, where supposedly foreign, external aggression is experienced by the analyst as if it were one's own (an internalization of the other's bad object), the mechanism never quite works unless it hooks on to some inner aggression in the analyst, there from childhood and now aroused in response to the patient's aggression and in partial identification with the patient's projected aggression.

The mechanism of identification with the aggressor, particularly the reversal of roles—attacking when anticipating attack and displacement to another from the original attacker—is clearly related but not identical with the first step in the type 1 constellation described earlier. The projection of inner aggression or projective identification, however, which plays only a minor role, if any, in the concept of identification with the aggressor, is a major aspect in the dynamics of the type 1 constellation, where aggression is then *perceived* as coming from the outside. Primary identification with an original *parental* aggressor, on the other hand, may play a major role in type 1, together with revenge against this primary aggressor.

Seduction of the Aggressor

The concept of seduction of the aggressor (Loewenstein, 1957) also is related to, but also different from, the mechanisms at work in patients A, B, and E, as described earlier. As postulated by Loewenstein, *seduction of the aggressor* or *protomasochism* is the first step in a sequence that may lead to true masochism. Protomasochism or premasochism is a normal childhood mechanism, involving the deflection of aggression from mother and of the child's own aggression by seduction of the mother in a game of teasing, provocation simultaneous with or followed by smiling appeasement—a game participated in by both child and parent. The threat of not being loved and its pleasurable removal almost coincide in the same act. Protomasochism prepares the child to deal with frustration and danger from the aggressor. In true masochism, pain and pleasure are inextricably connected and there is a seeking of pain, unpleasure, or humiliation for the sake of pleasure, where either the seeking or the pleasure may be unconscious (Brenner, 1959).

In patient A then, the sequence of attack and embrace could be likened to the normal childhood game of premasochism. However, it differs in that it is not a game for A or B. There is a great deal more destructive aggression in A than in a child, and there is no initial assumption of loving acceptance from the other (B), as there is in the child's expectation of its mother. The second step in A's maneuver—the smiling, loving reaching out to B—could be likened to the seduction of the aggressor, except at this point the other (B) is no longer perceived as an aggressor. In fact this genuine loving outreach by A can come about only when B is no longer perceived negatively, as described earlier. At best, then, it can be viewed as a *preventive* seduction of a *potential* aggressor. In B, his final enthusiastic response to A could be attributed to masochism—pleasure in pain—or relief of being reinstituted in A's good graces. Sometimes it may be just that. As discussed earlier, however, the character structures of the various B's (the objects of A's behavior) are too different to ascribe the response always to masochism only.

In E, meeting F's aggression with "goodness" might be seen as seduction of the aggressor and may involve that mechanism in some people. The result may look the same, but the mechanism I am addressing in E is not appeasement, seduction, or submission to aggression, but a dispersing or elimination of F's and E's own aggression. It comes from internal strength of good internal objects and self-images, not from weakness and helplessness, as does seduction of the aggressor or masochism, which have been called the weapons of the weak in the service of maintaining object relations, self-definition and survival, and narcissistic repair of lost omnipotence, as well as superego self-punishment for internal aggression.

In this chapter I have presented some of my considerations on the handling of aggression of everyday life—aggression from without and within. I have briefly reviewed some well-known defensive mechanisms and behaviors and have selected for in-depth discussion two additional complex mechanisms and behaviors I have observed and been intrigued by, one using overt aggression, the other dispersing or detoxifying aggression. There are other constellations, which I hope to be able to examine and present in the future.

REFERENCES

Arlow, Jacob. 1973. Perspectives on aggression in human adaptation. *Psychoanal. Q.* 42(2): 178–184.
Brenner, Charles. 1959. The masochistic character: Genesis and treatment. *JAPA* 7:197–225.
Eckstaedt, Anita. 1986. Two complementary cases of identification involving "Third Reich" fathers. *Int. J. Psychoanal.* 67 (pt. 3): 317–328.
Freud, Anna. [1936] 1946. *The ego and the mechanisms of defense.* New York: International Universities Press.
Freud, Sigmund. 1915. Instincts and their vicissitudes. *S.E.* 14:109–140.
———. 1920. Beyond the pleasure principle. *S.E.* 18:3–64.
———. 1924. The economic problem of masochism. *S.E.* 19:155–172.
Hartman, H., Kris, E., and Loewenstein, R. 1949. Notes on the theory of aggression. *P.S.C.*, 1–30.
Klein, Melanie. 1952. Some theoretical conclusions regarding the emotional life of the infant, in *Developments in psychoanalysis,* ed. J. Riviere, pp. 198–236. London: Hogarth Press.
Loewenstein, Rudolph. 1957. A contribution to the psychoanalytic theory of masochism. *JAPA* 5:187–234.
Mahler, M., Pine, F., and Bergman, A. 1975. *The psychological birth of the human infant.* New York: Basic Books.
Marcovitz, Eli. 1973. Aggression in human adaptation. *Psychoanal. Q.* 42(2):214–225.
McDevitt, John. 1983. The emergence of hostile aggression and its defensive and adaptive modifications during the separation-individuation process. *JAPA* 31:273–300. (Supplement on defense and resistance)
Moore, B., and Fine, B. 1990. *Psychoanalytic terms and concepts.* New Haven: Yale University Press.
Parens, Henry. 1973. Aggression: A reconsideration. *JAPA* 21(1): 34–60.
Rizzuto, A., Sashin, J., Buie, D., and Meissner, W. 1991. A revised theory of aggression. (Unpublished ms.)
Sandler, J., with Freud, A. 1985. *The analysis of defense: The ego and the mechanisms of defense revisited.* New York: International Universities Press.
Schafer, Roy. 1989. Narratives of the self, in *Psychoanalysis: Toward the second century,* ed. A. M. Cooper, O. Kernberg, and E. S. Person. New Haven: Yale University Press.
Trilling, Lionel. 1973. Aggression and utopia: A note on William Morris' *News from Nowhere. Psychoanal. Q.* 42(2): 214–225.

4

The Psychopathology
of Hatred

OTTO F. KERNBERG, M.D.

Affects and Drives

In this chapter I focus on hatred, a complex affect derived from rage, itself a primary affect at the core of the aggressive drive. Hatred, a universally present disposition like envy or disgust, occupies a central role in severe personality disorders that are characterized by the psychopathology of aggression. As background to my formulations regarding affects and drives, I shall recapitulate the ideas on which these formulations are based.

In earlier work (1984, chap. 14; 1990a, 1990b, 1990c), I proposed that libidinal and aggressive drives constitute a hierarchically supraordinate motivational system comprising affects that are their building blocks. Affects are psychophysiological behavior patterns that include a specific cognitive appraisal, a specific expressive facial pattern, a subjective experience of pleasurable (rewarding), or painful (aversive) quality, and both muscular and neurovegetative discharge patterns. The facial expression is part of a general communicative pattern that differentiates each affect.

Affects may be classified as primary and derived. The former make their appearance within the first two to three years of life; they have an intense, global quality, and their cognitive elements are diffuse and not well differentiated. Derived affects consist of cognitively elaborated combinations of the primary affects; unlike primary affects, they may not show all their original components with equal strength, and their experiential aspects gradually come to dominate the psychophysiological and facial communicative ones. For

This chapter is a modified version of a symposium paper published in the *Journal of the American Psychoanalytic Association* supplement, "Affect: Psychoanalytic Perspectives," vol. 39, pp. 209–238, 1991.

these phenomena I reserve the terms *emotions* or *feelings*, a distinction that derives from clinical observations of primitive affect states and emotional developments in the psychoanalytic situation. I use the term *affect state* to refer to the temporary activation of a particular affect. The term *primitive* refers to affects that are either primary or early derived ones, characterized by a relatively full-fledged presentation of all component features.

I also propose that early affective development is based on the fixation of early, affectively invested object relations in the form of affective memory. The empirical research of Robert Emde (1987; Emde et al., 1978), Carol Izard (1978), and Daniel Stern (1985) points to the central function of object relations in the activation of the infant's affects. Contemporary affect theory emphasizes the signaling function of affects in the relationship of the infant to the caregiver. This connection of object relations with the activation of affects supports the proposal that early affect states fixed in memory always involve an object relation. The activation of different affect states toward the same object takes place as the infant or child performs different developmental tasks and under the influence of biologically determined instinctive behavior patterns. The variety of affect states directed to the same object may provide an economical explanation of how affects are linked and are gradually integrated into a supraordinate motivational system that becomes the sexual or aggressive drive. Libido, or the sexual drive, results from the integration of positive or rewarding affect states such as elation and sexual excitement. Aggression as a drive results from the integration of negative or aversive affects, such as hatred, rage, and disgust. Rage may in fact be considered the central affect of aggression. It is under conditions of intense, peak affect states, both pleasurable and painful, that the infant's relationship to the caregiver is highlighted and determines the establishment of affective memory.

The unconscious integration of affectively invested early object relations requires assuming the existence of a higher level motivational system than that represented by affect states per se, a motivational system that is provided by the libidinal and aggressive drives. This concept of drives does justice to the complexity of the affective developments in relation to the parental objects. In summary, I propose that affects are the link between their biologically determined ("wired in") instinctive components, on the one hand, and their intrapsychic organization into the overall drives, on the other. The correspondence of the series of pleasurable or rewarding and painful or aversive affects states with the dual lines of libido and aggression makes sense both clinically and theoretically.

Memory structures acquired during peak affect states will be very different from those acquired during quiescent or low-level affect states. When the infant is in such an affect state, the memory structures established will be largely of a cognitive, discriminatory nature and contribute directly to ego development. Ordinary learning thus occurs under conditions in which alertness is focused on the immediate situation and tasks, with little distortion derived from affective arousal and no particular defensive mechanism interfering with it. These memory structures constitute the early precursors, we might say, of more specialized and adaptive ego functioning—the affective memory structures of early consciousness.

In contrast, peak affect experiences facilitate the internalization of primitive object relations organized along the axes of rewarding or "all good" and aversive or "all bad" objects. The experiences of self and object under the impact of extreme affect activation acquire an intensity that facilitates the laying down of affectively impregnated memory structures. These affective memory structures, constituted in essence of self and object representations in the context of a specific peak affect experience, represent the earliest intrapsychic structures of the symbiotic stage of development (Mahler and Furer, 1968). They mark the beginning of structure formation of internalized object relations, as well as the beginning of the organization of libidinal and aggressive drives. Peak affect states represent, by definition, extremely desirable (pleasurable) or undesirable (painful) experiences, which motivate wishes to repeat or avoid similar affective experiences. These wishes, gradually elaborated in unconscious fantasy, determine the motivational repertoire of what eventually constitutes the organized id.

This theory of peak affect states as the building blocks of drives resolves, I believe, some long-standing problems of drive theory. The concept of erotogenic zones, for example, as the source of libido may be replaced by that of a peak affect state that includes all physiologically activated functions and bodily zones that become involved in the affectively invested interactions of the infant and child with mother under condition of erotic, sensual arousal. I have in fact proposed that the central affect around which clusters the affective constellation of libido as a drive is the affect of sexual excitement (Kernberg, 1990c). It is curious but perhaps not surprising that sexual excitement as an affect has received much less attention from empirical research on early affect development than the other primary affects. It may well be, however, that sexual excitement, in its maximum intensity and definite form, requires a more complex and lengthier development than other primary affects.

The affect of rage, in contrast, the early characteristics and development of which have been documented extensively by infant researchers, constitutes, in my view, the essential affect around which clusters the complex affective formation of aggression as a drive. I focus next chiefly on the developmental vicissitudes of rage that lead to the dominance—in certain patients with severe character pathology—of hatred, which emerges as an overriding affect in the transference. This emergence permits the psychoanalytic exploration of hatred but also presents formidable challenges to the analyst's efforts to resolve the corresponding psychopathology in the transference. The basis for the formulations that follow includes, on the one hand, the relationship between the pathology of mother-infant relations in infants at high risk and the development of severe aggression in such infants (Massie, 1977; Gaensbauer and Sands, 1979; Call, 1980; Roiphe and Galenson, 1981; Fraiberg, 1983; Galenson, 1986; Osofsky, 1987) and, on the other hand, the psychopathology of severe aggression in the transference in patients with borderline personality organization and narcissistic and antisocial personality disorders (Winnicott, [1949] 1958; Bion, 1957, 1959, 1970; Green, 1986; Moser, 1978; Ogden, 1979; Krause, 1988; Krause and Lutolf, 1988; Grossman, 1991; Kernberg, 1989, 1990a). The observations of severe regression in patients who show predominance of hatred in the transference constitute the principal source for the formulations that follow.

Rage

Clinically, the basic affect state characterizing the activation of aggression in the transference is that of rage. Irritation is a mild aggressive affect that signals the potential for rage reactions, and that, in the form of a chronic mood, takes the form of irritability. Anger is a more intense affect than irritation, usually more differentiated regarding its cognitive content and the nature of the object relationship that is activated. In its overwhelming nature, diffuseness, and blurring of specific cognitive contents and corresponding object relations, a full-fledged rage reaction may erroneously convey the idea that it is a "pure" primitive affect. Clinically, however, the analysis of rage reaction—as is true also for other intense affect states—always reveals an underlying conscious or unconscious fantasy involving a specific relation between an aspect of the self and an aspect of a significant other.

Infant research documents the early appearance of rage as an affect and its primordial function to eliminate a source of pain or irritation. A later developmental function of rage is the elimination of an obstacle or barrier to gratification. Now, the originally biological function of rage, namely, signaling a state of pain to the caregiver to facilitate the elimination of the irritant, becomes a more focused appeal to the caretaker to restore a desired state of gratification. In the unconscious fantasies that develop around rage reactions, rage comes to signify both the activation of an all bad object relationship and the wish to eliminate it and restore an all good one. At a still later developmental stage, rage reactions may function as last-ditch efforts to restore a sense of autonomy in the face of severely frustrating situations unconsciously perceived as the threatening activation of all bad, persecutory object relationships. A state of narcissistic equilibrium is restored by a violent assertion of one's will, representing an unconscious identification with an idealized, all good, object.

Clinically, the intensity of the aggressive affects—whether irritation, anger, or rage—correlates roughly with the psychological function of the affects: to assert one's autonomy, to eliminate an obstacle or barrier to a desired level of satisfaction, or to eliminate or destroy a source of profound pain or frustration. The psychopathology of aggression, however, is not limited to the intensity and frequency of rage attacks. The most severe and dominant of the affects that jointly come to constitute aggression as a drive is the complex or elaborated affect of hatred. As we move from the transference developments of patients with neurotic personality organization to those of borderline personality organization, particularly those with severe narcissistic pathology and antisocial features, we are increasingly faced not only with rage attacks in the transference but with the development of hatred, which emerges along with certain typical secondary characterologic expressions and defenses against the awareness of this affect.

Hatred

Hatred is a complex aggressive affect: in contrast to the acuteness of rage reactions and the easily varying cognitive aspects of anger and rage, the cognitive aspect of hatred is chronic and stable. Hatred also presents with characterologic anchoring that includes powerful rationalizations and corresponding distortions of ego and superego functioning. The primary aim of one consumed by hatred is to destroy its object—a specific object of unconscious fantasy—and this object's conscious derivatives, an object who at bottom is both needed and desired and the destruction of whom is equally needed and desired. The understanding of this paradox is at the center of the psychoanalytic investigation of hatred. Hatred is not always pathological. As a response to an objective, real danger of physical or pathological destruction, a threat to the survival of oneself and those one loves, hatred is a normal elaboration of rage aimed to eliminate that danger; but unconscious motivations usually enter and intensify hatred, as in the search for revenge. As a chronic, characterologic predisposition, hatred always reflects the psychopathology of aggression.

An extreme form of hatred demands the physical elimination of the object and may be expressed in murder or in a radical devaluation of the object that may generalize in the form of a symbolic destruction of all objects—that is, all potential relationships with significant others, as clinically observable in antisocial personality structures. This extreme form of hatred may also sometimes be expressed in suicide, where the self is identified with the hated object and self-elimination is the only way to destroy the object as well.

Clinically, some patients with the syndrome of malignant narcissism (narcissistic personality, ego-syntonic aggression, paranoid and antisocial tendencies [Kernberg, 1989]) and *psychopathic* transferences (deceptiveness as a dominant transference feature) may consistently and ruthlessly attempt to exploit, destroy, symbolically castrate, or dehumanize significant others (including the therapist) to an extent that defies the therapist's efforts to protect or recapture some island of an idealized primitive, all good object relationship. At the same time, the transference may apparently be remarkably free from overt aggression; chronic deceptiveness, the search for a primitive all good self state that eliminates all objects (such as by means of alcohol or drugs), and unconscious and conscious efforts to coopt the therapist in the exploitation or destruction of others dominate the scene. The therapist's efforts to stand up against this diffuse, generalized destruction or corruption of everything valuable may be experienced by the patient (by projective mechanisms) as a brutal attack, which leads to the emergence of direct rage and hatred in the transference; we witness the transformation of a psychopathic into a *paranoid* transference. Paradoxically, this transformation is a frail hope for these patients.

At a less extreme level of severity, hatred takes the form of sadistic tendencies and wishes. Here the patient's wish, unconscious or conscious, is to make the object suffer, with a sense of profound conscious or unconscious enjoyment of that suffering. This sadism may take the form of a sexual perversion with an actual, physical damaging of the object; a characterologic sadism as part of the syndrome of malignant narcissism; a sadomasochistic personality structure; or, sometimes, of a rationalized, intellectualized form of cruelty that includes powerful wishes to humiliate the object. In contrast to the earlier, more extreme form of hatred mentioned, here the wish is not to eliminate but to maintain the relationship with the hated object in an enactment of an object relationship between a sadistic agent and a paralyzed victim. The desire and pleasure in inflicting pain are central here and represent an implicit condensation of aggression and libidinal excitement in inducing such suffering.

An even milder form of hatred centers around the desire to dominate the object, a search for power over it that may include sadistic components but tends to be self-limiting in the attacks on the object by the object's submission and the implied reconfirmation of the subject's freedom and autonomy by this very submission. Here, anal-sadistic components dominate the more primitive oral aggressive ones in the more severe form of hatred. The assertion of hierarchical superiority and "territoriality" in social interactions and the aggressive aspects of regressive small and large group processes are the most frequent manifestations of this milder level of hatred.

Finally, under conditions of relatively normal superego integration and within a neurotic personality organization with a well-differentiated tripartite structure, hatred may take the form of a rationalized identification with a strict and punitive superego, the aggressive assertion of idiosyncratic but well-rationalized systems of morality, justified indignation, and primitive levels of commitment to vindictive ideologies. Hatred at this level, of course, makes a bridge to the sublimatory function of courageous aggressive assertion at the service of commitment to ideals and ethical systems.

At this level of integration of hatred there is usually also a tendency toward self-directed hatred in the form of cruelty of the superego. Clinically we see a potential for a transformation of transferences from the primitive *paranoid* into the more advanced *depressive* type. Masochistic and sadomasochistic personality structures and mixed neurotic constellations, including paranoid, masochistic, and sadistic traits, may experience relatively sudden shifts between depressive and paranoid transference regression. In contrast, at more severe levels of the psychopathology of hatred the transference is overwhelmingly paranoid, except when psychopathic transferences defend the patient against the paranoid ones. Here, what dominates is the "paranoid urge to betray" (Jacobson, 1971).

Returning to the clinical characteristics of hatred, the entire spectrum of its corresponding affective and characterologic components may be observed in patients of the second level of pathology mentioned earlier who have at least a wish to preserve the hated object and in whom the full range of characteristics of this affect may be observed in the transference. The chronicity, stability, and characterologic anchoring of hatred is matched by the desire to inflict pain upon the object, characterologic (and sometimes sexual) sadism, and cruelty.

In addition, as I have pointed out in earlier work (1990a), primitive hatred also takes the form of an effort to destroy the potential for a gratifying human relationship and learning something of value in that human interaction. Underlying this need to destroy reality and communication in intimate relationships lies, I believe, unconscious and conscious envy of the object, particularly of the object not controlled from within by similar hatred.

It was Melanie Klein (1957) who first pointed to the envy of the good object as a dominant characteristic of patients with severe narcissistic psychopathology. I believe that such envy is complicated by the patient's need to destroy his or her own awareness of this envy because it would expose a terror over the savagery of the hatred of what, at base, the patient values in the object. Behind the envy of the object and the need to destroy and spoil anything good that might come from contact with it is also the terror of the unconscious identification with the originally hated, and needed, object. Envy may be considered both a source of a primitive form of hatred intimately linked with oral aggression, greed, and voracity, and a complication of the hatred that derives from the fixation to trauma that I will refer to later.

At the surface, the hatred of the unconsciously, and consciously, envied object is usually rationalized as the fear of the object's destructive potential. This destructive potential of the hated object derives from both actual aggression inflicted by essentially needed objects in the patient's past (in patients who have been severely traumatized) and the projection of their own rage and hatred upon that object.

Tendencies toward chronic and potentially severe self-mutilation and non-depressive suicidal behaviors frequently accompany the syndrome of malignant narcissism, where these manifestations of intense primitive hatred are dominant. Self-mutilation typically reflects unconscious identification with a hateful and hated object. Hatred and intolerance of communication with the object may protect the patient from what might otherwise emerge as a combination of cruel attacks by the patient onto the object, paranoid fears of that object, and self-directed aggression in identification with the hated object.

Clinically, the transference characterized by a combination of arrogance, curiosity, and pseudostupidity (incapacity to reflect on what the therapist says), described by Wilfred Bion (1957), illustrates the acting out of patients' envy of the therapist, destruction of meaning, and sadism.

One of the most consistent features in transferences dominated by the acting out of severe hatred is the patient's intense involvement with the therapist: the extraordinary dependence manifest simultaneously with an aggression toward the therapist, an impressive demonstration of the "fixation to the trauma." At the same time, in the patient's fantasies and fears, there is also the assumption that unless the patient consistently fights off the therapist, the patient will be subjected to a similar onslaught of hatred and sadistic exploitation and persecution by the therapist. Obviously, by means of projective identification, the patient is attributing to the therapist his or her own hatred and sadism, but, by the same token, the total situation illustrates the intimate link between the persecutor and the persecuted, master and slave, sadist and masochist—all referring in the last resort to the sadistic, frustrating, teasing mother and the helpless, paralyzed infant.

Basically, what the patient is enacting is an object relationship between persecutor and victim, with alternating identifications with these roles while projecting the reciprocal role onto the therapist. In the most severe cases, it is as if the only alternative to being victimized is to become a tyrant, and the repetitive assertion of hatred and sadism would appear to be the only form of survival and meaning, aside from murder, suicide, or psychopathy. In less severe cases, the psychopathology of envy of the good object emerges as an additional dynamic factor, the intolerance of the good object who escapes from that savagery and who is hated because of the willful withholding (as the patient fantasizes) of what could transform the object from a persecuting one into an ideal one. Here, the search for an ideal object, in the last resort an ideal mother, lies behind the unending, repetitive onslaught of hatred in the transference.

In still less severe cases, where more sophisticated and elaborated types of sadomasochistic behaviors dominate within a neurotic personality organization, we discover the unconscious potential for pleasure in pain, the temptation to experience pain as a precondition for experiencing pleasure, in the context of castration anxiety, unconscious guilt over oedipal strivings, and as the ultimate transformation of passively experienced pain into an active compromise solution of the corresponding unconscious conflicts.

All these dynamics may emerge intimately condensed and combined in many cases, with differences in degree and proportion. What they have in common, however, is an intense motivation for maintaining the link with the hated object, a link that gratifies these various primitive transferences and is responsible for, in my view, the powerful fixation to this traumatic relationship.

Fixation to the Trauma

I believe that peak affect states organize internalized object relationships not only under conditions of love, the elation that corresponds to a primitive idealized fusion between an all-good self and all-good object, but also under conditions of rage, in the internalization of originally undifferentiated all-bad self and object representations, which are gradually sorted out into the typical object relationship under the domination of hatred. An extremely powerful link to the traumatizing object—under the dominance of hatred—has been observed in the study of battered children, infants at high risk, and even in the fixation to extremely traumatic circumstances, such as the "Stockholm syndrome" of hijacked airplane passengers who end up defending their captors. Research by Selma Fraiberg (1983) and Eleanor Galenson (1986) is particularly instructive regarding infants' internalization of the aggressive behavior of mothers toward them and these infants' replication of their mothers' behavior in relationships with her and with other objects.

The intense attachment to the frustrating mother is the ultimate origin of the transformation of rage into hatred. The ultimate cause of this particular transformation is the fixation to a traumatic relationship with a fundamentally needed object that is experienced as all bad and as having destroyed or swallowed up the ideal, all-good object. The revengeful destruction of this bad object is intended magically to restore the all-good one, but in the process, it leads to the destruction of the very capacity of the self to relate to the object. This transformation takes the form not of simply identifying with the object (mother), but with the *relationship* to her, so that the hatred of her as victimizer, with its painful, impotent, and paralyzing implications, also is transformed into the identification with the mother as the cruel, omnipotent, and contemptuously destructive object, while a search develops for other objects onto whom the attacked, depreciated, teased, and mistreated self can be projected. In identifying with both suffering self and sadistic object, the subject is himself swallowed up by the all-encompassing aggression in the relationship.

Hatred as a reversal of suffering is a basic type of revengeful triumph over the object, a triumph also over the terrifying self-representation achieved by projective identification, and the symbolic revenge for past suffering condensed in the fixation to sadistic behavior patterns. Consequently, these patients mistreat others sadistically because they experience themselves as mistreated, once more, by sadistic objects. Unconsciously, they become their persecutory objects while sadistically attacking their victims, the dissociated and projected victimized self. Fundamentally, they cannot escape being both victim and perpetrator at the same time. As victimizer, they cannot live without their victim—the projected, disowned persecuted self; as victims, they remain attached to their victimizers internally, and sometimes in behavior shocking to an observer, to external persecutors as well.

Extremely contradictory, unreliable behaviors on the part of the mother probably reinforce the psychopathic end of the spectrum of hatred in the patient by interpreting the mother's behavior as a betrayal by the potentially good object that becomes unpredictably and overwhelmingly bad. In identifying himself or herself, in turn, with a betraying object, the patient thus initiates the path to a revengeful destruction of all object relations. Here probably lies the ultimate source of Edith Jacobson's (1971) "paranoid urge to betray." The most severe psychopathology of attachment behavior has been described in infants with mothers whose behavior combined abandonment, violence, chaos, and a teasing overstimulation together with chronic frustration (Fraiberg, 1983; Galenson, 1986).

Elsewhere I have described (1990c) a fundamental function of sexual excitement, namely, the inclusion of an aggressive component—the aggressive implication of penetrating and being penetrated—as a means to incorporate aggression at the service of love, using the erotogenic potential of the experience of pain as a crucial contributor to the gratifying fusion with the other in sexual excitement and orgasm. This normal capability for transforming pain into erotic excitement miscarries under conditions of severe aggression in the mother-infant relationship and is probably a crucial bridge to the erotic excitement with the induction of suffering in others that consolidates the pleasurable characteristics of sadistic hatred. If, at the same time, as Denise Braunschweig and Michael Fain (1971, 1975) have suggested, the alternatingly erotically stimulating and withdrawing attitudes of the mother toward her infant originate its unconscious identification with a teasing mother as well as with being teased, and activate, in the process, its own sexual excitement as a basic affect, then severely traumatizing mothers whose behavior includes exaggerated teasing of the infant may orient its hatred particularly toward the more severe sadomasochistic perversions as an expression of this hatred.

More generally, the induction of severe pain in the infant and small child leads to rage first, and then, by the identificatory and transformational mechanisms mentioned, to the development of hatred. Thus, as William Grossman (1989) has proposed, pain may lead, by a series of intrapsychic transformations, to the intensification and psychopathology of aggression as a major drive.

Excessive activation of aggression as a drive (to which characterologically fixated hatred contributes fundamentally) interferes with the normal integration of the mutually dissociated, all good and all bad internalized object relations at the conclusion of the developmental phase of separation-individuation and therefore with the initiation of object constancy and the advanced stage of oedipal development. Excessive aggression, in disrupting these processes, leads to the fixation at a lack of integration of all good and all bad internalized object relations, while self and object representations within each of these all good and all bad object relationships are differentiated. These developments constitute the psychostructural conditions of borderline personality organization, characteristic of severe personality disorders where preoedipal and oedipal aggression are dominant.

Under more favorable circumstances, integration of all good and all bad internalized object relations may proceed, and object constancy may develop, which leads to the integration of the definite ego and superego structures and the establishment of repressive boundaries separating ego from id: the definite tripartite structure consolidates. Here, the psychopathology of hatred is absorbed by the superego. The integration of early sadistic superego precursors with the preoedipal ego ideal, on the one hand, and of oedipal prohibitions and demands with those earlier superego structures, on the other, leads to sadistic superego demands, depressive-masochistic psychopathology, and secondarily rationalized, characterologic sadism correlated with the integration of cruel and sadistic ethical systems. Otherwise, various sexual pathologies, including perversions at a neurotic level of personality organization, may contain hatred as a relatively harmless, erotized perverse symptom.

The induction of shame in and the humiliation of others as characterologic traits are other manifestations of hatred potentially integrated into superego-mediated characterologic features. Obsessive-compulsive patients need to control and dominate others to feel protected against threatening outbreaks of aggressive rebelliousness and chaos in others, thus enacting their identification with a hated object and their projection of unacceptable, repressed, and projected aspects of their self at a relatively high level of psychic functioning. The intense fixation to specific hated objects may therefore be seen along the entire spectrum of psychopathology and illustrates, sometimes in almost caricatural ways, attachment to the enemy or persecutor. It says something about the profound commonality of the basic affects of rage and sexual excitement in their role of fixating object relationships, that it is under conditions of intense hatred and intense love that the highest tendency exists for sustained mutual gaze.

Clinical Illustrations

Mrs. A

Mrs. A, a housewife with borderline personality organization, a narcissistic personality disorder displaying the syndrome of malignant narcissism, was in intensive, long-term, psychoanalytic psychotherapy. She had a history from early childhood of an intense relationship with an antisocial father who encouraged and colluded with her in deceiving her mother. Abuse of hypnotics, sedatives, and analgesics was rampant in the home: the patient and her siblings as well as her mother swallowed pills casually at times of frustration or unhappiness. Mrs. A's self-mutilating symptoms had brought her close to death several times, and she had managed to burn herself with cigarettes to the extent of suffering third degree burns on various parts of her body. Serious suicidal attempts punctuated her life throughout late adolescence and into her twenties, when she started her treatment.

At a certain point of her psychotherapy, she managed to obtain anxiolytic and analgesic medications from several physicians by providing them with false information. She also became engaged in several sexual relationships while professing concern over her husband's serious illness and his failure to be appropriately concerned about this illness. She had married shortly before starting psychotherapy. She had also joined a social group active in proselytiz-ing against the use of drugs; Mrs. A gave speeches protesting drug abuse while abusing them herself. In psychotherapy, she evinced an attitude of provocative indifference toward what the therapist was communicating to her, alternating with paranoid suspiciousness to any change of routine in the sessions.

Mrs. A showed an inordinate talent for finding the weaknesses of others that would then justify her exploitation or mistreatment of them. Her dreams reflected extremely sadistic fantasies, such as her participation in the mass murder of inmates of psychiatric hospitals, her being a member of the prison guard of Nazi concentration camps, and her throwing couples to their death from balconies of high-rise buildings. Although she gave no evidence of rage in her daily life or in the transference, she seemed aloof and indifferent.

Any efforts the therapist made to confront her with the emotional implica-tions of her behavior brought about intense paranoid developments in the transference, micropsychotic episodes in the hours, with quasi-hallucinatory experiences during and in between sessions, and suicidal behavior. In the case of Mrs. A, the predominance of psychopathic over paranoid transferences (her chronic deceptiveness in relation to her therapist) indicates the most severe kind of activation of the psychopathology of hatred in the treatment situation. The behavior that symbolically reflected the defensive dismantling of all ob-ject relationships protected her from activation in the transference of the intense hatred manifest in her dreams. Consistent clarification, confrontation, and interpretation of the deceptiveness toward the therapist, the other physi-cians, her husband, and the social organization in which she worked, shifted that psychopathic transference into a paranoid one. At first she projected her hatred onto the therapist and reacted with intense suspiciousness and even psychoticlike regression in the sessions. Only later could she tolerate the direct awareness of the intense hatred that dominated all her object relation-ships, including her attitude toward the healthier aspects of her own person-ality. The sequence of psychopathic to paranoid to depressive transferences is typical for the transformation and resolution of severe hatred in the transfer-ence.

Miss B

Miss B, in her early thirties, is a patient with a narcissistic personality functioning on an overt borderline level, severe suicidal tendencies without depression, failure in her intellectual pursuits in spite of high intelligence but without antisocial features. Miss B, who had been subjected to severe physical abuse by her stepmother throughout her early childhood, had only a vague memory of her father, who died before she entered elementary school. She presented intense rage attacks in the early stages of her treatment, efforts to control the therapist's life by refusing to leave his office at the end of the sessions and by insistent telephone calls. With sufficient structuring of the treatment situation, however, she was able to reduce gradually the direct expression of violence in the sessions and in her daily life outside the sessions. At the same time, she used the sessions to acquire knowledge from the therapist that she would then elaborate herself to deal with her problems, while carefully avoiding any actual collaborative work with him. As a result, his interpretations seemed to be vaguely related to a gradual improvement she showed outside the sessions but were consistently rejected by her within the sessions themselves.

In the fourth year of this psychotherapy and with a marked reduction in the acting out outside and in the sessions, it was possible to explore a silent but consistent relationship that the patient evinced in the hours spent with him, characterized by a combination of arrogance, curiosity (about him, not herself), and the pseudostupidity described by Bion (1957). The activation of a pathological grandiose self identified with an omnipotent, sadistic, and envious image of her stepmother finally clarified the nature of the unconscious, sadistic destruction of everything coming from the therapist silently occurring in the sessions and gradually led to the emergence of direct hatred, death wishes, and sadistic triumph over the therapist in the sessions.

Only after consistent and painstaking analysis of the paranoid transferences that emerged as a consequence of the efforts to analyze the narcissistic resistances in the transference was this patient finally able to acknowledge the pleasurable aspect of her aggression: her intense hatred of the therapist's capacity to be able to help her. She was then able to reduce the acting out of unconscious envy together with a reduction of the paranoid transference and a beginning capacity for guilt feelings in the session—the initiation of depressive transferences. Miss B did not show psychopathic transferences; she started with paranoid ones that eventually changed to depressive ones.

Miss C

Miss C, in her late twenties, suffered from a chronic paranoid schizophrenic illness. Her relationship with her mother had been characterized by intense ambivalence since early childhood, great dependency upon this dominating and overwhelming mother, and intense rebelliousness against her, which culminated during late adolescence in Miss C's abrupt departure from home. The father maintained a warm and somewhat erotized relationship with her but avoided becoming involved in her conflictual interactions with the mother; she experienced him as pleasing her and secretly on her side but weak and overtly abandoning her in her fight with the mother.

After several unhappy love affairs, Miss C had entered psychotherapy, in which she regressed and became overtly psychotic for the first time. She experienced acute depersonalization, ideas of reference, and unusual powers of perception. Impulsive moves from one part of the country to another helped her to keep her psychotic symptoms from destroying intimate relationships. She eventually developed multiple auditory and visual hallucinations, chronic delusions of bodily and thought control, and intense psychomotor agitation, which required hospitalization. Over a period of one year in the hospital, she gradually compensated with the help of moderate doses of neuroleptics but without abandoning some basic psychotic convictions, particularly the idea that other people, particularly women, were attempting to steal her "energy."

She entered psychoanalytic psychotherapy with me while psychophar-macological maintenance with low-dose neuroleptics permitted her to function outside the hospital and to resume a position in computer programming. The patient was aware that she had to control and keep to herself her convictions that women were stealing her energy, and in the sessions this symptom became a major transference pattern. Characteristically, at times when she treated me as the benign, impotent, yet seductive father, she became very suspicious in the sessions, watched my every movement, and interpreted minor shifts in my position as an indication that I was now stealing energy from her and therefore weakening her capacity to think—to the extent of blocking all her thought processes.

It gradually emerged that these developments occurred at times when she felt sexual feelings toward me, unconsciously implying sexual feelings to her father, and projected these feelings onto me with the fear that I would want to rape her. Then she experienced me as acquiring powerful hostile capabilities leading to my enriching myself at the cost of robbing her of her physical and mental energy. Simultaneously, it also became clear that she experienced herself as in an intense rivalry with the secretaries of the office suite where I saw her, and she eventually experienced these secretaries as engaged in a conspiracy against her, making fun of her, and also attempting to steal her energy.

Still later, she was able to become aware of her intense hatred of these secretaries as representing maternal figures and was able to tolerate fantasies of attacking and destroying them. She was able to experience intense hatred against me because I had not protected her against the "sadistic" female nursing staff, as she saw it, who allegedly were trying to destroy her capacity to think and to become independent while she was in the hospital.

Miss C now became aware of a confusion in her feelings toward me, a shift between erotic feelings and hatred that was so intense that she could no longer recognize the very nature of her feelings, nor whether she or I or both of us had these feelings.

At one point, in bringing all these elements together, I interpreted that confusion as derived from her fear to experience sexual fantasies and wishes toward me as a symbolic father because it would lead to her mother's immediate aggressive destruction of her mind, an aggression from her mother that was particularly dangerous because, as she saw it, her mother was aware of the patient's own murderous rage against her. As the patient became less afraid to experience her feelings of hatred against her mother and motherly representatives in my office and at her job, the enactment of the delusion of my and other people stealing her energy gradually subsided.

This case, in my view, illustrates severe hatred condensing preoedipal and oedipal issues under an overriding oedipal structure, projective identification of that hatred with a lack of differentiation between herself and her object, and the effort to deal with her hatred by psychotic projection onto threatening maternal objects. Miss C had been subject to severe rage attacks when she was in frank psychotic regression. As she became able to function more appropriately in reality and her psychotic symptoms became more circumscribed to the transference, the chronicity and intensity of her hatred of her mother emerged as a major source of the regressive nature of her oedipal conflicts, the defensive refusion with an idealized but erotically threatening father image, and the return of the projected aggression in the form of delusions of bodily influence.

Miss D

Miss D had a depressive-masochistic personality structure with strong paranoid features, and a chronic, characterologic depression that brought her to treatment. She was in standard psychoanalysis, four sessions a week. In the third year of her psychoanalysis, a severe depression developed related to the activation in the transference of the relationship with her deeply disturbed, drug-addicted mother. The mother, during Miss D's childhood, under the influence of drugs, would reject the patient and treat her in a sadistic and neglectful way, and while engaged in severe conflicts with the equally drug-addicted father, she would let the patient in on all the sexual and nonsexual intimacies of the relationship between the parents.

In the first two years of treatment the transference remained at an advanced oedipal level, with a nonsexualized idealization of the therapist as an ideal father and a repression of underlying sexual feelings. After two years the transference changed, with the activation in Miss D of a sense of being misunderstood, mistreated, controlled, and brainwashed by the analyst. Her complaints of mistreatment by the therapist alternated with angry, sarcastic outbursts in the sessions and abrupt storming out of his office. What is significant here is the moralistic tone in which hatred was expressed in the treatment situation in the form of superego-determined, rationalized blaming of the analyst for not living up to the patient's expectations of perfection, oscillating with severe self-depreciation of the patient, also reflecting cruel, exaggerated, and infantile superego attacks, all of them illustrating the absorption of hatred within her masochistic personality structure.

Now the sadomasochistic relationship with mother was enacted in the patient's alternation between masochistic complaints and sadistic attacks on the analyst in an escalating violence that at times made it practically impossible for the analyst to say anything without triggering in her a rageful affect storm. Gradually, the repeated interpretation that she was recreating in the sessions the chaotic situation and the hateful relationship with mother—in alternation with the enactment of the identification of the analyst with her mother while she became her infantile self, with the projection of her infantile self representation onto the analyst while she enacted her mother's image—permitted a clarification of this situation over a period of time. It became clear that the defensive activation of this relationship with her mother protected her against more deeply lying positive sexual feelings toward the analyst as oedipal father.

Some Further Comments about Treatment

What follows are some general considerations regarding the treatment of patients with severe psychopathology of aggression, particularly intense hatred in the transference. In an earlier paper (1990a), I pointed to the importance of interpreting consistently and in depth the nature of the unconscious fantasies implied in the activation of rage in the transference and particularly the importance of interpreting secondary defenses against acknowledging the pleasurable aspects of rage. Here, in broadening my focus and considering the entire spectrum of the psychopathology of hatred, I stress first the countertransference consequences of this affect.

I have pointed out (1975, 1984) that what the patient hates, particularly the narcissistic patient with antisocial features, is what he or she most needs from the therapist: the therapist's unwavering dedication to him. The patient also hates because he envies the creativity involved in the therapist's efforts to gain understanding and to communicate this understanding to the patient. The analyst's sense of being exhausted, of his efforts going to waste, of the enormity of the patient's lack of gratitude may bring about complications in the countertransference that tend to perpetuate or even obscure the patient's acting out of hatred and envy.

The therapist may attempt to escape from his discouragement by an emotional disconnection from the patient. The restoration of the therapist's tranquility may be at the cost of an internal giving up that, not surprisingly, is often perceived by the patient but is easily tolerated by him or her because it is rightly experienced as the therapist's defeat. An uneasy equilibrium may ensue, in which a surface friendliness obscures the "parasitic" (Bion, 1970) nature of the therapeutic relationship.

The therapist may enter into a collusion with splitting processes in the patient, facilitate the displacement of aggression elsewhere, and foster the creation of a pseudotherapeutic alliance that assures a friendly surface relationship in the transference while aggression is acted out outside the treatment sessions.

Another solution frequently adopted by the therapist may be to absorb the patient's aggression, with full awareness of what is going on but without finding a way to transform this acting out into viable interpretations. This development amounts to a masochistic submission to "impossible" patients, sometimes quite consciously engaged in by a therapist who believes that with sufficient love most things can be cured. The counterpart to such a masochistic submission to the patient, however, is often the eventual acting out of aggression in the countertransference with a sudden disruption of the treatment, dismissal of the patient, or an enactment by the therapist unconsciously geared to provoking the patient to leave treatment.

Most frequently, however, it is likely that the therapist, even a highly experienced therapist, may shift in his or her internal stance from day to day, from session to session, oscillating between efforts to resolve analytically the activation of hatred in the transference and times of giving up or withdrawal. These natural oscillations may actually reflect a reasonable compromise formation, which permits the therapist to step back and evaluate the effects of various interventions, grants some breathing space to reevaluate the situation and then return once more to an active interpretative stance.

In all cases, I think it is extremely important to diagnose secondary defenses against hatred at the most severe end of the spectrum of aggression in the transference, that is, the development of antisocial or psychopathic transferences referred to earlier. The patient's conscious or unconscious corruption of all relationships, particularly the therapeutic one, must be examined consistently, with the therapist fully aware that such an examination will probably shift the apparently "quiet" psychopathic transference relationship into a severely paranoid one, with the activation of intensive hatred in the transference. The therapist's normal superego functions, his being moral but not moralistic (E. Ticho, personal communication), will be experienced by patients with antisocial tendencies as devastating attacks and criticism.

It is important to interpret the patient's paranoid reaction as part of the interpretation of the antisocial transferences. In other words, an interpretation might go as follows: "I am under the impression that, if I point out to you that I believe (such and such behavior) is an expression of your profound need to destroy (a certain relationship), that you might interpret my comment as a savage attack on you, as if I were attacking you rather than trying to help you understand what I consider a very important aspect of your difficulties at this time."

Once the transferences have shifted from a dominantly antisocial into a paranoid mode, the general technical approach to severe paranoid regression is indicated, the characteristics and management of which I have discussed elsewhere (1984). Here, I want only to stress the open acknowledgment to the patient who is convinced of a paranoid distortion of reality that the therapist sees that reality in a completely different way but respects the temporary incompatibility of the patient's and the therapist's perception of reality: in other words, a *psychotic nucleus* is identified, circumscribed, and tolerated in the transference before working on its interpretive resolution. It is usually only at advanced stages of the treatment of patients with severe psychopathology that integration of idealized and persecutory internalized object relations can take place, with a corresponding shift of paranoid transferences into depressive transferences—that is, the emergence in the patient of guilt feelings, concern over the dangerous effects of aggression, and wishes to repair the psychotherapeutic relationship.

Where the sadistic elements are particularly marked, it is important that the patient become aware of his or her pleasure in hatred (Kernberg, 1990b). This awareness requires that the therapist be able to empathize with the pleasure implied in the patient's aggression. When power relations are the dominant issue in the transference and hatred is expressed as an inordinate need for the assertion of power and autonomy, the analysis of this aspect of the transference is usually facilitated by the fact that ordinary anal-sadistic components are involved and the therapist then is dealing with the "healthier" end of the spectrum of the psychopathology of aggression.

Again, the most difficult cases are those in which extremely severe aggression goes hand in hand with extreme psychopathology of superego functioning, so that internal constraints against dangerous enactment of aggression are missing and the therapist may be realistically afraid of unleashing destructive forces beyond the capacity of the treatment to contain them. This applies to some patients who present the syndrome of malignant narcissism and is probably a major reason for the unapproachability with psychoanalytic modalities of treatment to the antisocial personality proper. It is important that the therapist have a reasonable sense of security that the analysis of powerful aggressive forces will not create new risks for the patient or others, including the therapist. A realistic assessment of this possibility and a realistic structuring of the treatment situation to protect patient, therapist, and others from inordinate and dangerous, potentially irreversible effects of the acting out of aggression are preconditions for successful work in this area.

REFERENCES

Bion, W. R. 1957. On arrogance, in *Second thoughts: Selected papers on psycho-analysis*, 86–92. New York: Aronson, 1967.

———. 1959. Attacks on linking, in *Second thoughts: Selected papers on psycho-analysis*, 93–109. New York: Aronson, 1967.

———. 1970. *Attention and interpretation*. London: Heinemann.

Braunschweig, D., and Fain, M. 1971. *Eros et Anteros*. Paris: Payot.

———. 1975. *Le nuit, le jour: Essai psychanalytique sur le fonctionnement mental*. Paris: Payot.

Call, J. D. 1980. Attachment disorders of infancy, in *Comprehensive textbook of psychiatry*, vol. 3, ed. H. I. Kaplan et al., 2586–2592. Baltimore: Williams & Wilkins.

Emde, R. 1987. Development terminable and interminable. Plenary Presentation at the 35th International Psycho-Analytical Congress, Montreal, Canada, 27 July 1987.

Emde, R., Kligman, D., Reich, J., and Wade, T. 1978. Emotional expression in infancy: 1. Initial studies of social signaling and an emergent model, in *The development of affect*, ed. M. Lewis and L. Rosenblum, 125–148. New York: Plenum.

Fraiberg, S. 1983. Pathological defenses in infancy. *Psychoanal. Q.* 60:612–635.

Gaensbauer, T., and Sands, K. 1979. Distorted affective communications in abused and neglected infants and their potential impact on caretakers. *J. Amer. Acad. Child Psychiat.* 18:236–250.

Galenson, E. 1986. Some thoughts about infant psychopathology and aggressive development. *Int. Rev. Psycho.-Anal.* 13:349–354.

Green, A. 1986. Conceptions of affect, in *On private madness,* 174–213. London: Hogarth Press.

Grossman, W. I. 1991. Pain, aggression, fantasy and concepts of sadomasochism. *Psychoanal. Q.* 60:22–52.

Izard, C. 1978. On the ontogenesis of emotions and emotion-cognition relationships in infancy, in *The development of affect,* ed. M. Lewis and L. Rosenblum, 389–413. New York: Plenum.

Jacobson, E. 1971. Acting out and the urge to betray in paranoid patients, in *Depression,* 302–318. New York: International Universities Press.

Kernberg, O. F. 1975. *Borderline conditions and pathological narcissism.* New York: Aronson.

———. 1984. *Severe personality disorders: Psychotherapeutic strategies.* New Haven: Yale University Press.

———. 1989. The narcissistic personality disorder and the differential diagnosis of antisocial behavior, in *Psychiatric clinics of North America: Narcissistic personality disorder,* vol. 12, 553–570. Philadelphia: Saunders.

———. 1990a. Hatred as pleasure, in *Pleasure beyond the pleasure principle,* ed. R. Glick and S. Bone. New Haven: Yale University Press.

———. 1990b. New perspectives in psychoanalytic affect theory, in *Emotion: Theory, research and experience.* Emotion, Psychopathology and Psychotherapy, ed. R. Plutchik and H. Kellerman, 115–130. New York: Academic Press.

———. 1990c. Sadomasochism, sexual excitement, and perversion. *J. Amer. Psychoanal. Assn.* 39:333–362.

Klein, M. 1957. *Envy and gratitude.* New York: Basic Books.

Krause, R. 1988. Eine Taxonomie der Affekte und ihre Anwendung auf das Verstandnis der frühen Störungen. *Psychotherapie und Medizinische Psychologie* 38:77–86.

Krause, R., and Lutolf, P. 1988. Facial indicators of transference processes in psychoanalytical treatment, in *Psychoanalytic process research strategies,* ed. H. Dahl and H. Kachele, 257–272. Heidelberg: Springer.

Mahler, M., and Furer, M. 1968. *On human symbiosis and the vicissitudes of individuation.* New York: International Universities Press.

Massie, H. 1977. Patterns of mother-infant behavior and subsequent childhood psychoses. *Child Psychiat. Human Devel.* 7:211–230.

Moser, U. 1978. Affektsignale und aggressives Verhalten. Zwei verbal formulierte Modelle der Aggression. *Psyche* 32:229–258.

Ogden, T. 1979. On projective identification. *Int. J. Psychoanal.* 60:357–373.

Osofsky, J. D. 1987. Affective exchanges between high risk mothers and infants. Plenary Presentation at the 35th International Psycho-Analytical Congress, Montreal, Canada, 27 July 1987.

Roiphe, H., and Galenson, E. 1981. *Infantile origins of sexual identity.* New York: International Universities Press.

Stern, D. N. 1985. *The interpersonal world of the infant.* New York: Basic Books.

Winnicott, D. W. [1949] 1958. Hate in the countertransference, in *Collected papers,* 194–203. New York: Basic Books.

5

The Early Determinants
of Penis Envy

LUCY LAFARGE, M.D.

Penis envy bears a complex relation to the concepts of rage, power, and aggression. In this chapter I will attempt to place penis envy and other feminine experiences of the absence of a penis within a developmental framework and to demonstrate the continuing, active presence of very early fantasies surrounding the anatomical difference between the sexes in adult women at all levels of character structure. I believe that these early meanings originate at the time when the girl first reacts to the anatomical genital difference, an event that we can date through child observational data (Galenson and Roiphe, 1976; Roiphe and Galenson, 1981) approximately at the age of eighteen months. The absence of a penis acquires a range of potential meanings for the girl linked to the evolving psychic structure of this early developmental phase. The affective climate of this phase, particularly the presence of rage and heightened hostile aggression, strongly determines the predominant early meaning assigned to genital difference. This meaning in turn influences the further structuring of aggression at both preoedipal and oedipal levels and the integration of genital difference with female sexuality and with fantasies of power and powerlessness.

My focus on the girl's early experience of not having a penis does not imply a return to Freud's view of the girl's discovery of the genital difference as the prime organizer of her femininity. The wish for a penis, and the many meanings of not having one, constitute a fantasy system that parallels and impinges upon the girl's complex experience of her own femininity and female genitals. Similarly, my emphasis on the early meanings of genital difference is intended to enrich rather than to replace our knowledge of the important later meanings that genital difference assumes for the girl in the context of oedipal dynamics and of the broader culture.

For the three women I will describe, meanings of genital difference were enmeshed with fantasies and experiences of the early maternal relationship. For each of the three, one meaning of the absence of the penis was that of an important loss, and for each, this loss resonated with the fantasied loss of the mother. Each woman, however, experienced this loss differently. For the neurotic woman whose case I will present, fantasies of having and losing a penis were associated with sadness and guilt. These fantasies incorporated earlier meanings of object loss but acquired their most important meaning as a defense against oedipal conflicts. For the borderline woman, the fantasy of losing a penis was closely associated with rage and with the fantasied loss of a mother who formed an essential part of the self. This fantasy contributed to the experience of oedipal conflict as catastrophically dangerous. The fantasy of having a penis retained a central defensive function in conflicts over separation and loss. For the psychotic woman, the absence of a penis was felt as *identical* to the loss of the mother as part of her psychic structure, with the consequent emergence of rage and disorganization. Oedipal unfolding was impeded, and a fused, delusional structure warded off the awareness of any absence or loss.

Freud's View of Femininity

Freud viewed the discovery of the difference between the sexes as the central organizer of both the girl's sense of femininity and her entry into the Oedipus complex. He thought that until the phallic phase, boys and girls developed in parallel, experiencing themselves and all others as masculine. Both sexes became aware of the anatomical genital difference in the context of an early genital organization, which, he believed, developed at approximately age three to five (Freud, 1923). In this *phallic-oedipal* phase, penis and clitoris became the leading zones of sexual excitement, and awareness of genital difference acted as a crucial organizer of further development, pushing the girl and boy into different developmental pathways.

Following her discovery of genital difference, the girl began to develop a sense of herself as feminine, viewing femininity as defective masculinity. Her disappointment led to a loosening of her tie to her mother. Her wish for a penis was displaced onto a wish for a baby, and she took her father as love object in the hope that he would give her a child. Her sense that the clitoris was inferior to the penis led her to abandon clitoral masturbation and opened the way to the discovery of vaginal sexuality at puberty (1925, 1931).

For each sex, awareness of the anatomical genital difference led to a differential structuring of aggression. For the girl, Freud believed, anger and envy were primary and universal reactions (1925). The girl's subsequent development reflected her attempts to master, undo, and compensate for her painful sense of injury. For the boy, awareness of the girl's "lost" penis stirred fears that his own penis could be lost as well. The boy used the turning of aggression against himself, in the form of superego identifications with powerful parental figures, particularly the oedipal father, as a way of mastering oedipal strivings and their attendant castration anxiety. What analagous process could be seen for the girl? Already castrated, she had little motive for the demolition of the Oedipus complex, which she only slowly repressed or abandoned under the influence of parental wishes (1925). Although he viewed phallic-oedipal events as decisive for superego formation, Freud noted that preoedipal experiences were particularly important for the girl. The girl's oedipal attachment to her father was often built upon a long and powerful earlier attachment to her mother (1931). For the girl, preoedipal maternal identifications were more critical than oedipal ones (1933).

Freud's late dating of the girl's discovery of the anatomical genital difference, his conviction that all girls shared a uniform reaction to this discovery, and his close linkage of castration anxiety and superego internalization led to difficulties in his conceptualization of the structuring of aggression in women. Convinced that a single reaction to genital difference was primary, Freud saw the broad range of meanings that genital difference assumes for women as defensive fantasies and hence failed to observe the complex factors, and particularly the early vicissitudes of aggression, that determined subjective meaning. Similarly, because Freud viewed castration anxiety as the central motivation for superego internalization, he saw little motivation for this later structuring of aggression in women. Interpreting his data to fit his model, he saw the feminine superego as weak and undeveloped and failed to give sufficient weight to other factors, particularly the triadic nature of oedipal conflicts, that motivate superego internalization in both sexes.

Early critics of Freud's psychology of women took issue with his view of penis envy as a primary and universal reaction to the girl's discovery of the anatomical difference between the sexes and as the central organizer of femininity. Karen Horney (1924, [1926] 1971) noted the large contribution of culture to the meaning assigned to genital difference and questioned the significance of the girl's discovery of the anatomical genital difference. The girl did feel a sense of inferiority at the time of her discovery, Horney argued, but penis envy acquired its main meaning and function later, as a defensive regression from oedipal conflict. Marie Bonaparte observed that the girl's further development stemmed not from the anatomical genital difference itself but from the psychological meaning, which she attributed to it (Person, 1974). Melanie Klein ([1928] 1981) questioned Freud's hypothesis of a long period of parallel development for girls and boys as well as his insistence that the penis was seen by both as the sole organ of genital pleasure. She felt that oral frustration led both sexes to a search for new aims and objects in the first and second year of life—and consequently to early oedipal wishes in which genital and pregenital aims were mingled—and to early genital awareness, which included vaginal awareness for the girl. Early oedipal wishes incorporated different fantasies for the boy and the girl and led to different danger situations for each, with the boy fearing punishment by castration and the girl fearing the destruction of the interior of her body.

Fifty years after Freud's final formulation, much of his psychology of women has been thrown into question. The relation between the girl's recognition of the anatomical genital difference and her entry into the Oedipus complex remains controversial. Henri Parens (1976) sees varying paths of entry into the oedipal phase; Roiphe and Galenson (1981) report an erotic turn toward the father as a frequent result of the girl's discovery of genital difference at rapprochement; Edgcumbe and Burgner (1975) see the later consolidation of that discovery as a prerequisite for oedipal unfolding.

The girl's castration reaction is no longer seen as the unique organizer of feminine identity (Blum, 1976). Current psychoanalytic thought would consider the development of a feminine self representation as a complex, multifaceted process that begins long before the integration of the anatomical genital difference and continues throughout life. Somatic experiences (Greenacre, 1952), parental expectations and handling (Money and Erhardt, 1972), cognitive factors (Kleeman, 1971, 1976), and the affective transmission of maternal sexuality and fantasy (Grunberger, 1970; Olivier, 1989) all make important contributions to the early development of the sense of femininity.

As development proceeds, complex identifications with the mother and with the ideals of both parents become important determinants of the feminine self representation (Blum, 1976; Bernstein, 1983). The mother's attitude toward her own femininity, and particularly toward her genitals, colors the girl's self experience. Finally, the girl's experience of femininity is affected by identification with attitudes toward women in the broader culture.

The Developmental Context of Feminine Castration Reactions

Child observation (Galenson and Roiphe, 1976; Roiphe and Galenson, 1981) has shown that an early phase of genital arousal occurs for both sexes far earlier than Freud believed, at approximately age sixteen to eighteen months. Both sexes become aware of the anatomical genital difference at this time. The psychological impact of this awareness, however, is seen to be quite different for the two sexes. Most of the boys in Roiphe and Galenson's study did not manifest powerful reactions to their discovery of genital difference at this early phase. For boys, castration reactions become significant only later, under the impact of oedipal strivings, as Freud postulated. By contrast, most girls showed significant early castration reactions. Girls were often envious and resentful, a finding also noted by Margaret Mahler's group (Mahler, Pine, and Bergman, 1975). Their hostility toward the mother was intensified, and they showed a regression to earlier oral and anal satisfactions. In addition, many of the girls studied manifested an adaptive surge in symbolic thought, with an expansion in symbolic play and fantasy. Where conflict was marked, an inter-ference with an already existing capacity for symbolization was evident in a deterioration of both language and play.

Eleanor Galenson and Herman Roiphe's observations can be understood in the context of Mahler's (Mahler, Pine, and Bergman, 1975) concepts of sepa-ration and individuation. For both boys and girls, the dawning awareness of self as separate from mother appears to be a developmental prerequisite for the discovery of genital difference. Those children who were observed to be delayed in the milestones of separation and individuation were subsequently delayed in reaching anal, urinary, and genital awareness as well. The girl's regressive clinging to the mother after her discovery of genital difference, or alternately her surge in symbolic play, reflects the impact of this discovery upon the evolving object world of rapprochement.

At the earlier level of organization found in rapprochement, pleasurable representations of the self are closely associated with pleasurable represen-tations of the mother, and these good representations of self and mother together serve to ward off painful experiences of the self-mother dyad (Jacob-son, 1964; Kernberg, 1976). The presence and emotional availability of the mother and a positive feeling tone between mother and child, support the stability of pleasurable representations and, because these representations are central to the ego, of ego functions as well.

The mother's absence, and other painful affect states, threaten the stability of these representations. The perceived loss of the mother at this phase is not experienced as an absence but as the painful emergence of bad experiences of self and object (Klein, 1940; Isaacs, [1952] 1989). The child's anger at the mother is felt as particularly dangerous because it directly threatens the sta-bility of the positive maternal representation and, less directly, because the child associates his or her anger with the experience of the mother's absence and, by projection, with the mother's anger at him.

At this early phase, power might best be conceptualized as the power to survive hostile aggression—that is, as the power of the parent to survive the child's anger, and, more important, as the power of good self and object representations to endure anger, transient loss, and pain.

As rapprochement proceeds, the mother's presence or a positive feeling tone between mother and child supports the integration of good and bad aspects of self and object representations and the establishment of a separate self representation. The mother's absence or the child's anger may slow devel-opment or may lead to a regressive fusion of self and object representations or to a heightened defensive use of splitting between good and bad representa-tions.

The child's establishment of a separate self representation is felt in part as a loss of the mother as an omnipotent extension of the self. Power at this midphase might be conceptualized as the capacity for omnipotent action, which the child experiences in his union with the mother.

As object constancy becomes secure, the distance of the mother, now experienced as separate, no longer threatens the child with regression and with the catastrophic loss of the representations of good self and good object. Instead, the child's anger or the mother's distance threatens the child with sadness, with a loss of self-esteem, and with the perceived loss of the object's love. The loss of the sense of omnipotence that accompanies separation of self and object is compensated at least in part by complex, realistic identifications with the mother. Power might now be conceptualized as the power of restraint and of competent—rather than omnipotent—action in reality, a power acquired through partial identifications with the parents.

Because development at rapprochement follows an oscillating course with higher levels of organization repeatedly gained and lost, the girl's awareness of the anatomical genital difference is potentially experienced at each level of organization found at this phase. At the most primitive level, the girl's discovery of something missing that could be there at the site of heightened erotism triggers a reverberating cycle of loss and anger. The absence of a penis is felt as a catastrophic loss. Rage and pain threaten the stability of good self and object representations and the consequent emergence of a persecutory experience of self and object. The girl's anger at the mother for failing to protect her from this loss (and, by projection, the girl's experience of her mother's anger at her) further endangers the survival of representations of good self and good mother. In effect, the absence of the penis in this primitive object world is experienced as identical to the loss of the mother: either threatens the girl with the loss of a vital psychic structure, the world of good objects that protects her against bad objects, pain, and rage.

With the girl's progress toward object constancy, her more advanced and complex recognition of genital difference is integrated as part of the nascent separate self representation. The girl's continued awareness of the absent penis parallels her awareness of the loss of the mother as an omnipotent extension of the self. These losses are no longer experienced as intimately connected, but they continue to resonate in one another. The narcissistic loss involved in the loss of union with a mother experienced as powerful and good stirs a strong current of envy of the mother, an envy that is mingled with envy of the lost penis.

With the achievement of object constancy, the girl's castration reaction has shifted from a threat of instability of self and object to a much more focused threat of anger and sadness experienced by a stable self toward a more stable representation of the mother. If the absence of a penis is still perceived as a loss, it is felt as a sign of the loss of the mother's love. This loss is balanced by emerging positive realistic identifications with the mother and the mother's genitals. Identification with a mother who is perceived as powerful repairs, at least in part, the narcissistic injuries of loss of union with the earlier mother and loss of the penis.

A heightening of hostile aggression at rapprochement, which tilts the fluctuating course of this phase toward regression, will also lead to a predominant integration of the girl's awareness of genital difference at the earlier levels of object relations found in this phase. In this case, experiences of genital difference may become linked with the primitive defensive structures, which ward off catastrophic loss and envy. The regressive refusion of representations of self and mother will come to be fused with a representation of the penis as well. A heightened defensive split between good and bad representations will become linked with a split between masculine and feminine representations of the self.

In a reverberating system, the girl's castration reactions, which are influenced by the reorganization of the object world at rapprochement, also influence the unfolding of this phase. Particularly intense anger at the discovery of genital difference may slow the course of rapprochement or increase recourse to pathological defenses. Early castration reactions are only one factor contributing to girls' observed greater difficulty in negotiating the rapprochement subphase. Individual differences are great. Mothers have particular difficulty in separating from daughters (Bergman, 1987). An upsurge of forceful activity, often accompanied by anger, provides an important impetus in both sexes to the developmental shift from passivity to activity and to the unfolding of the separation-individuation process (McDevitt, 1983). Girls tend to use the motor apparatus for the direct expression of both hostile and nonhostile aggression far less than boys. The cause for this is controversial. Constitutional factors may be significant; parents tend to restrict daughters' direct expression of aggression far more than sons'. These early factors, which antedate separation and individuation, are compounded at rapprochement by the girl's heightened awareness of the possibility of object loss, engendered by her experience of the loss of her penis.

Penis Envy and Symbolic Thought

As I have described, at the most primitive level of organization found at rapprochement the girl's awareness of the loss of the penis is experienced as identical with the loss of a positive bond with the mother; each is felt as the emergence of a catastrophically painful experience of self and mother. As rapprochement proceeds, the girl comes to experience the two losses as distinct, and with the growing capacity for symbolic thought that accompanies the shift toward object constancy, she is able to use the penis as a symbol of the mother. The fantasy of having a penis comes to serve a defensive function in the management of anxieties concerning anger, separation, and loss in the maternal relationship.

This early use of the penis as symbol supports the development of object constancy. Envy of the penis is the first of a series of transformations that deflect aggression outside the mother-child pair. Klein ([1957] 1977) describes the girl's displacement of destructive envy from the maternal breast to the father's penis, which the mother is felt to contain within herself, then to the penis as part of the father, and finally to the father as a whole object. Displacement protects the maternal bond and facilitates the working through of hostile aggression.

When the quota of hostile aggression at rapprochement is too great and progress toward object constancy is hindered, this symbolic expansion cannot take place. The perceived loss of the penis continues to be felt as the loss of the positive maternal representation—a loss of psychic structure that cannot be mastered via symbolization and fantasy. At the most severe level, conflicts over hostile aggression and loss lead to the formation of psychotic structures in which experiences of fusion with mother and penis serve as protection against rage, pain, and loss. At a highly concrete but nonpsychotic level, the fantasied presence of the lost or feared-for penis must be guaranteed by a fetish. Phyllis Greenacre (1969, 1970) describes the use of fetishes by children of both sexes at this age as a protection against the loss of both penis and mother. She aptly describes the fetish as "congealed anger" (1969, 333), indicating the intensity of rage that must be contained by such a concrete and durable defensive structure.

Next in ascending capacity for symbolic transformation would be women's experience of penis envy as concrete and their reification of the analyst's interpretations of it as a screen for early narcissistic concerns (Grossman and Stewart, 1976). The more metaphorical transformations of penis envy, so often seen in women, are of course strongly influenced by later defensive functions, by identification, and by culture. Nevertheless, I believe that these retain some trace of their earliest defensive function, evident in their special tendency to be concretized.

Sadomasochistic Fantasy

The progression toward object constancy is accompanied, for both sexes, by a growing capacity for the elaboration of sadomasochistic fantasy (Parens, 1979; McDevitt, 1983). I believe that for both sexes, but particularly for girls, the heightened hostile aggression of rapprochement, to which early castration reactions contribute, leads to the potential for a sadomasochistic structuring of the experiences of separation and reunion that are central to this phase. When hostile aggression is moderate and the progress toward object constancy steady, this sadomasochistic structuring takes the form of fantasies surrounding object loss, with the object's withdrawal experienced as punishment or sadistic withholding. A masochistic tilt in these fantasies, with anger projected onto the mother, protects the mother from the girl's aggression.

With a greater heightening of hostile aggression, this early elaboration may take the form instead of a sadomasochistic structuring of the instability of object relations and affects. Affective swings become charged with painful excitement. Experiences of boundary loss and of the extinguishing of individual proprioception and cognition in the service of primary identification are erotized and elaborated as fantasies of surrender. These early erotized experiences of loss of the sense of self form a substrate for later masochistic fantasies of sexual submission and self-destruction.

I would place in this category the women described by Janine Chasseguet-Smirgel (1986) as suffering from "primary passivity"—women who suppress all anxiety and affect in order to preserve a symbiotic relationship with the mother and who later court death at the hands of lovers. I would agree with Chasseguet-Smirgel that this psychopathology originates in the service of a primitive early maternal relationship but feel that this suppression of differentiated self-experience gains force through early erotization.

For boys, an equally high quota of hostile aggression in the rapprochement subphase more often takes the form of an unstable body image and fantasies of femininity (Galenson, 1988). As Freud observed in "A Child Is Being Beaten," fantasies of transformation into a woman afford the boy a permutation of self-directed aggression that is not available to the girl. In latency, such fantasies of femininity permit the boy to retain in consciousness core beating fantasies that the girl must repress (Freud, 1919, 190). Similarly, earlier fantasies of feminine transformation afford a masculine mode of structuring masochistic fantasy different from the feminine one.

Genital Difference and Oedipal Dynamics
The girl's predominant integration of genital difference at rapprochement strongly influences her experience of oedipal dynamics and the later structuring of aggression, female sexuality, and experiences of power and powerlessness that occur with the internalization of the superego. Because loss of the mother is a central danger of oedipal rivalry for the girl, feminine oedipal desires tend to revive earlier anxieties and fantasies surrounding maternal loss, fantasies that are enmeshed with fantasies about castration and genital difference. Hence, the girl's oedipal phase fantasies of having a penis condense the wish to satisfy the mother sexually in a negative oedipal romance: the wish to be a boy in order to avoid dangerous feminine wishes for sexual union with the father and through the earlier equation of penis with mother, a wish for assurance that the mother has not been and cannot be lost. Freud's view that the girl, already castrated, had little motivation for the resolution of the Oedipus complex and the internalization of the superego is not consistent with current psychoanalytic thinking. The danger that the girl's oedipal rivalry will lead to the loss of the mother, to the loss of her love, or to her retaliation are sufficient motives for superego internalization.

With the internalization of the superego, fantasies about genital difference are incorporated in much more complex, less personified and less representational structures. Because parental superego and ego ideal form a major part of the child's superego identifications, gender-related parental values are particularly important at this phase. An ego ideal of feminine "weakness"— suppression of open displays of aggression and self-assertion, of self-abnegation, and contextual morality—may represent for the girl not a failure of superego internalization, as Freud thought, but a particularly strong internalization of parental superego values (Blum, 1976; Bernstein, 1983). Similarly, a *maternal ego ideal* consisting of devotion, nurturance, and self-sacrifice often does not represent a weak and masochistic adaptation but rather an identification with a mother experienced as powerful and highly valued (Meyers, 1988). The reworking of the superego at adolescence permits a further integration of culturally held values of phallic power and feminine submission, or, conversely, in a changing society, the possibility of some change in the conservative conscience of society and its expression in feminine values.

The experience of genital difference at the highest level that I have described, where female genitals and femininity are integrated as part of a loving, complex identification with the mother, will lead to an oedipal situation in which each parent is loved as a whole and complex object and the female genital is valued as part of a loving relationship with the father. The wish for a penis also acquires meaning as a part of whole object relationships, representing for the girl a means of loving the mother sexually and a gratifying identification with the father as well as a defensive structure that wards off positive oedipal strivings. Earlier meanings of maternal loss and the earlier equation of mother with penis are incorporated within this oedipal framework.

CASE 1: the analysis of Mrs. D, a married woman in her forties who came to analysis with complaints of depression and constant self-criticism

The central event of Mrs. D's childhood had been the death of a sister during Mrs. D's latency. From the beginning of her analysis, Mrs. D frequently voiced a belief that men had the better deal, claiming attention more freely from both men and women. In her own family, her father had been catered to and competed for by Mrs. D and her mother.

The fantasy of having a penis came into focus in the third year of Mrs. D's analysis. At that time, Mrs. D's relentless self-criticism had abated somewhat. She began the first of the sessions I describe here by saying that she wished she could be closer to me. She felt like a lame duck, left out and unwanted. She connected this feeling with the death of her sister Mary and the depression that she and her parents had felt afterward. Speaking of this, she felt a "deep sadness." She wished that she could explore this with me, saying that all I knew of her was "the tip of the iceberg." At the same time she wanted to ignore her sadness.

She recalled a dream: She was a Jewish man, hiding from the Nazis, who were torturing people with matches. They found her and demanded her papers, and she offered to show them her genitals instead, saying, "See, I have never been circumscribed!" She thought about her substitution of the word "circumscribed" for "circumcised." How she hated to be circumscribed, restrained! She felt that her father had controlled her. I pointed out that she herself kept her sadness circumscribed. Yes, she agreed, she was especially afraid of weeping; that, she felt, would be opening a real "Pandora's box." It was funny that the man had offered to show his genitals as proof when he was really circumcised. He counted on the Nazis not looking closely. Exposing his genitals was like exposing her feelings—a great danger: her fear was that I might abandon her if she were too sad.

This session reveals the first of a series of linkages between Mrs. D's fantasy of having a penis and her fantasies and feelings about Mary's death. Mrs. D had already devoted many sessions to her rivalry with Mary for their mother's attention and her intense guilt when Mary had been removed by death from the mother-daughter triangle. (This piece of analysis had resulted in the lessening superego pressure reflected in Mrs. D's lessening self-criticism.) The fantasy of having a penis protected Mrs. D from the positive oedipal meaning of Mary's death and the associated affects of guilt and sadness. Mrs. D had experienced Mary as a rival for the father and Mary's death as an oedipal triumph. If Mrs. D had a penis, then she had not wished for sexual union with her father and was not responsible for Mary's death. Mrs. D's image of herself as a man with a circumcised penis reflects a weakening of her wish to have a perfect, unmarked male genital and the beginning exposure of the female genital underneath. This exposure in turn draws the attack of Mrs. D's still harsh superego (the Nazis).

In the sessions that followed, Mrs. D's associations were with something "concrete" that was missing. A dream image of a mother and two daughters linked this thought to the memory of Mary. At the next session, Mrs. D's associations turned to her envy of men. She began this session by saying that she was disappointed that I was not wearing slacks. She remembered a "snatch of a dream": she was watching men playing tennis and felt humiliated. Men played tennis better than she did, she said; they had a "nice rhythmic stroke." She felt angry at men today; the "bottom line" was that they wanted to lord it over her. She felt dissatisfied with me and the analysis. "Bottom line," she repeated, I had given her nothing concrete. Perhaps responding to the concreteness of Mrs. D's language, I made an uncharacteristically concrete interpretation, saying that she seemed to associate having something concrete with having a penis. Mrs. D agreed: men had it all. She felt angry and humiliated by my interpretation, though, as if I did not think she was special. Sadly, she spoke of concrete things she wished she had had: if she had been allowed to go to Mary's funeral, that would have been something. . . . She wished that she had been breast-fed.

For several sessions after this, Mrs. D spoke of feeling hopeless. The penis was just a metaphor, she realized. She had begun the analysis hoping that I would transform her by magic into a different person, one who had not had the losses that she had had. Now she saw that the hope of a magical transformation was "a fallacy." If she were not like her father, then she was like her mother, and she did not want to look deeper into that. She felt that looking deeper would hurt both her mother and herself and she would be to blame. She had wanted to be like her father as he was before Mary's death, not the depressed father that she had known later. If she could not be this earlier father, then no one was; and the time before Mary's death seemed more lost to her.

This material demonstrates several further linkages between Mrs. D's fantasy of having a penis and fantasies and feelings surrounding Mary's death. The predominant danger had shifted from guilt over Mary's death to pain and sadness at her loss. Mary was again equated with the mother, and her loss linked with preoedipal meanings of maternal loss (the breast-feeding) as well as oedipal ones. In this context, the fantasy of having a penis serves multiple defensive functions: Clearly, it wards off positive oedipal wishes for the father. In addition, I believe, it draws upon an earlier linkage of penis and mother, which originated at rapprochement, and through the equation of penis, mother, and Mary provides concrete assurance that Mary and mother cannot and have not been lost. This phallic buttress against loss and grief is reinforced by an identification with the father of the era before Mary's death.

As this material was analyzed, Mrs. D spoke of feeling softer, more feminine, and less critical of her mother. She thought of her father after Mary's death; she wondered if he might have been sexually attracted to her as she grew older. Mrs. D began a session a few weeks later by saying how uncomfortable she felt when she thought about competing with me. Then she reported another dream: She had gone to a department store to buy a baby blanket like the one she had had when she was little. Suddenly, she was afraid that she would miss her appointment with me. She hurried back for the blanket, but there was none; she could find only a tuft of wool. Then, in a hospital, she saw some doctors fussing over a sick patient. "I wish I had something that people paid attention to," she thought. She took a swivel chair out of the hospital. In the doorway was a blanket and champagne spilling onto it out of a bottle.

Mrs. D's associations were with a woman friend to whom she felt inferior. "I wanted something I could show off," she said. "You're a doctor. You have something concrete." The blanket was like a replacement for all that she had lost. Thinking of it, she felt sad, like crying, but even her tears were "a drop in the bucket"—not like the flow of the champagne. Without concrete replacements, she felt doomed to be envious of me and all that I had. Something to show would be something to be seen—assurance that she would not be forgotten. Although the doctors were paying attention to the sick patient, she felt that Mary might have died because she was forgotten and unprotected. Without something to show, she might be swept away too; and being recognized just for having something would mean that she had not had to struggle to survive. She knew how much she had wanted to live; she would have been willing to struggle to the death with Mary if she had had to. "Something to show" meant that there had been no struggle, that her life had not been at the expense of Mary's.

A further function of Mrs. D's fantasy of having a penis is revealed here as a defense against the fear of being like Mary and vulnerable to a sudden, inexplicable death. Mrs. D's oedipal rivalry with her analyst continued to threaten her with guilt and with the dual loss of penis and mother. Each of the two central images of the dream—the blanket and the champagne bottle—condensed both potential losses and together reflected an intermediate phase in the working through of the meanings of the two fantasied losses. The fetishistic bottle reflected an earlier need for a durable defense against grief and pain that Mrs. D experienced as intolerable. The blanket, with its connotation of transitional object, represented a loss that could be tolerated and mourned. As the analysis progressed, Mrs. D's experience of herself as a feminine and sexual woman and her capacity to mourn Mary's death continued to develop in tandem.

A predominant integration of the awareness of genital difference at a somewhat lower level and its linkage with split representations of self and object will lead to the unfolding of a pseudo-oedipal situation in which genital difference is used to anchor a split between the two parents. A full oedipal unfolding, which would entail an integration of each parental representation and the experience of a loving attitude toward each as a whole object, is impeded. Oedipal victory is felt to be catastrophically dangerous because loss of the mother may be felt as the loss of a vital piece of psychic structure. Similarly, the awareness of feminine genitals in the oedipal relation to the father threatens the emergence of anger, envy, and the consequent loss of psychic structure.

CASE 2: Miss L, a woman in her thirties who came for treatment because she felt chronically depressed and empty

For Miss L, the level of closeness she experienced with her objects was far more significant than their sex. In her masochistic affairs with men and submissive friendships with women, she felt that she lost her identity if she became too intimate, while distance and separation threatened her with rage and paranoid regression.

Early in the analysis, Miss L attempted to control the distance between us, trying to please me with enthusiasm and support without giving way to intimate revelations. In this early phase, Miss L had what I believe was the fantasy of being someone else's penis. When she felt competent, she saw herself as an athletic team player, the "tool" of the coach. This fantasy reflected an identification with Miss L's father, whom she saw as athletic and steadfast, but in the main it seemed to represent the loss of Miss L's individual identity in the service of maintaining a symbiotic connection to her mother. Initially, she felt little suffering at her surrender. The fantasy of a union with me (with myself as mother, Miss L as my penis) warded off these painful feelings.

Gradually, Miss L's self-experience as my phallic extension faded, and she began to feel that her submission to me was a painful surrender but one that was required to guarantee my presence. She felt that I would not tolerate her separate existence. She tolerated her own rage at my separate existence poorly, and my absence or perceived disinterest often led to paranoid regression or to renewed fantasies of fusion.

The fantasy of *having* a penis appeared for the first time in the third year of Miss L's analysis. After a vacation when she had experienced a severe regression, Miss L began to express her rage at my abandonment much more openly than she had before. She reported a dream filled with fiery imagery of murder and suicide. Her associations were to her anger at me and the excitement that accompanied it. She reflected that she thought that we would both survive.

The next day, Miss L reported another dream: A man had given her a ring with a large pink stone. She was flashing the ring around, showing off. The ring was a cheap dime store one and the stone was wobbly, but she felt proud and admired. As she associated to the dream, Miss L seemed gay and giddy. Then she paused and said that she was worried about becoming a "tool." Her associations slowed; she seemed sad and said that she felt empty. It was as if she had brought in the exciting dream to make up for being such an empty person, one who did not have enough to hold me. I said that the dream was like the ring, which excited people when she showed it off. Miss L agreed. The excitement, she said, covered her sadness and loneliness, a feeling of pain and loss that she could hardly bear to "open up."

Miss L's growing capacity to tolerate both her rage at my absence and the excitement that resulted from her erotization of that rage had led to a heightened awareness of genital difference. Miss L, however, experienced the loss of both penis and analyst (experienced as the mother in the transference) as a threat of unbearable loneliness and emptiness—the loss of a part of her inner world which she could not afford to lose. The fantasy of having a penis, represented by the pink stone of the dream, warded off both losses. Secondarily, the stone acquired negative oedipal significance as a means of exciting and holding the mother. The intensity of Miss L's anxiety and underlying rage is reflected in the fetishistic quality of this image. The wobbliness of the stone reflects the insecure status of the phallic defense, and, indeed, in the session Miss L first returns to the earlier symbiotic defensive fantasy of being a penis and then experiences the pain that the stone was intended to ward off.

In the sessions that followed, Miss L spoke of feeling like two people, one active and connected, the other defective and alone. Her anger at me was often overt, but it quickly turned to anger at herself. Speaking of feeling unhelped by me, she recalled a dream of a fake gold necklace that her mother had given her as a gift. She liked it even if it was a fake, she said. If she was disappointed with me and the analysis, it was her own fault. "I'm the fake necklace! I'm the one with nothing to give!"

The experience of feeling split that Miss L described reflected a defensive attempt to ward off her rage at me and the defective image of herself, which accompanied the experiences of separateness and genital difference. The "fake necklace" dream indicates the breakdown of Miss L's fetishistic defense. The stone/penis, which represented in the dream an unstable means of holding her object's love, had quickly become condensed with images of the actual object (her mother or myself) and herself. In effect, the anger and pain evoked by separation interfered with Miss L's capacity to develop a stable symbolic displacement, which would have helped her to master them.

In the weeks that followed, Miss L's associations turned to oedipal fantasies with an apocalyptic tone. She distanced herself from the anger manifest in her fantasies, calling them "weird" and "foreign." In this context, she reported a dream in which she was alternately a man and a woman: "A couple was drinking together in a dark room. Then they separated. They went in separate cars. First I was her driving; then I was him driving. She was driving fast and laughing, coming in and out of his vision. She went faster and faster, out of control. Her car crashed and burned. Then I was him at her funeral."

Miss L observed that this was a new kind of dream for her, a driving dream where she was not being driven. "Whether I was the girl or the boy, I was driving." The boy and the girl were two sides of her, Miss L said. The boy was sober and level-headed and sad. The girl wanted things and was out of control with excitement. She felt sad at the thought of their being separated. As a boy, Miss L could not control her losses; she could not hold on to what she wanted most, but she survived. She wished that she could be both sides, that she could allow herself to want things without being so endangered. As a girl, her manicky excitement might excite others and hold them. This relationship, too, was dangerous and hollow, an empty show of relating.

This session reflected an oedipal situation strongly colored by preoedipal fantasies related to the dangerousness of separation and feminine sexuality. The initial romantic liaison of the dream, with the implied threat of the loss of an oedipal mother, quickly shifts to a sexualized drama of separation whereby the mother who is lost is an earlier mother who forms an essential part of the psychic structure. Losing this mother as she takes the driver's seat, Miss L is unable to control either excitement or aggression and rides to a fiery death. An identification with the man in this primal scene warded off dangers at an oedipal level by averting the competition that threatens the loss of the mother. At a preoedipal level, through the equation of penis and mother, the "sober" man has recaptured the psychic structure necessary for the control of affects and impulses.

Miss L erotized experiences of fusion (as masochistic surrender) and of the loss of control that she experienced at separation. Her spinning out of control represented both the emergence of overwhelming sexual desire and a hypomanic, giddy excitement, which she often used to ward off the loss that she experienced at times of separation. The fantasy that her hypomanic excitement excited others represented a further defensive exploitation of her experience of being out of control. The total bodily excitement represented in this dream was an experience often reported by Miss L, not unlike the overflow of somatic excitement from zone to zone described by Greenacre (1952) in children with a predisposition to anxiety. Perhaps its association in the dream with fantasies of separation and of an object tie reflect attempts to incorporate this feeling of being overwhelmed within a defensive fantasy structure.

A predominant experience of castration reactions at the most primitive level, where they are associated with a catastrophic loss of good representations of self and object, leads to a tenuous integration of genital difference within self and object representations and to an unstable unfolding of triadic object relationships. As Klein (1957) describes, at this level the girl's flight from rage and envy of the mother leads to a tenuous idealization of the paternal penis and the father. This split between the two parents is unstable; idealization of the father soon becomes infiltrated with envy and rage as well. At this level, a psychotic, fused structure of self, mother, and penis may be used to ward off catastrophic object loss and envy of both sexes. As Klein (1957) notes, a fused parental representation gains meaning in the oedipal situation as a representation of the parental couple joined in intercourse. The fusion of the self representation with the representations of the parents protects the child from envy of the couple as well as envy of the parent of each sex.

CASE 3: Miss S, a woman in her late twenties with a history of binge eating, chronic feelings of emptiness, and frequent, prolonged psychotic episodes

I treated Miss S face to face, in psychotherapy three times a week. During periods of regression, mingled with complaints of emptiness and of being destroyed, Miss S would manifest an unusual psychotic symptom. She would declare that she was "not Ashley Hayes" (a well-known fashion model at that time). A tall, striking woman, Ashley Hayes had only to be seen to be admired. She was physically perfect. Miss S's Ashley Hayes was explicitly a combination of man, woman, and penis. Miss S described her as "masculine" and "hard." Slender and erect, Ashley was envied by men and women alike. Miss S envied beautiful women; she was also envious of men because she felt they "lorded it" over women. As Ashley, she would turn the tables and dominate men who would be wild with desire for her.

Miss S's "Ashley" symptom reflected a wish to *be* a penis, but unlike Miss L's fantasy of being my "tool," Miss S's fantasy did not appear to guarantee a connection with me. Instead, Miss S's symptom seemed to isolate her from me altogether. As Ashley, she was inferior to no one and needed no one.

Miss S did not wish to be *like* Ashley Hayes; she wished to *be* Ashley Hayes. I soon came to understand that her complaint was meant as an accusation: despite her apparent improvement in therapy with me, I had not helped her to be Ashley Hayes, and as this was her only real goal, I had done nothing for her. My interpretations of her demand for a magical transformation as a defense against terrible anxiety about her real state and as an attack on me and the real help that I gave her were intolerable to her. She felt any discussion of her wish to be Ashley as toxic because it meant that she really could not be Ashley.

The meaning of this symptom became much clearer in a series of sessions in the third year of Miss S's treatment. By now her psychotic episodes had become briefer, less frequent, and more clearly linked to negative transference reactions. She had begun to look for a job for the first time. She began one session by announcing that she had applied for a job and thought she might get it. This theme soon began to alternate with the familiar idea that she wished to have an exciting, glamorous life and that I wished to force her to give up her hopes. I interpreted her internal conflict as being that between beginning to hope and function in reality and attacking her hopes and regressing. Miss S continued to attack me. Why did I not want her to be beautiful and admired? She felt humiliated at taking a routine job.

Then Miss S came late for one session and sat looking away from me. She said that she was ugly and had to be beautiful. If I really wanted to help her, I would help her to become a beautiful model. In response to this material, I had an extremely intense countertransference reaction, unlike any I have ever had. I was aware of feeling anxious, but my main experience was a bizarre somatic one. I felt as if I were going to starve if I did not eat something immediately. I literally felt as if Miss S were destroying my body and that I was going to die. As I listened to Miss S, who did not speak in a particularly angry tone, I considered my reaction and felt that it was a response to the tremendous rage at me underlying her words (a complementary identification) and a (concordant) identification with Miss S's own desperate frustration and her fantasy of being destroyed inside, which she experienced somatically and for which she needed to compensate with a fantasy of perfect beauty.

I told Miss S that her wanting me to transform her in this way was an attack on me and all that we had actually done together. Somewhat to my surprise, her mood shifted; she said that she did feel angry at me but did not know why. She thought that she would take the job. On this note, she left.

In the following session, Miss S, said that she had not wanted to come. After our last meeting, she had had a "terrible" dream: she was destroying my office, throwing the books off the shelves, and breaking everything. I said that it might be better to hurt my office than to hurt me. Miss S said that she had wanted to hurt me physically or kill me at the last session. She had never been so angry at anyone. She felt that she had given up everything for me and that I wanted her to have no pleasure or excitement, nothing at all outside of myself and the therapy.

She appeared at our next session nicely dressed and looking happier. She said that she had taken the job and was looking forward to starting. She reflected on the feeling she had had that she could have nothing outside of therapy. Now she saw that she had *wished* to have nothing outside of therapy. Instead of having her own life, she had wanted to be absorbed into mine. When she saw that another person had something she wanted, she felt that she could never get what that person had by trying and felt unbearably envious. Then she would become absorbed in that person—"like an extension who is just the same." When she had wanted me to transform her into Ashley Hayes, she said (explaining this phenomenon for the first time in a way that I could understand), she had not meant that she, Miss S, would become different but that she would surrender her identity as Miss S to the envied Ashley. She felt the same with me. She envied me and wanted to become part of me, to lose her identity in an exciting act of surrender. She fought this wish to be absorbed all the time. Right now she felt less like that. After admitting her anger toward me, she felt more able to be someone herself and less need to be absorbed.

The "perfectly beautiful" Ashley Hayes represented for Miss S a fusion of the idealized surface of her own body with the idealized surface of her mother's body. Donald Meltzer and Meg Harris Williams (1988) have described the idealization of the surface of the mother's body with a projection to the interior of aggressive fantasies of the mother-child relationship. For Miss S, the scale of her rage and pain at loss or disappointment in her objects required a delusional construct. Her splitting of experiences of "perfect beauty" and being "destroyed inside" exploited the disjunction in feminine experience, noted by Greenacre (1952), between a visible body surface and the sensations arising within a vaguely delineated body interior.

The delusional structure formed by the fusion of body surfaces was also fused with a representation of the penis. Annie Reich ([1953] 1973, 1954, 1960) describes patients with severe narcissistic pathology for whom concrete archaic identifications with idealized infantile objects, experienced as phallic, serve as pathological nuclei of the ego ideal and ward off rage and hypochondriasis. For Reich's patients, these identifications represented focal deficits in reality testing in distorted but nonpsychotic ego structure. Miss S's grandiose identification was a psychotic structure. This was evident in her more generalized psychotic symptoms, her disorganization and cognitive regression, and in the concreteness of her experience of being absorbed.

For Miss S, the loss of either mother or penis posed a catastrophic threat of rage and disintegration. In effect, Miss S could not tolerate wanting anything that she did not have. The experience of delusional fusion with me protected her from any contact with me in reality and from the shattering jolts of wanting, not having, and envying. Miss S had erotized the experience of fusion as a "painful, exciting absorption."

Miss S was unable to form the symbolic chain that I have described: from breast to penis and outward. Both beauty and internal damage were completely concrete for her. Her delusion of an idealized surface that contained and concealed a disturbing interior reflected her inability to repress or transform her painful experiences. They were either there or, when they were concealed, not there. Earlier in the treatment, my countertransference to her Ashley symptom mirrored this situation: I was expected to act upon it in some way, but this could not be done; it was either there or not there.

It was when Miss S made significant moves toward separation—by looking for a life "outside the therapy"—that this delusion came into focus in the transference. Her rage, envy, and humiliation as we moved apart fueled a psychotic demand to be Ashley. Her growing ability to tolerate anger in the transference, however, and to experience me as separate led to a series of unprecedented events: Miss S was able to project her "destroyed" experience onto me. My tolerance of her projection and my interpretation of it supported her growing ability to tolerate awareness of her rage, to represent it in a dream, and finally to reflect on it and on the delusional Ashley construct that surrounded it. This sequence marked the fading of Miss S's Ashley symptom; when it reappeared in subsequent months, it was transient and weakly held.

For the three women I have described, penis envy and the fantasy of having a penis had widely different meanings and defensive functions. For each of the women, the fantasies drew upon early, preoedipal meanings of genital difference, but the quality of these early meanings, the affects with which they were associated, and their relation to later, oedipal meanings, were different at different levels of character structure.

For Mrs. D, genital difference and the fantasy of having a penis acquired their principal meanings in the context of oedipal conflicts. Mrs. D had experienced the death of her sister Mary during latency as the destruction of an oedipal rival, equated with the death of the oedipal mother. The fantasy of being a man warded off the oedipal significance of Mary's death and Mrs. D's consequent guilt over her triumph. The loss of Mary as an oedipal rival also revived earlier, preoedipal fantasies of the loss of the mother, fantasies that were entwined with Mrs. D's experience of the loss of a penis. These losses did not pose the threat of rage and disintegration but rather of profound sadness. On this level, the fantasy of having a penis served as a reassurance that the mother had not been lost and warded off Mrs. D's painful grief. Similarly, fantasies of power and powerlessness assumed their central meanings in relation to Mary's death, with the fantasy of being a powerful but passive man serving as assurance that Mrs. D, unlike Mary, would survive, and warding off Mrs. D's guilty self-experience as an active and powerful woman.

For Miss L, genital difference and the fantasy of having a penis acquired central meanings in relation to preoedipal fantasies of separation and object loss. The perceived loss of either penis or mother threatened Miss L with the loss of the psychic representation of a good mother and the consequent emergence of rage and uncontrollable excitement. The fantasy of *being* the mother's penis and then, as Miss L's capacity to tolerate separateness grew stronger, the fantasy of *having* a fetishistic penis protected Miss L from these catastrophic losses. Power also acquired meaning in relation to these experiences, with power identified as masculine and seen as the power to survive and control impulses. Preoedipal fantasies regarding genital difference strongly colored Miss L's experience of oedipal conflict. The oedipal wish for the father, which led to genital excitement and rivalry with the mother, revived preoedipal meanings of the loss of penis and mother as the loss of vital psychic structure. In this context, the fantasy of being a man warded off anxieties on an oedipal level, by defending against feminine sexual wishes, and on a preoedipal level by guaranteeing that mother and penis had not been lost. Only later in the analysis, when these preoedipal meanings of genital difference and object loss had been worked through, did a less dangerous and catastrophic oedipal situation emerge.

In the case of Miss S, preoedipal meanings of genital difference were vastly more important than later ones. For her, the rage and envy stirred by the recognition of separateness or difference were intolerable. A delusional structure in which idealized aspects of self, mother, and penis were fused helped her to conceal and deny these painful affects and obliterated her experience of real objects who might evoke them. Power, for Miss S, bore the meanings of perfection and omnipotence. Although this meaning is not manifest in the clinical material, we might speculate that oedipal-phase frustrations and envy of both parents reinforced this delusional defense.

For all three women, early meanings of genital difference were closely linked to early fantasies and affects surrounding separation and object loss. These data are in accord with the data of childhood observation, which place the girl's discovery of genital difference at the rapprochement subphase. In the two cases where oedipal dynamics clearly emerged, early meanings of object loss and genital difference colored the experience of oedipal conflict.

These findings have important implications for our understanding of the structuring of aggression in feminine development. Freud believed that penis envy was the girl's uniform reaction to the discovery of genital difference at ages three to five. He saw castration anxiety consequent to the discovery of genital difference as the primary motivation for superego internalization in boys, but felt that anxiety associated with genital difference provided little motivation for superego development in girls and hence that the female superego was weak and undeveloped.

We would now see the recognition of genital difference as an important factor in the structuring of aggression in both sexes but as a factor that operates differently in each. For the boy, Freud's scenario was largely correct: oedipal desires trigger an awareness of the implications of genital difference; castration anxiety and fear of the loss of the oedipal rival motivate superego internalization. For the girl, the experience of separateness at rapprochement triggers awareness of genital difference. The balance of aggression at rapprochement, which strongly determines the girl's experience of separateness, also determines her predominant experience of genital difference. Early reactions to genital difference, in turn, influence the further vicissitudes of aggression as rapprochement proceeds. At the oedipal phase, rivalry with the mother and heightened genital excitement revive the linked fantasies regarding genital difference and maternal loss that have been integrated at rapprochement. These fantasies influence oedipal unfolding and, together with fear of loss of the oedipal mother, motivate superego internalization.

REFERENCES

Bergman, A. 1987. On the development of female identity: Issues of mother-daughter interaction during the separation-individuation process. *Psychoanalytic Inquiry* 7: 381–396.

Bernstein, I. 1983. Masochistic pathology and feminine development. *J. Amer. Psychoanal. Assn.* 31:467–486.

Blum, H. 1976. Masochism, the ego ideal, and the psychology of women. *J. Amer. Psychoanal. Assn.* 24 (suppl.): 157–190.

Chasseguet-Smirgel, J. 1986. Submissive daughters: Hypotheses on primary passivity and its effects on thought mechanisms, in *Sexuality and Mind*, 45–59. New York: New York University Press.

Edgcumbe, R., and Burgner, M. 1975. The phallic narcissistic phase: A differentiation between preoedipal and oedipal aspects of phallic development. *Psychoanalytic study of the child*, vol. 30, 161–180.

Freud, S. 1919. A child is being beaten: A contribution to the study of the origin of sexual perversions. *S.E.* 17.

———. 1923. The infantile genital organization: An interpolation into the theory of sexuality. *S.E.* 19.

———. 1924. The dissolution of the Oedipus complex. *S.E.* 19.

———. 1925. Some psychical consequences of the anatomical distinction between the sexes. *S.E.* 19.

———. 1931. Female sexuality. *S.E.* 21.

———. 1933. New introductory lectures on psycho-analysis. *S.E.* 22.

Galenson, E. 1988. The precursors of masochism: Protomasochism, in *Masochism: Current psychoanalytic perspectives*, ed. R. Glick and D. Meyers, 189–204. Hillsdale, N.J.: Analytic Press.

Galenson, E., and Roiphe, H. 1976. Some suggested revisions concerning early female development. *J. Amer. Psychoanal. Assn.* 24 (suppl.): 29–58.

Greenacre, P. 1952. Anatomical structure and superego development, in *Trauma, growth and personality*, 149–164. New York: Norton.

———. 1969. The fetish and the transitional object, in *Emotional growth*, 315–334. New York: International Universities Press.

———. 1970. The transitional object and the fetish: With special reference to the role of illusion, in *Emotional growth*, 335–352. New York: International Universities Press.

Grossman, W., and Stewart, W. 1976. Penis envy: From childhood wish to developmental metaphor. *J. Amer. Psychoanal. Assn.* 24 (suppl.): 193–212.

Grunberger, B. 1970. Outline for a study of narcissism in female sexuality, in *Female sexuality*, ed. J. Chasseguet-Smirgel, 68–83. Ann Arbor: University of Michigan Press.

Horney, K. 1924. On the genesis of the castration complex in women. *Int. J. Psychoanal.* 5:49–65.

———. [1926] 1971. The flight from womanhood: The masculinity-complex in women as viewed by men and women, in *Women and analysis*, ed. J. Strouse, 171–186. New York: Grossman.

Isaacs, S. [1952] 1989. The nature and functions of phantasy, in *Developments in psychoanalysis*, ed. J. Riviere, 67–121. London: Karnac Books.

Jacobson, E. 1964. *The self and the object world.* New York: International Universities Press.

Kernberg, O. 1976. *Object-relations theory and clinical psychoanalysis.* New York: Aronson.

Kleeman, J. 1971. The establishment of core gender identity in normal girls. 2 vols. *Archives of sexual behavior* 1:103–129.

———. 1976. Freud's early views of female sexuality in the light of direct child observation. *J. Amer. Psychoanal. Assn.* 24 (suppl.): 3–28.

Klein, M. [1928] 1981. Early stages of the Oedipus conflict, in *Love, guilt and reparation and other works, 1921–1945*, 186–198. London: Hogarth Press.

———. 1940. Mourning and its relation to manic-depressive states, in *Love, guilt and reparation and other works, 1921–1945*, 344–369. London: Hogarth Press.

———. [1957] 1977. Envy and gratitude, in *Envy and gratitude*, 176–233. New York: Delta.

Mahler, M., Pine, F., and Bergman, A. 1975. *The psychological birth of the human infant.* New York: Basic Books.

McDevitt, J. 1983. The emergence of hostile aggression and its defensive and adaptive manifestations during the separation-individuation process. *J. Amer. Psychoanal. Assn.* 31 (suppl.): 273–300.

Meltzer, D., and Williams, M. H. 1988. *The apprehension of beauty: The role of aesthetic conflict in development, art and violence.* Perthshire, Scotland: Clunie Press.

Meyers, H. 1988. A consideration of treatment techniques in relation to the functions of masochism, in *Masochism: Current psychoanalytic perspectives*, ed. R. Glick and D. Meyers, 175–188. Hillsdale, N.J.: Analytic Press.

Money, J., and Erhardt, A. 1972. *Man and woman, boy and girl.* Baltimore: Johns Hopkins University Press.

Olivier, D. 1989. *Jocasta's children.* London: Routledge.

Parens, H. 1976. On the girl's entry into the Oedipus complex. *J. Amer. Psychoanal. Assn.* 24 (suppl.): 79–108.

———. 1979. *The development of aggression in early childhood.* New York: Aronson.

Person, E. 1974. Some new observations on the origins of femininity, in *Women and analysis*, ed. J. Strouse, 250–261. New York: Grossman.

Reich, A. [1953] 1973. Narcissistic object choice in women, in *Psychoanalytic contributions*, 85–94. New York: International Universities Press.

———. 1954. Early identifications as archaic elements in the superego, in *Psychoanalytic contributions*, 209–235. New York: International Universities Press.

———. 1960. Pathological forms of self esteem regulation, in *Psychoanalytic contributions*, 288–311. New York: International Universities Press.

Roiphe, H., and Galenson, E. 1981. *Infantile origins of sexual identity.* New York: International Universities Press.

6

Assertiveness, Anger, Rage, and Destructive Aggression: A Perspective from the Treatment Process

PAUL H. ORNSTEIN, M.D.
and ANNA ORNSTEIN, M.D.

There is no need to marshal evidence for the ubiquity and pervasiveness of intractable violence, murderous rage, and widespread destructiveness. Their expressions in individuals and in large segments of entire populations regularly impinge on our daily lives. Questions relate only to their sources of origin and possible ways of management, in individuals as well as in groups.

As psychoanalysts, we have compelling empirical data about human behavior and motivation—including the propensity for violence, rage, and destructiveness—only from within the treatment process. Although this provides a rather narrow perspective for a comprehensive assessment, it does offer a unique window on pathogenesis and psychopathology in individuals. Yet, rightly or wrongly, we expect to be able to extrapolate from these indepth observations of individuals to the family, small groups, large groups (ethnic groups and nations), and even to mankind as a whole.

Heinz Kohut (1973), for instance, in a wide-ranging article on the potential significance of the insights of clinical psychoanalysis, was adamant in his belief that psychoanalysis should be ultimately applicable on a larger scale if it was to maintain a place of importance in contemporary society. Essentially, he stated that, if psychoanalysis remained restricted to the treatment of a few, and if its insights could not contribute to the solution of the leading sociopsychological problems of our time, it would remain an isolated, ever-more esoteric, individual treatment method of little or no sociocultural consequence.

He was particularly interested in and keenly aware of what psychoanalysis needed to, and in fact could, contribute to the understanding and management of the various forms of destructive aggression. Although he could demonstrate the effectiveness of his ideas only in the clinical situation—in his thought experiments, in his application of psychoanalytic ideas outside of the

102

clinical setting (Kohut, [1960] 1978), and in his imaginative extrapolations—
he offered a broadly applicable approach that could now be tested on a larger
scale (Kohut, [1972] 1978, 1973, [1975a] 1978, [1975b] 1978). Testing such
propositions is a means to safeguard against unwarranted, highly speculative,
extrapolations.

In this chapter we focus on what we have learned from the clinical situation,
pointing briefly to its possible broader relevance. We begin by highlighting
the essentials of the clinical method; we put the theory and treatment of
aggression into historical perspective; we then turn to a self-psychological
conception of normal aggression and *narcissistic rage*, followed by a self-
psychological perspective on the treatment process (including two clinical
vignettes); and conclude with a sharper delineation of healthy aggression
(here self-assertiveness or self-assertive ambition) from destructive aggression—focusing on the implications of this view for the individual as well as for
society as a whole.

On Observing the Experience of Rage

Our title speaks of assertiveness, anger, rage, and destructive aggression, yet
in clinical psychoanalysis or psychotherapy we can meaningfully consider only
the experiencing of assertiveness (or the assertive person); the experiencing of
anger (or the angry person); the experiencing of rage (or the raging person);
and the experiencing of aggressive-destructiveness (or the aggressive-
destructive person), and we can apply this to violence and murder. This
distinction is not merely one of language. There are at least two advantages to
the emphasis: first, by calling attention to the experiencing self, we convey an
attitude that invites the empathic observational stance in the therapist vis-à-vis
such persons and experiences; second, by calling attention to the experience
or the experiencing person, we clearly imply that each of these nouns—
assertiveness, anger, rage, and destructive aggression—refers to innumer-
able, subtly different qualities and meanings; that each is embedded, in each
instance of its occurrence, in a highly idiosyncratic configuration of experience that requires an immediate as well as a broader context for its understanding and explanation. For example, anger and rage can hide or compensate for momentary feelings of helplessness, or each can be evoked by an acute
injury to the self (*narcissistic injury*) and reflect attempts to regain power and
punish the offender; anger or hate can momentarily, or over a longer period,
cover unacceptable feelings of love; the list is endless. These subtle and varied
meanings are ultimately more important for clinical work as well as broader
extrapolations than whether these affects are drive-derivatives or not. Yet,
whether we consider them to be drive-derivatives or not will greatly influence
the focus and manner of intervention. In any case, a contemporary view of
affects challenges the notion that they are drive-derivatives and postulates

them as independent motivational structures (e.g., Basch, 1976; Stern, 1985; Lichtenberg, 1989).

Thus, since all of the affects mentioned always become part of a larger configuration of experience, our general comment has to do with the range and limitations of empathy—the only "direct" access to inner experience, of which these affects are a part. At a recent discussion, we talked about some of these issues, and a colleague raised the question of the limitations of empathy in interviewing a Vietnam veteran who had frequently killed suspected Vietcong (in cold blood, as wanton murder). Our colleague attempted to grasp, he said, how this soldier felt at the moment of killing his victims and what it was that he suffered now, in his reminiscences. He suggested to the patient that it must have been a horrifying experience to watch people die at your own hands. Whereupon the man responded: "Doctor, you don't understand, I was in ecstasy at those moments, I had an orgasm!" Our colleague said with some exasperation, "With that I could not empathize," illustrating the serious limitations (in this instance, the failure) of empathy.

In our view, this example is not a failure of the empathic mode of observation. Our colleague appears to have made an honest effort to assume a vantage point from within the patient's perspective. That he did not "read" the patient's inner experiences correctly is not the issue here. The issue is that, once our colleague assumed the empathic observational stance and offered his tentative understanding, the patient could immediately correct him and supply his own answer. Once the patient described the nature and context of his experiences, he made it easier for all of us to understand what it was like for him (and not for us!) to be in that situation.

What is meant by empathy clinically is the taking up of an observational vantage point imaginatively within the inner world of the other. To do that requires the help of that other; to obtain that help in the clinical situation, the patient has to experience the therapist as making the effort to understand what the particular subjective experience was for him or her and for no other.

We go so far as to suggest (somewhat tongue in cheek) that it is better to offer an incorrect understanding from an empathic vantage point than a supposedly correct one as an external observer. The patient might then more easily have a chance to lead us on to the right track. From such an empathic perspective, we would be more receptive to the patient's own ideas about the nature of his or her inner experience than we otherwise could be. Assuming the empathic vantage point is not to be confused with condoning a particular behavior, which is a frequent misconception in grasping what empathy is about.

What was important in the above example has to do with the fact that the therapist said something that reflected the patient's inner experience. This comment indicated to the patient the direction of the therapist's thinking: his effort to understand what it was like for the patient to have experienced killing someone. Once the direction toward the subjective experience was taken by the therapist, the patient followed it and helped the therapist to get to know more accurately what the experience was really like for him.

Our point has to do with the fundamental issue that such experiences can, in principle, be understood from within (i.e., empathically). This does not mean that we, too, have to feel orgastic in the process, but only that we should know and have a sense for the fact that the patient did. Freud offered us at least two reasons why every human experience is potentially open to empathic perception by other human beings. He quoted the age-old adage many times: "Nothing human is alien to me" (and killing other human beings is, with or without sexual excitement, obviously a human activity), and he frequently referred to the fact that poets, writers, novelists, biographers, playwrights (we can now add, film makers) have empathically understood an endless variety of even the most bizarre human experiences. For instance, in his play *The Balcony*, the French playwright Jean Genet depicted from within and understood thoroughly the meaning and function of many a sadomasochistic perversion, similarly to the way in which, from a self psychological perspective, we would understand them today. Such literature, added to wide-ranging clinical experiences and the various psychoanalytic or other formulations about such experiences, can certainly expand our highly individual, innate, and now professionally trained, capacity for empathy. Without such expansions, few of us would get along in the field of psychoanalysis and psychoanalytic psychotherapy.

The empathic approach, rather than being actually dangerous or a masochistic exercise in moral superiority—as some think—on the part of the therapist who believes he can empathize with a murderer or any other criminal, is the sine qua non for a fundamentally analytic and potentially successful treatment procedure. More than this, a psychoanalytic approach that places empathy in a central position as its observational method can more readily be applied beyond the clinical situation. We need only think of the biographer's and the historian's comparable prolonged empathic immersion in their subjects to recognize the validity of this claim. Sustained empathy outside the clinical situation can thus meaningfully enlarge and expand the psychoanalytic empirical database and enable us to make less speculative extrapolations to sociocultural and historical processes (Kohut, [1972] 1978, 1973, [1975a] 1978, [1975b] 1978; P. H. Ornstein, 1978, 1979, 1990).

A Historical Perspective on Theory and Treatment

A condensed historical survey, integrating the evolution of both the theoretical and clinical aspects of the problem of rage, aggression, and related affects, should serve as a backdrop against which to examine our current treatment approaches and the theories that guide them.

A convenient starting point is the moment when Freud found it not only clinically necessary but also theoretically preferable to speak of the dual drives as sex and aggression and to speak on a more abstract, metapsychological level of the libidinal and aggressive energies that fuel them as emanating from the life-instinct and death-instinct, respectively. The prior classification of sexual and self-preservative drives gave way to conceiving of aggression as primary and separate from both the sexual and the self-preservative drives.

As Freud marshaled his clinical evidence to buttress his new conception of the drive theory, he assigned the role of self-preservation not to a basic drive but to the ego. This final dual-drive theory, postulating sex and aggression as the basic drives and self-preservation as a function of the ego, drastically changed Freud's view of man, psychopathology, and the treatment process. We need not recount here the details of these changes in Freud's conceptualizations, the validity of the clinical evidence, the pro's and con's for a dual-drive theory or for a drive theory itself. What interests us are the consequences of the dual-drive theory upon the treatment process and, more particularly, upon the treatment of anger and related affects.

When aggression is seen as a primary drive, all its latent (i.e., unconscious or preconscious) and manifest expressions have to be traced back to their original phase-specific sources, such as oral, anal, and phallic aggression and their vicissitudes. This process of tracing back the manifestations of drive-derivatives to their original sources is referred to as the analysis of aggression. In this view, what is drive-related is at the deepest intrapsychic level: it is rock bottom and cannot be further analyzed; only the manner in which one deals with aggression is amenable to analysis. Aggression in this context is a given.

The implications of this theory for the interpretive process are manifold. When derivatives of aggression as a drive are only hinted at, viewed as displaced, disavowed, repressed, or hidden by reaction formation or other defense mechanisms, the therapist is guided by the theory to "free" the aggression by bringing it into consciousness; to have it abreacted and thereby "dissolved" or "spent"; to have one's own rage "accepted, but contained," "integrated and thereby controlled," "tamed or civilized," "sublimated or neutralized"; and "channeled into constructive pursuits"—all of these amount to renouncing unneutralized aggression. Interpretations that have the above aims willy-nilly apply "moral pressure" in attempting to channel aggression into adaptive behavior.

The therapist's search for the hidden anger very often cannot be confirmed by the patient. Relentless, albeit gentle and tactful, pursuit of the hidden anger tells the patient, however, that he or she does not know what he or she feels, but the therapist does. In any case, this is how many patients hear it. Some patients experience this response as a narcissistic injury, disturbing enough to them, so that they do get angry. Therapists may then take this anger as proof that the interpretation was indeed correct, that they have discovered and freed up the *hidden* anger.

When anger is expressed directly or indirectly at the therapist, its interpretation (guided by the above assumptions) implies that such feelings are misdirected, inappropriate, and anachronistic—hence not in tune with current reality in the treatment situation. From the point of view of the therapist who experiences himself or herself as their undeserving target, these angry feelings are manifestations of *transference distortions*. Some patients, when told that their reaction is based on distortions get furious, and the therapist is again right.

There is, furthermore, an inherent (and apparently unalterable) contradiction in the approach just described. The patient is encouraged to experience and express anger since repressed anger is assumed to be the motive force behind various forms of psychopathology. In this view, it is the child's unexpressed anger that finds an outlet in neurotic symptoms. Then, when anger is experienced and expressed in the transference, it is considered inappropriate because of its (inevitable but unwarranted) displacement from the past to the present, from the parental imagoes to the therapist. By focusing on its anachronistic nature, anger is thus deprived of its legitimacy in the here and now in the patient's current psychic reality. More important, since in this theoretical frame of reference anger in childhood is considered a projection of drive-related fantasies, the proper interpretation of anger in the course of analysis would require that it be traced back to the original childhood fantasies. Jacob Arlow (1963) clearly called for such a reconstructive interpretation: "In clinical practice, it is most important to be able to uncover the precise way in which the unconscious instinctual wish is given form in the fantasy" (p. 21).

Before we turn to a self psychological conception of aggression and *narcissistic rage* and to its correlated treatment approach, let us restate some essential points. One of the most significant consequences of the assumption of a primary aggressive drive is that aggression and related affects are always intrinsic, primary givens, embedded in the structure of the various forms of psychopathology. Since the therapist "knows" that anger, either disavowed or repressed, has become part of the patient's symptoms, he or she has to search for it actively in order to accomplish the interpretive task. As always, we need to consider the unspoken or unintended implications of such a message. It might be, in effect, that "anger must be there. You have split it off from where it belongs. You will have to get it out into the open in order to resolve your problems."

What is disregarded in this approach is that even if the anger would be there *hidden* (repressed), the patient could not possibly simply express or acknowledge what he or she is not feeling. Its mere intellectual acknowledgment leads nowhere. Even if the anger were felt, expressing it or acknowledging it might still be impossible, if the acknowledgment threatened the emotional bond to the therapist that the patient needed and desperately tried to maintain by keeping the anger hidden or unexpressed.

Might it not be analytically more cogent and helpful to focus on the patient's need to keep the anger hidden or unexpressed (if its presence is suspected) in order to ward off the disruption of this connectedness to the therapist in the transference? The interpretive approach depends on what we consider to be primary: the need to feel connected to the selfobject-analyst or the aggressive drive. Self psychology, in fact, assumes a primary need for feeling connected and conceives of healthy as well as pathological forms of aggression as arising out of this self-selfobject matrix during the vicissitudes of development and in treatment.

With this last statement, we have introduced a self psychological perspective on the treatment process. We should preface its further elaboration, however, with an overview of a self psychological conception of aggression and narcissistic rage.[1]

A Self Psychological Conception of Aggression and Narcissistic Rage

Narcissistic rage is a complex mental state with a number of distinctive features (Kohut [1972] 1978). It therefore cannot simply be reduced to an underlying biological drive—a recognition central to Kohut's theories. Furthermore, our grasp of Kohut's theoretical conception of and clinical approach to narcissistic rage can only be properly understood if we recognize that he considered the needs of the self as primary and the drives as basic (biologically given) constituents of the self—building blocks of this larger, complex configuration of experience. Drives as constituents of the self are normally smoothly embedded within the cohesive structure of the self. They become secondarily intensified and appear to dominate the clinical picture in isolated form when the self loses its cohesiveness, when it "falls apart" in response to traumatic injury. Such experiences are related to the vulnerability of the self owing to developmental defects or deficits in its structure. It is important to add here that narcissistic rage is one of many possible outcomes of the enfeeblement or fragmentation of the self. For instance, "when the self is weak . . . [and] crumbles in the face of traumatic experiences, we witness the emergence of intensified drivenness, either of sexuality or of aggression, or both" (Ornstein and Ornstein, 1986; cf. Leider, 1990), as well as many other forms of psychopathology, as "disintegration products of the self."

Narcissistic rage, whether acute or chronic, thus arises from a matrix of preexisting self-pathology, which is what makes it so complex and multifaceted. It is always an enfeebled, fragmentation-prone or protractedly fragmented (archaic) self, a self vulnerable to ridicule, shame, and humiliation that reacts with this most destructive form of rage. Kohut described human aggression in the form of narcissistic rage as originating in injuries to archaic grandiosity and exhibitionism on the one hand, and in painful, traumatic

1. The drive theory of aggression has not successfully resolved the question of what transforms healthy aggression into its pathological form. Self psychology postulates self-assertiveness (the equivalent of normal aggression) as a function of a well-structured bipolar self. This may be compared to the replacement by Freud of the self-perservative drive with self-preservation as a function of the ego (containing a modicum of normal aggression).

disappointments in archaic, omnipotent, idealized selfobjects, on the other (Kohut, [1972] 1978). This is understandable if we recognize that the grandiose self demands admiration and complete control over its archaic surround (which it experiences as a part of itself), and that the idealized, omnipotent selfobject is expected to live up to the archaic needs for perfection, power, and omniscience. The rage response to narcissistic injuries in either of these two realms is what Kohut considers to be most destructive, violent, and murderous. He goes on to say that "the need for revenge, for righting a wrong, for undoing a hurt by whatever means, and a deeply anchored, unrelenting compulsion in the pursuit of all these aims, which give no rest to those who have suffered a narcissistic injury—these are the characteristic features of narcissistic rage in all its forms and which set it apart from other kinds of aggression" ([1972] 1978, 637–638; see also Terman, 1975; Ornstein and Ornstein, 1986; Wolf, 1988; Leider, 1990). The dangerousness may escalate even further, "in [the] typical forms [of narcissistic rage, where] there is utter disregard for reasonable limitations and a boundless wish to redress injury and to obtain revenge" (Kohut [1972] 1978, 640). This is then explained by further reference to the specific circumstances that lead to the explosive rage: "the most intense experiences of shame and the most violent forms of narcissistic rage arise in those individuals for whom a sense of absolute control over an archaic environment is indispensable because the maintenance of self-esteem— and indeed of the self—depends on the unconditional availability of the approving-mirroring selfobject or of the merger-permitting idealized one" (ibid., 644–645).

Kohut considered narcissistic rage as the prototype of *destructive* aggression. He viewed the latter as consisting of many different bands on a wide spectrum that begins with "such trivial occurrences as a fleeting annoyance . . . [and goes on] to such ominous derangements as the furor of the catatonic and the grudges of the paranoiac" (Kohut, [1972] 1978, 636). Somewhere in this spectrum there is a specific band of aggression (already described) to which the term narcissistic rage more specifically applies. But Kohut also uses the term to "refer to all points in this spectrum as narcissistic rage, since with this designation we are referring to the most characteristic and best known of a series of experiences that not only form a continuum, but, with all their differences, are essentially related to each other" (ibid.).

Two important implications of this suggested nomenclature should be made explicit. One of them is that the spectrum of destructive aggression stretches from the mildest to the most severe form. This spectrum does not include mature aggression, which, as indicated earlier, is one of the basic capacities or building blocks of a cohesive bipolar self. Kohut prefers to call this innate capacity for mature aggressive action *self-assertiveness*, or *self-assertive ambition* (constituting one pole of the bipolar self), to underline its a priori healthy character and the fact that in this context self-assertiveness is not conceived of as a tamed or sublimated aggression. The other implication is the reactive nature of all forms of aggression in this spectrum. Weaknesses or specific defects or deficits in either or both poles of the self will *secondarily*, in response to even some of the most (to the external observer) innocuous traumata, bring forth various forms of narcissistic rage.

Self-assertiveness has its own line of development,[2] beginning with the archaic grandiose-exhibitionistic self, whose felicitous developmental and maturational transformations form the self-assertive pole of the bipolar self. This self-assertive pole embodies the capacities for self-esteem regulation, enjoyment of mental and physical activities and the pursuit of goals and purposes. Healthy competitiveness (which includes oedipal competitiveness)[3] is a part of this self-assertiveness.

Internalized values and ideals (constituting the other pole of the bipolar self) play a decisive role in affect-regulation and thus participate in the maintenance of the cohesiveness of the self. Traumata to this pole of the self further undermine both the expression and containment of all affects.

The claim that narcissistic rage is secondary—and clearly observable as such in the transference—does not lead us to minimize its significance or disregard it in our interpretive approach. It does not diminish our appreciation of its potential destructiveness, nor of the difficulties that may arise in dealing with it therapeutically. It does, however, give us a decisive direction in the treatment process. This direction is expressed in our focus on the *narcissistic matrix*, from which the rage arises. Such a focus serves as a guiding principle in the interpretation of both individual and group aggression—without in any way sidestepping or actively dampening its acute or chronic manifestations. In fact, when a loosening of rigid defenses in the course of treatment make the appearance of undisguised narcissistic rage possible, we welcome it as a sign of therapeutic progress.

2. Infant research in the last decade had confirmed this clinical assertion. Stechler (as quoted by Lichtenberg, 1989) in a series of articles (1982, 1985, 1987; Stechler and Kaplan, 1980) concluded that assertion and aggression have different origins in our biopsychosocial heritage, that they serve different functions in our lives, and are accompanied by different affective experiences. According to Stechler, a central feature of assertion is that it is activated by an optimal level of variety and its function is greatly enhanced when the actions of the infant are effective in producing an alteration in the environment. These activities are associated with affects of interest, excitement, and joy—very different from the affects associated with the dysphoric affects of fear, distress, and anger that are associated with aggressive behavior.

Stechler maintains that the central feature of aggression is that it is a reaction to a perceived threat to the integrity of the individual and that it operates through self-protective functions, such as an attack aimed at destroying or driving off the perceived source of the threat.

Assertion and aggression, however, are frequently combined in fantasy and action. Whether or not these two motives of behavior become combined depends on the environment's ability to recognize the infant's and child's intent. Because of the ease with which assertion may become contaminated with aggression, infants are heavily influenced by the handling they receive (Lichtenberg, 1989, 171–172).

3. It goes without saying, in the present context, that healthy competitiveness (including oedipal competitiveness) becomes the seed of future psychopathology on the soil of a profound underlying oedipal (or earlier) self-pathology.

A Self Psychological Perspective on the Treatment Process
(with Two Clinical Vignettes)

With the basic assumption of a primary need for feeling connected, we have already indicated a decisive shift in emphasis away from a primary interest in the uncovering of hidden affects and motives to the importance of maintaining the cohesiveness of the self through the cohesiveness of the transference. This definitely does not signal a neglect or disregard of hidden or manifest negative (hostile-aggressive) affects as they emerge in the transference. The question is how such affects should be interpreted without threatening the patient's precariously (and often desperately) maintained emotional connection to the therapist-selfobject, who, in his assigned role, is to accept and understand the patient's anger.

If this anger is accepted, understood and interpreted as an expectable reaction to actual or fantasied slights in the transference, it "legitimizes" the patient's reaction in the context in which it occurred. This response aids the establishment and maintenance of the selfobject transference and deepens the therapeutic or analytic process. This interpretive focus enhances cohesion of the patient's self and leads to one of its most important consequences: it increases introspection and lessens the need to maintain repression or disavowal (and other defenses) that had kept negative affects inaccessible to the patient.

Once anger is expressed, a major obstacle to its experience has been (intrapsychically) removed: the fear of abandonment and the fear of retaliation, which are threats to the establishment and maintenance of the selfobject transferences and thus to the integrity of the self.

Whatever is expressed through anger and related affects is complex and varied in its sources, contexts, and meanings and calls for an empathic grasp of its idiosyncratic configuration. This is best achieved if we deal with the expression of anger and related affects as communication that conveys the nature of the patient's immediate experiences. We have to tune in on these experiences, including the manner in which the patient has learned to deal with negative affects, but not remain focused in our interpretations on the particular defense mechanisms involved, such as disavowal, displacement, or repression. The focus on the patient's subjective experience of anger and not on the question, Against whom does he or she feel it? will also protect us from experiencing ourselves to be its immediate targets and respond with expectable countertransference reactions. Immersing ourselves in the patients' subjective experiences promotes an understanding of what it feels like to experience those affects, what might have led to their emergence, and what purpose they might serve at a particular moment in the patient's emotional experience. The interpretive focus can then more easily shift to the broader context of the experience from which the anger or rage arises and to the immediate (or long-term) functions anger or rage serves for the angry or enraged person.

Attention to the current precipitating events and experiences, along with the patient's reactions to them, are important because they echo earlier, similar experiences (the narcissistic injuries of infancy and childhood) as well as the patient's lifelong, habitual ways of dealing with them. Thus, they reveal both the original sources and current meanings of the experience. Recognizing the current meanings or functions of anger as an affect must be distinguished from "liberating" anger from repression in order to interpret it as a displacement. In other words, when empathically grasped, anger is a symptom and a form of communication that shows the way to the basic problem—to its narcissistic roots or to its roots in the patient's oedipal or archaic self-pathology.

The aim of our interventions in this context is not to prove the patient wrong (by focusing on so-called transference distortions) but to prove him or her right by acknowledging that his or her reaction—namely, the rage response to some perceived slight by the therapist—is understandable. For instance, if the patient feels insulted by the therapist, it is understandable that he or she would feel enraged, irrespective of whether or not the severity of the "insult" would warrant such a response to an external observer. The particular sensitivity and rage-proneness can then, at a later point, be traced back to its earlier antecedents. What the therapist's avowed intentions were is immaterial—and not the proper focus of investigation; it is the patient's subjective experience that is the target of further inquiry.

Two clinical vignettes illustrate this perspective on treatment:

A. A dream and a few associations revealed a patient's profound yearning for unconditional acceptance in analysis (with P. Ornstein). Up to the time of analysis, the patient had repeatedly searched in vain for the hidden, bottled-up, unconscious rage in himself—which he was sure could dangerously explode at any moment. He "knew" he had to be enraged at his parents and siblings because of unspeakably horrible childhood experiences, but he could not *feel* the rage. We already knew that many of his "dysfunctions" (as he called them) contained or expressed his rage in that he "revengefully refused to do certain everyday tasks." He had a "powder-keg-theory of rage" in mind, when his dream and associations directed us to another view.

In his dream, the patient was in some kind of a competitive game with his siblings. He must have done something for which they banished him to sit on the front stairs of the house all by himself. He felt lonely and sad. After a while they came to ask him to rejoin the game. He promptly did and felt relieved and happy. In his associations he recounted the brutal exclusion he frequently suffered at the hands of his older siblings. Sitting on the front stairs alone and in despair was a familiar feeling from his childhood. He recalled that he would have had to humiliate himself in front of his siblings, admit defeat, and beg for forgiveness as the price of readmission to the game. He would rather sit there on the stairs forever than do that. That was his stance to that very day—hence the various dysfunctions that expressed it.

In the dream, however, something different happened: the patient was readmitted to the game without the demand that he apologize and mend his ways. Once reinvited, he felt relieved and happy to join them. Where was the rage? It seemed, he said, that having been asked to rejoin his siblings without preconditions, he now felt accepted *as he was*. This acceptance on his own terms allowed him to give up his defiant, painful, and lonely brooding on the stairs, actually without a trace of lingering rage, and he could enjoy being part of the game. He understood now that the dream—as no other experience in his life before—gave him an idea of what made it possible for him to rejoin his siblings' game. He realized that what could dissipate the rage most quickly and profoundly was the feeling that he was accepted and valued as he was and not only as his siblings wanted him to be. He now felt that the dream portrayed a lifelong wish and a current hope for unconditional acceptance by the analyst as fulfilled.

B. A thirty-four-year-old divorced man, in brief focal psychotherapy (with A. Ornstein), had just been jilted by his fourth girlfriend (in as many years) and reacted to this last trauma with an acute depression and disorganization. It became clear early in the treatment that the patient thought and felt that it was the "pushiness" of a tall and strappy rival that had cost him the loss of his girlfriend and not the fact that she had fallen out of love with him. For a short while he entertained the fantasy of provoking a fight with this man. He plotted a violent attack on him using his boxing skills, which he thought would compensate for his own short and comparatively frail stature.

As it turned out in the course of treatment, the patient's anger and fantasies of violence served the purpose of distracting him from the pain of abandonment by his girlfriend. In considering the other man the culprit, the patient was protected (for a short time, at least) from experiencing the more painful realization that it was his girlfriend who had betrayed him, an affect that would have been potentially much more disorganizing than anger. The manifest fantasy of violence protected the patient against the devastating feeling of betrayal and provided him, instead, with a sense of power. It was the acceptance, understanding and ultimate explanation of the protective function of the violent fantasy that permitted the emergence of the feeling of betrayal and its consequences. Recognizing and interpreting the protective function of rage led the patient to wonder about his own behavior, which might have contributed to his losing women so quickly.

These clinical vignettes only hint at the various meanings that anger, rage, and destructive aggression may have in the treatment situation. Anger appears in many forms, shapes, and disguises: anger can be talked about in a cold and calm fashion, as if the affect belonged to a third person; anger can be acutely felt in recounting an event that provoked the angry affect; and it can be thoroughly embedded in a complex set of compulsive rituals. On the whole, anger is commonly thought of as a destructive affect—destructive in the sense that it either constitutes the nucleus of various forms of psychopathology or it is acted out in a destructive fashion. As we have seen, however, although anger may escalate into destructive rage vis-à-vis the external environment, it may simultaneously serve important self-protective functions. Since anger (or rage) sometimes provides a sense of power (most recognizable in narcissistic rage fantasies), it may in these instances function to preserve or attempt to restore, rather than destroy, self-cohesion. It is this internal self-protective function that we need to focus on if we aim at fundamental alterations in a patient's proneness to narcissistic rage.

In the therapeutic situation, it is useful to distinguish between anger that is experienced consciously and whose sources are explored jointly with the therapist, and rage reactions that disrupt, or threaten to disrupt, a silent merger transference. Under these latter circumstances the patient has to be able to "use" the therapist to regain inner calm and control. Only after the rage subsides can its genesis be explored and interpreted within the transference. The therapist's function in such situations is comparable to that of the parent who is witnessing a child's temper tantrum: it is not to add insult to injury by demanding that the patient stop the expression of the powerful affect, or even to understand its function or meaning. The best action is to provide protection for the patient and for oneself—and wait until the storm subsides. This type of disruption often indicates that the deepening of the transference inevitably and regularly increases the patient's feelings of vulnerability in the therapeutic situation relatively independently of the nature of the patient's pretherapeutic psychic organization. Although both qualitative and quantitative aspects of the patient's vulnerability have their specific genetic antecedents, it is this increasing vulnerability vis-à-vis the therapist as selfobject that leads to the frequent and painful disruptions of the transference and becomes the pivotal point of the therapist's reconstructive interpretations.

The increasing vulnerability in the treatment situation exposes the structural deficiency of the self, a deficiency that becomes manifest in difficulties regarding tension regulation, the capacity for self-calming, self-soothing, and the experiencing and containment of intense affects. Such defects or deficits help to explain the ever-present fear of overstimulation, fragmentation, and disintegration. Thus, in a person with an already low frustration tolerance, the balance can easily be tipped toward a fragmentation of the self by the slightest injury, which brings narcissistic rage to the fore as its breakdown product (Kohut, [1972] 1978; Ornstein and Ornstein, 1986; Wolf, 1988; Leider, 1990).

In the treatment process there is usually mounting evidence that the slow, stepwise firming up of the self (through transmuting internalization) leads to a visibly improved capacity for tension regulation, and with it, containment of the rage reactions that still occur upon frustration and disrupt the transference. The specific precipitants for such disruptions always reveal—often by bringing back actual memories of their antecedents—their genetic sources. The tracing back of current experiences to their childhood and infantile precursors often leads to insight on the road toward the belated acquisition of structure, an insight that deepens even further and gains in dynamic effectiveness after significant structure building has taken place, and more important, as a consequence of it.

Self-Assertiveness and Destructive Aggression: Implications for the Individual and Society

A further deepening of our understanding of the nature of narcissistic rage will accrue from its comparison and contrast with normal aggression. A scrutiny of the vicissitudes of the transformation of narcissistic rage into normal aggression within the treatment process reveals that it is the underlying self-pathology from which the rage has arisen that is ameliorated or "cured" and that the manifestations of narcissistic rage change *secondarily*. Thus, strictly speaking, it is not the narcissistic rage that is affected but the underlying structure—the self becomes firmed up, cohesive, and regains its vitality. This enables the self to use its capacity for mature aggression, that is, self-assertiveness, to accomplish its goals and actively remove the obstacles it encounters on its way toward its goals. Once the self has become firm and cohesive, mature aggression can blend harmoniously with its structure. Mature aggression usually subsides after attacking the source of injury, in contrast to narcissistic rage, which may turn into a sustained, chronic (often variously disguised) form of rage.

After introducing his theory of narcissistic rage—especially of chronic narcissistic rage—Kohut ([1972] 1978) soon applied it on a broader sociocultural and political scale (Kohut, 1973) and later illustrated its heuristic value in attempting to understand the rise of Nazi Germany and the horrors perpetrated by the Nazis (Kohut, [1969–70] 1990, [early 1970s] 1990, 1978). The assumptions of a *group-self, group-cohesiveness,* and a *disintegration of the group-self*—assumptions that are carefully considered and amply justified in these writings—permitted Kohut to transfer successfully some of the insights gained in the analysis of the transference to the understanding of group-formation and group-disintegration as well as the emergence of narcissistic rage in groups.

One of his telling examples involves the identification of the preexisting pathology in the German group-self before Germany lost World War I and the subsequent trauma of the treaty at Versailles. Kohut added a significant psychoanalytic perspective to numerous social-psychological, historical, economic, political, and sociocultural explanations. He not only increased our understanding of that particular historical process but also offered a method that psychologically sophisticated historians could profitably incorporate into their own approach. His illustrations of the explanatory power of a self psychologically sophisticated applied analysis (and especially its method) have not yet been adequately discussed or debated in our literature.

One of his many conclusions can be illustrated with a personal anecdote. In considering the psychological matrix of the Arab-Israeli conflict after the Six-Day War in 1967, Kohut remarked in conversation how the Israelis, from their position of strength, ought to provide the Arabs with a small victory in order to allow them to regain self-esteem. This gesture would undoubtedly encourage them, he thought, to come to the negotiating table and discuss matters face to face. We recoiled with considerable annoyance from this suggestion. What?! we thought, to offer the Arabs even a small victory after decades of their refusal to sit down with the Israelis?! After countless terrorist attacks, instigating three wars, decades of economic boycott? This was to us an impossible and unfair expectation. At the suggestion, we had reached the limits of our own empathic capacity and were therefore unable to extend our self psychological perspective to this most painful and long festering dangerous conflict.

The test came a few years later, when after the 1973 war President Anwar Sadat of Egypt, and the Egyptian people, apparently felt sufficiently rehabilitated from previous humiliating defeats to arrange Sadat's stunning journey to Jerusalem. The rest is history. The lessons need not be spelled out (see Wolf, 1988, 82–84). Suffice it to say that both the understanding and management of even international conflicts may benefit from understanding their narcissistic matrix and thus the role of national humiliation versus national pride in the sensitive task of their diplomatic management.

We have surveyed here a self psychologically based psychoanalytic approach to narcissistic rage in individuals and in larger groups. It is our experience that the treatment approach dictated by these ideas has already revitalized psychoanalytic psychotherapies and increased their therapeutic leverage. Far from neglecting aggression and rage, the approach aims at a fundamental alteration of the basic self-pathology, the soil from which rage arises. Rather than bypass or suppress hidden or manifest expressions of rage, the self psychologically informed clinician works toward an amelioration of the basic psychopathology that would diminish or eliminate the proneness to rage reactions.

Claims such as these remain private convictions unless they can be substantiated at first by many individual clinicians who are drawn to apply them, and later by rigorous, formal research studies. The same applies to the extrapolation to larger groups. Interdisciplinary studies, involving clinicians, historians, anthropologists, and political scientists (to name only a few) could scrutinize the relevance as well as the usefulness of clinically gained knowledge for understanding the actions and experiences of larger groups, as well as contributing to their ability to deal with them. Current, explosive ethnic strife in Eastern Europe, the conflicts of the Middle East and elsewhere are the natural laboratories for such studies on a large scale—as our anecdote illustrates. It is in these larger arenas—beyond the bounds of the basic rule (Kohut, [1960] 1978)—where the explanatory and the therapeutic power of such psychoanalytic theories and treatment principles could profitably be studied and tested.

REFERENCES

Arlow, J. 1963. Conflict, regression and symptom formation. *Int. J. Psycho-Anal.* 44:12–22.

Basch, M. F. 1976. The concept of affect: A re-examination. *J. Amer. Psychoanal. Assn.* 24:759–777.

Kohut, H. [1960] 1978. Beyond the bounds of the basic rule: Some recent contributions to applied psychoanalysis, in *The search for the self,* ed. P. H. Ornstein, vol. 2, 275–303. New York: International Universities Press.

———. [1969–70] 1990. On leadership, in *The search for the self,* ed. P. H. Ornstein, vol. 3, 103–128. Madison, Conn.: International Universities Press.

———. [early 1970s] 1990. On courage, in *The search for the self,* ed. P. H. Ornstein, vol. 3, 129–182. Madison, Conn.: International Universities Press.

———. [1972] 1978. Thoughts on narcissism and narcissistic rage, in *The search for the self,* ed. P. H. Ornstein, vol. 2, 615–658. New York: International Universities Press.

———. 1973. Psychoanalysis in a troubled world, in *The annual of psychoanalysis,* vol. 1. New York: International Universities Press.

———. [1975a] 1978. The future of psychoanalysis, in *The search for the self,* ed. P. H. Ornstein, vol. 2, 663–684. New York: International Universities Press.

———. [1975b] 1978. The psychoanalyst in the community of scholars, in *The search for the self,* ed. P. H. Ornstein, vol. 2, 685–724. New York: International Universities Press.

———. 1978. Self-psychology and the sciences of man, in *The search for the self,* ed. P. H. Ornstein, vol. 3, 235–260. Madison, Conn.: International Universities Press, 1990.

Leider, R. J. 1990. Aggression, anger, rage and hate: A self psychological perspective. (Unpublished ms.).

Lichtenberg, J. 1989. *Psychoanalysis and motivation.* Hillsdale, N.J.: Analytic Press.

Ornstein, P. H. 1978. The evolution of Heinz Kohut's psychoanalytic psychology of the self, in *The search for the self,* ed. P. H. Ornstein, vol. 1, Introduction, 1–106. New York: International Universities Press.

———. 1979. Remarks on the central position of empathy in psychoanalysis. *Bulletin of the Association for Psychoanalytic Medicine* 18:95–105.

———. 1985. Sexuality and aggression in the bipolar self. Presented at the Eighth Annual Conference on the Psychology of the Self, New York City. In *Progress in self psychology,* vol. 9. (In press).

———. 1990. The unfolding and completion of Heinz Kohut's paradigm of psychoanalysis, in *The search for the self,* ed. P. H. Ornstein, vol. 3, 1–78. Madison, Conn.: International Universities Press.

Ornstein, P. H., and Ornstein, A. 1986. The functional integrity of the self: Understanding its disintegration products. *Psychiatric Annals* 16:486–488.

Stern, D. 1985. *The interpersonal world of the infant.* New York: Basic Books.

Terman, D. M. 1975. Aggression and narcissistic rage: A clinical elaboration, in *The annual of psychoanalysis,* vol. 3. New York: International Universities Press.

Wolf, E. S. 1988. *Treating the self.* New York: Guilford Press.

II

Children and Their Development

From adult psychoanalytic work, we move to *Children and Their Development.* In important, intriguing, and often elusive ways, "The child is father [and mother] of the patient we treat" and of crucial dimensions of the theories we apply in our work. The treatment and the observational studies of developing children increasingly offer critical assessments of those formulations that have profoundly influenced adult psychoanalytic clinical and theoretical efforts.

Henri Parens's "Rage toward Self and Others in Early Childhood" takes up the question of drive, frustration, and self organization from a developmental psychoanalytic perspective that draws on his direct observations of work with troubled children and their mothers in a therapeutic nursery. Parens believes there is an inherent aggressive drive and that anger, a drive derivative, is a normal affective response mobilized to reduce unpleasure. If, however, an infant's anger is ineffective in modifying unrelenting frustration, a pathological process ensues in which anger becomes hostility that over time consolidates into hate. By observing how children deal with and organize their angry responses to frustration, Parens postulates the pathological integration of abnormal hostile destructiveness with normal assertiveness and mastery.

Does direct experimental observation of infants support the concept of an aggressive drive underlying rage? Michael Lewis, in "The Development of Anger and Rage," draws on experimental studies of the developing child to address this question. Starting from the idea of frustration-engendered anger, Lewis looks (quite literally) at the child contending with experimentally controlled frustration situations. From his observational perspective, anger is an affect that expresses the intention to overcome a frustrating obstacle; when effective, this becomes an expression of assertiveness, which in turn is a critical experience of the development of the self. Lewis is able to demonstrate anger in infants as young as eight weeks, as the child attempts to reestablish a pleasurable experience that was interrupted. By contrast, rage in his view is not a response directed toward the return of pleasure but rather a non-directed affect explosion, reflecting a desperate attempt to defend the child's emerging sense of itself against catastrophic threat. His observations suggest that shame is the threat to this fragile developing self; rage is the danger of feeling shame. Whereas anger is part of a mobilization to reestablish pleasure, rage reflects an attempt to eliminate the source of the shame. His work offers suggestive support to certain self psychological as well as object relational formulations.

7

Rage toward Self and Others in Early Childhood

HENRI PARENS, M.D.

Aggression is not only a complex and powerful motivator of behavior, it also manifests itself in varying types of behaviors suggestive of aggression trends of differing characteristics. Many models have been proposed from psychoanalysis (e.g., Freud, 1920, 1930; Storr, 1968, 1972; Rochlin, 1973; Marcovitz, 1973; Parens, 1973, 1979a; Kohut, 1977) and academic and clinical psychology (e.g., Dollard et al., 1939; Moyer, 1968; Berkowitz, 1969a, 1969b; Feshbach, 1970; DeWit and Hartup, 1974; Patterson, 1982) to biology (e.g., Aring, 1973; Reis, 1973; Ginsberg, 1982), animal behavior (e.g., Scott, 1958; Lorenz, 1966), and transdisciplinary scholarship (e.g., Hamburg and Trudeau, 1981).

Our depth-psychological direct observational studies[1] have led to the conceptualization of aggression as an instinctual drive comprising three trends, two of which are primary (inborn)—namely, *nondestructive aggression* and *nonaffective destructiveness*—and a third, *hostile destructiveness,* which is generated by excessive unpleasure (Parens, 1973, 1979a, 1979b, 1987, 1989a; Parens et al., 1986; Parens et al., 1989). This latter hypothesis is especially compatible with that of John Dollard and his colleagues, and with those of Anthony Storr, Gregory Rochlin, and Otto Kernberg (1976, 1982), Heinz Kohut, Meyer Gunther (1980), and others. Thus, affective experience influences the development of drive.

1. The Early Child Development Program (ECDP) of the Infant Psychiatry Section, Henri Parens, director and principal investigator, Department of Psychiatry, Medical College of Pennsylvania/EPPI. Program described in Parens (1979a). Research staff of ECDP included Peter Bennett, M.D., Andrina Duff, M.S.S., Rogelio Hernit, M.D., Leafy Pollock, Ph.D., Elizabeth Scattergood, M.A., William Singletary, M.D., and transient contributors-trainees in Psychiatry and Psychology.

Primary-trend, nondestructive aggression, which fuels the thrust to autonomy and assertiveness, is essential for healthy development and adaptation,
and for the achievement of autonomy and one's goals (Parens, 1979a, 1989b;
see also Kohut, 1977; Gunther, 1980). Hostile destructiveness—which when
excessive creates disruptions of healthy psychic structure formation and object
relations and leads to excessive sadism, masochism, guilt, and depression—
in moderate doses also fuels adaptive ego functioning, including protecting
one's autonomy and rights, oneself and one's love-objects, property, and goal
achievement, and is a major determiner of that great socializer, conscience
formation (via ambivalence).

In this chapter, I focus on some of the influences of hostile destructiveness,
its affects, especially of rage, and on the development of self in the context of
object relatedness during the early years of life.

A Temper Tantrum

The following vignette comes from our observational studies. David seemed
beside himself! It had been building, yet his outburst seemed sudden, as if at
one moment the efforts to contain his mounting distress and rage were suddenly overpowered. Typically for him, thirty-eight-month-old David seemed
on edge when his mother rolled him and his eleven-month-old sister in a
stroller into the observational setting this morning. For reasons not known
to us, his mother did not immediately respond to his impatient, pressured
need to get out of the stroller. He squirmed vigorously, vocalizing bursts of
effort and complaint, conveying his intolerance of the restraint and the inability to be on his feet, to do, it seemed, what he felt driven to do. Alert to his state,
the mother tried to judge when to turn him, did so, and pulled him caringly out
of the stroller, trying to calm him by acknowledging his eagerness to get out;
meanwhile he complemented her effort with his own dysphoric, eruptive
movements to get out.

Phew! He could now move where he wished. He darted to the fruit on the
table; smiling, he signaled to his mother that he had noticed it was there. He
went to the toys, briefly interacted with two peers there, and busily manipu-
lated toys, making them move. During this time, the mother had gotten to his
sister, a much calmer and easier child, and helped her out of the stroller. Ten
minutes had passed when David brought an apple to his mother; it was not
clear if he wanted her permission to eat it or simply to inform her that he was
doing so. The mother did not want him to have it because he had complained
of stomach pain, and she feared, she told him, it might upset his stomach
more.

He erupted! Virtually at once his face evidenced intense pain and rage, with
crying and blustering nonverbal vocalizations, and he dropped to the floor,
kicking and pushing away, all the while flailing at the mother who had just
taken the apple from him. Mother looked pale, embarrassed (in the group
setting), and moderately bewildered—she had been through this with him
many times before—as she tried sympathetically to calm him, tell him why she

had prohibited the apple for now. His kicking and flailing made her pull away slightly, but as he calmed a bit, she came closer and continued her effort to explain and calm him further. Within thirty seconds he let her hold him, and she, now seated in a soft chair, continued her efforts. Both child and mother looked pale, drained, and tensely in pain still—both, it seemed, trying to contain David's still palpable potential for eruption.

About one minute into the calming phase, as another child picked up the wooden car with which he had been playing, David erupted again, not as harshly, nor with flailing or kicking. As he ragefully complained and demanded the return of the toy, he picked up a block and threw it toward and nearly hit, not the child who was playing with the car, but another group mother, a person totally uninvolved in the event. David, further frustrated by the second child's resistance in returning the toy, in quick sequence grabbed his sister's bottle, which was at hand, threw it at her, picked up another block, and threw it at me (the parenting group instructor), nearly falling off the chair in doing so. He looked at me anxiously, more surprised than enraged as I told him I was sorry he was feeling so bad but that I did not want him to throw things at me or to fall off the chair. I wished he could talk to his mommy or me about the things that were making him so upset. Simultaneously, his mother was gently telling him not to hit his sister, that Dr. Parens had not done anything to him, and made good efforts again to calm him, telling him he could not throw things at people. With his mother's help, the second child returned the car to David, and David became calm as his mother continued to talk to him. Both David and his mother now looked exhausted and pained.

As usually happens with a tantrum, the focus of the group was on this pair, parents and children subdued, the children playing quietly, occasionally looking at David and his mother, at times at me, as if to see how I was reacting or what I would say or do. (This is to be expected since in group-parenting work, a point is made of focusing on and talking about problematic behaviors and how to handle them in growth-promoting ways [Parens, Pollock, and Prall, 1974; Parens et al., 1987; Parens, 1988].)

As he recovered gradually, David began to annoy his sister by taking the toy with which she was playing, looking at his mother as he did so, smiling provocatively. The teasing continued and intensified into taunting; the mother now became angry with him. At the moment when he was on the verge of going too far, David abruptly changed his activity, asking his mother to take out his letter cards and play with him at identifying the letters of the alphabet. David and his mother continued to look emotionally drained, and David seemed vulnerable to a recurring eruption of rage by his lowered threshold of irritability, resulting from the traumatic state produced by the tantrum.

During this alternately waxing and waning tantrum and after, the disruption of a rich learning-promoting, exploratory sensorimotor activity of a child of this age was observed, as well as the discharge of hostile destructive behaviors produced by David's posttantrum state. Evidence of the powerful motivation effected by the rage itself could be seen and felt, as well as David's (the ego's) various reactions and efforts both to gratify the rage and cope with it. First, there was the eruptive direct attack on the mother, soon followed by a displacement of David's rage by varying means onto another mother, his sister, and me, associated with his directing some of the rage onto himself (in nearly falling off the chair). After some calming, he teased and taunted his sister and mother, which he then abruptly interrupted, turning to play with a toy, evidence not only of mastery activity but also of sublimation. On a number of occasions a young child has been seen to turn away abruptly from a pressured discharge of rage or sexual excitation in an effort at sublimation. In addition, the inference is that David now experienced a lowered threshold of irritability, probably produced by an overload of the ego with rage, mounting stress, and the threat of explosion, the first sudden outburst having been followed by a period of tenuous "quiescence" and efforts at mastery. There was evidence of the re-emergence of a second component of tantrum, and David's efforts to maintain mastery, albeit waveringly, could be inferred. Last, there was evidence in David's behavior of the intensely painful affect he had experienced during the tantrum, especially during its waning components, and from such evidence the potential for traumatization from the tantrum experience can be inferred. This is so not only for the child, who looks "washed out" and painfully exhausted during the waning period of a tantrum episode, but for the mother as well.

The Hostile Destructive Affects

While a variety of affect models are advanced, psychoanalysts agree that affects are principally reactive experiential phenomena that have specific inborn patterns discernible in expression (facial, vocal, etc.) and behavior. They are reliable windows to psychic experience. Affects occur along a pleasure-unpleasure experience continuum and for our considerations here, one can usefully draw (perhaps somewhat simplistically) a pleasure-unpleasure affects dichotomy.

Affects, being reactive phenomena, are not vegetatively generated. Their potential for activation, however, is inborn. Rage, like other affects, does not occur spontaneously; it is not vegetatively generated as might be assumed by proponents of the death-instinct theory or by parents desperate to explain away their children's rage reactions. I have found its potential to exist in all the children I have observed, albeit with different thresholds of activation, facilitation, and levels of reactivity. Although rageful crying and lashing out do not occur spontaneously, they are not taught to the newborn; rage is not a learned reaction.

Rage on the Spectrum of Hostile Destructive Affects

Direct observational work led me as early as 1973 to question the then long-held death-instinct-based psychoanalytic theory of aggression and to postu-

late that rage is experience-dependent, a component affect of hostile destructiveness, and that hostile destructiveness is most commonly generated by
experiences of excessive unpleasure (Parens, 1973, 1979a, 1989a, 1991).[2]
Unpleasure *is* psychic pain, whether mild or intense. From one child to another and in each child from day to day and even hour to hour, the reactions to
what they experience as unpleasurable and emotionally painful vary.

The degree of unpleasure determines the range and quality of affect experienced and the adaptive behavior it activates. Mild unpleasure will disrupt the
existing affective state, induce alertness (ego function), and may lead to adaptive reactions of mastery such as eliminating the offending stimulus, learning,
and so forth, or the erection of a defense, such as avoidance (gaze avoidance
even in infants [Brazelton, 1981]). In young children, when the unpleasure
mounts or persists, *irritability* (fussiness, whimpering, etc.) may become evident. From about six months of age, as unpleasure mounts, it elicits crying,
and as it approaches the threshold of being experienced as excessive, *anger* is
elicited and may be directly expressed, or it may, in turn, elicit a psychic
defense. I have proposed that, also from about six months of age, when the
infant's unpleasure is *experienced as excessive*, it effects a critical experiential
change and begins to activate the hostile destructive affect, *hostility* (Parens,
1979a, 110-111). When such excessive unpleasure experiences persist, occur
frequently enough, and are sufficiently intense from the middle of the second
year on, they stabilize into *hate*, a more enduring feeling of self-object-
attached hostile destructiveness (McDevitt, 1983).

When excessive unpleasure mounts sharply, unless the ego's activity
(defense) can mediate its experiencing, a *rage* reaction will be triggered
(Rochlin, 1973; Parens, 1979a, 1987, 1991). Commonly, when hostile destructiveness resulting from past trauma accumulates and stabilizes intrapsychically at high levels (whether manifest or contained by defenses), acute
peaks of fresh, excessively felt unpleasure may more easily trigger rage reactions; this may occur even if the stimulus is of low intensity. In this model then,
the affects from irritability and anger to hostility, hate, and rage are all reactive
to unpleasure experiencing determined by the intensity, frequency, and duration of such experiencing, each containing an increasingly intense level of
hostile destructiveness (Parens, 1991).

Rage Reactions and Tantrums

Rage reactions can be engendered in young children by inducing sufficiently intense unpleasure (psychic pain) of varying kinds—most commonly
by deprivation and hostile caregiving, including physical pain or threat, but
eventually most readily by a perceived injury to autonomy and narcissism
(Storr, 1972; Kohut, 1972, 1977; Rochlin, 1973; Parens, 1973, 1979a, 1987,

2. Exceptions are the rage reactions associated with specific physiological disordered states, as
occurs in seizure disorders (e.g., temporal lobe epilepsy), acute alcohol intoxication, and so forth.

1989a). Eliciting rage is greatly facilitated by existing heightened levels of accumulated and stabilized hostile destructiveness. Due to the confluence of an already present load of hostile destructiveness and an overburdened ego (which lowers the threshold for rage elicitation or defense against it) in some children, as with David, just a spark of further stress can trigger a rage reaction.

In early childhood, the experience of rage manifests itself in two basic forms, in rage reactions and in temper tantrums (Parens et al., 1987). These forms differ particularly along three parameters: (1) in their manifest experiential forms, (2) in ego functional characteristics, and (3) in what we infer to be their varying potential for psychic traumatization.

First, in terms of their respective manifest forms, a rage reaction appears as a single outburst of varying duration and intensity. In contrast, a tantrum is a prolonged, sustained series of ragelike reactions patterned in waves (Parens et al., 1987; see fig. 7-1).

Observing children closely, whether six weeks or three years old, one often finds that following a period of increasingly felt unpleasure and crying, when the source of unpleasure has not been removed, distress continues to mount and may turn into rage reactivity. Usually, the first sign of a tantrum is a ragelike reaction of moderate intensity. After a period of quieting, it is soon followed by another, more intense, wave of ragelike feelings, which are then followed once again by quiet. Waves of this kind increase in intensity until a tantrum becomes continuous, much stronger, and more difficult to subdue. In other words, "superimposed on the major curve of a tantrum is a secondary curve constituted of waves of tantrum episodes which, as they climb the major curve, become more and more intense" (Parens et al., 1987, 102; see fig. 7-1). In children like David, who have low thresholds of irritability and rapid reactivity patterning, and in those primed by traumatizing experiencing, a tantrum may start more suddenly, almost explosively. It will then continue if not mitigated, in a wavelike pattern. A tantrum can be brought to a close by caregiving that is effectively calming. It can also be interrupted by threatening caregiving.

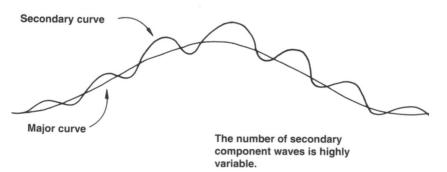

Figure 7-1. Temper Tantrum Model

A tantrum wave can also be triggered by a new unpleasure-inducing event of external or, as is common, internal (memory or fantasy) origin.

Rage reactions and temper tantrums, then, both have structure. A rage reaction tends to be a unitary experiencing of intense unpleasure, which elicits rage in a characteristic wavelike form that commonly has a climbing limb, a crest, and a descending limb. This episodic structure characterizes both a rage reaction and each component episode of a tantrum (see fig. 7-2). While a rage reaction tends to be a single episode, the structure of a temper tantrum consists of a series of such component episodes.

Second, there are distinguishing psychic-functioning characteristics within the outburst of a rage reaction and those of temper-tantrum-component episodes. In an experience-derived rage reaction—while suffering an intense amount of excessive unpleasure and therewith hostility—the child remains in contact with the environment, reality testing seeming age-adequately intact, and direction can be given to the hostile destructive discharge, which is commonly directed toward an object (animate or inanimate), and sometimes, subsequently, toward the self. At the peak of the tantrum, during the climbing limb of each component episode, the child commonly experiences an altered state of consciousness, the boundaries between self and other fade, and inner disorganization and a sense of helplessness prevail. At the crest of the wave (episode) and during the descending limb of each component episode, there is a return to better psychic organization and age-adequate reality testing. In other words, childhood temper tantrums bring with them a greater level of psychic-functioning disorganization than do rage reactions, being accompanied as they are by an altered state of consciousness, regression in age-adequate reality testing, and a relative loss of self-object differentiation. Temper tantrums occur more readily at a younger age because of the immaturity of the ego and its lesser capacity to mediate extreme hostile destructiveness, which is why we are more likely to see, instead, rage reactions in adolescents and adults.

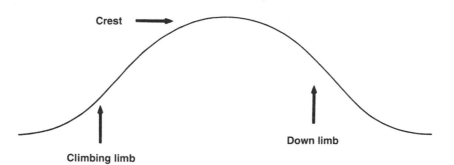

Figure 7-2. Temper Tantrum Model: Component Wave of Second Curve

Third, direct observation of young children suggests that temper tantrums are potentially more traumatizing to the child (and the primary caregiver) than rage reactions. Many rage reactions have adaptive value by virtue of the expression (discharge) of affect overload, by the discharge of the hostile destructive affect experienced, and by the results these may yield. It is not so for tantrums. The greater experience of disorganization, helplessness, and regression in ego function, side by side with the more prolonged and recurrent episodes of excessive unpleasure and hostile destructive affect experience, contribute to the greater traumatic effect of temper tantrums.

In addition, each rage reaction and tantrum has its own specific underlying psychodynamics. These dynamics also contribute to whether or not a rage reaction, and even a tantrum, will be traumatizing or will serve constructive adaptation; that is, we have seen tantrums and rage reactions arise in conjunction with a primary caregiver's limit setting, which, as with David, was felt to be clinically traumatizing. In another child whose mother set limits too restrictively, the child's rage reactions served to protect his autonomy in demanding less restrictiveness, which in our parenting education effort (Parens et al., 1974; Parens, 1988), we were able to help the mother understand. We have seen such reactivity also in reaction to a narcissistic injury (e.g., a bigger boy takes Johnny's truck), as well as in reaction to being teased and, interestingly, in association with a child's incapacity to master a situation. It was not surprising to find that traumatizing rage reactions or tantrums were associated with limit setting, narcissistic injury, and with being teased and taunted. It was surprising, however, to see what I felt to be a very painful tantrum caused by a child's experiencing as excessively unpleasurable her incapacity to master a situation. We found such a tantrum more difficult to assess for its traumatizing potential.

Rage: Powerful Motivator of Behavior

Professionals and nonprofessionals alike know, as David's case illustrates, that rage is a powerful motivator of behavior. It was so powerful in three-year-old David that he needed his mother's help to contain it; it motivated directly expressed attacks on the mother and, by displacement, onto another mother, his sister, and an observer—none of whom had discernible ill intentions toward him. Furthermore, the attacks also became directed against himself. In addition, for at least an hour after its acute activation, this three-year-old was vulnerable, as if primed, to rage being reactivated by even minor stimuli.

Two questions follow from the consideration that rage is a powerful motivator of behavior: (1) What factors combine to make it so powerful? and (2) What factors make it more or less powerful and facilitate or reduce its activation, generation, and stabilization in the psyche?

What Factors Combine to Make Rage So Powerful a Motivator of Behavior?
The details of the David vignette illustrate that an experience of excessive

unpleasure triggered a tantrum—that of the mother thwarting David's wish to eat an apple. Our research group's impression was that David experienced this unpleasure as excessive and beyond his tolerance, a reactivity we recognized in him as manifesting a low tolerance for frustration. Although David was observed only weekly for $1\frac{1}{2}$ half hours from about two years of age, his development since birth had not been followed, nor had he been seen therapeutically; we inferred that his low frustration tolerance came primarily from inborn factors. We learned from his mother that he had been an infant with a low threshold for irritability, with a pattern of rapid reactivity to unpleasure-inducing events with quick progression to rage, and he reacted with a high measure of aggression—all of which made his ability to organize the experience of unpleasure difficult and his mother's ample ministrations of limited success. Children with such inborn diatheses experience unpleasure as excessive more quickly than others. Further complicating their lives from the outset, many such children cannot be as easily comforted or soothed by even good caregivers. Mother-child interaction is then often established well beneath an optimal level and eventually becomes internalized. Parents who understand their children's greater vulnerability to experiencing unpleasure as excessive, as David's mother did, are better able to try to soothe and calm and to take more time to help the child organize the experience, in spite of the greater demands on them for such help and the early failures of their efforts. Rage reactions and tantrums are never easy for parents to deal with, but knowing the nature of their children's inborn susceptibilities and knowing whether or not they need more help in coping constructively with unpleasure-inducing events often elicits a better effort.

Superimposed on whatever vulnerabilities, tolerances, and coping capabilities children are born with, experience in the context of human interaction (object relations) most determines how much hostility and rage is generated in children. Pertinent to this assertion is the hypothesis that excessive unpleasure activates the mechanism that generates hostile destructiveness (Parens, 1979a, 1984, 1989b). This hypothesis underscores that unpleasure of whatever origin, when experienced as excessive, generates hostile destructiveness and that the intensity, frequency, and duration of the excessively felt unpleasure generates and mobilizes a commensurate degree and form of hostile destructiveness, which in time becomes patterned, part of structure formation, personality, and object relations (Parens, 1979a, 115-117). In its essentials, the "frustration-aggression" hypothesis of Dollard and co-workers (1939) is subsumed in my hypothesis, which corrects some of the major problems of the frustration-aggression model: there are sources of unpleasure other than frustration, and the hostile destructiveness generated is not always discharged (outwardly) and may, therefore, not be immediately manifest.

As noted earlier, when unpleasure mounts, a child's affective experience may traverse the spectrum of hostile destructive affects, moving from mild irritability to rage (Parens, 1992). Above all, the *intensity, duration,* and *fre-*

quency of unpleasure experiences determine the hostile destructive affect activated and its cumulative intrapsychic structuring. Of course, intensity, duration, and frequency of unpleasure are influenced by the "meaning" of what causes unpleasure: the psychodynamic parameter of rage and its intrapsychic structuring. If I, an observer, had told David that he could not have an apple because it might upset his already upset tummy, there is a good chance he would not have erupted into a rage (A. Freud, 1963). Because his mother, his prime libidinal object, did so, it had an altogether different meaning and was a powerful determiner of the greater unpleasure David experienced. Object relatedness and the quality of that relationship give specific meaning to an event and greatly determine the degree of unpleasure experienced. We can speculate that there are at least three factors operative: (1) the mother denying David the apple, by virtue of her meaning much more emotionally to him than an observer, was experienced as inflicting a much greater narcissistic injury, emotional deprivation, and loss; (2) David experienced the disallowing of his wishes many times before (as is the case for every three-year-old child), more with his mother than with me; and (3) specific psychodynamic disappointments were effected, probably of both emerging oedipal and existing preoedipal wishes, at the center of which the mother featured prominently. There is more at stake, much more pain, excessive unpleasure more readily experienced, and hostile destructive affect more powerfully activated in being deprived by one's beloved mother than by some "nice enough" but only modestly emotionally invested person.

Another factor inherent in making the affect rage a powerful motivator of behavior is that rage partakes of aggression, specifically of hostile destructiveness. First, aggression is best explained when conceptualized as an instinctual drive. A number of writers have argued against the usefulness of this concept—some because of problems inherent in classical drive theory's energic concept; some because of its limiting drive-discharge formulation; and some for other valid and less valid reasons. Most noteworthy among psychoanalytic aggression theorists, Gregory Rochlin (1973), in linking narcissistic injury to the generation of hostile destructiveness, rejects drive theory but does so describing it only in Freud's earliest, now long-discarded hydraulic model of drive, disregarding Freud's 1915 revisions (including his observation that the drives have great plasticity) and the evolving nature of his psychosexual development model, both of which speak to the influence of *experience* on drive and the fact that drive *develops*. In other words, Rochlin's discarding of the concept of instinctual drive is based on his considering drives solely as the inborn hydraulics of psychic energy, thinking that has been abandoned for decades.

The seeming vagueness of my statement that rage partakes of aggression lies in the problem created by the existence of varying definitions of *aggression*. By aggression I do *not* mean only hostile destructiveness or rage (1979a). Academic psychology deliberately speaks of aggression as meaning hostility.

What psychoanalysts speak of as *nonhostile aggression,* academic psychologists label *assertiveness.* Psychoanalytic clinicians from Freud on, however, have pointed to the inherent common source of assertiveness, hostility and hate, nondestructive aggression, and hostile destructiveness—a commonality that makes possible the assumed transformation of one to the other, mainly that hostile destructiveness by some modifying process of "neutralization" can be converted to nondestructive aggression. This warrants their being conceptualized as pertaining to one drive. In sum, by aggression I mean the umbrella concept (Marcovitz, 1973) that subsumes nondestructive aggression and hostile destructiveness (Parens, 1979a, 1984, 1989a). I find the explications of aggression as instinctual drive useful in both clinical and observation settings, especially in terms of understanding the contributions of hostile destructiveness and rage in the psyche as both drive (in conflict and character formation) *and* affect (in experience) (Parens, 1973, 1979a, 1982, 1989a; see also Kernberg, 1976, 1982).

The second line of thought that contributes to an explanation of what makes rage a powerful motivator of behavior is that the impact of a noxious stimulus on the organism creates a self-preservative reaction of "aggressively ridding" the self of the noxious agent, and the more the stimulus is experienced as noxious, the more intense the aggressive-ridding reaction. Elsewhere I have drawn metaphorically on the biological assumption that proposes that irritability of the protoplasm is reactive to noxious stimuli or agents, as a model for unpleasure-induced aggression, that is, hostile destructiveness (Parens, 1979a, 110-111).

An affect should not be assumed to be that which aggressively rids the self of a noxious agent. The noxious agent, threatening the steady state and survival of the organism, simultaneously activates the affect (from irritability to rage) and the more or less vigorous aggressive, ridding action, which bespeaks an act of aggression. The affect in the experience of rage arises from the excessive unpleasure experienced.

When I suggest that rage partakes of aggression (hostile destructiveness), here is how I think it does so. Following the physiological model referred to earlier, it became necessary to ask by what step the aggressive, ridding impulse inferable in the physiological reaction becomes a hostile destructive impulse. It would seem that the important factor that modifies the aggressive, ridding impulse into a hostile destructive impulse is the part played by unpleasure. The inference from observations is that excessively felt unpleasure introduces an all-important qualitative character into aggression: this painful affective condition qualitatively changes the aim of aggression, which then becomes hostile and "ridding" aggression, or hostile destructive aggression. Nondestructive aggression affectively modified by excessively felt unpleasure acquires the aim of inflicting pain and harm upon and destroying the object (Parens, 1979a, 111). The widely ranging affective experience of unpleasure, then, plays a cardinal part in transforming the nondestructive trend of aggression into hostile destructiveness, which in its most intense range manifests itself as rage. It is by virtue of the cumulative, excessive unpleasure experiencing, which progressively becomes structured into a constant source of inner pressure to inflict pain and destroy the source of pain (that is, as instinctual drive [Parens, 1989b]), that rage becomes so powerful a motivator of behavior.

What Increases and Lessens the Generation and Stabilization of Rage in the Psyche?

As noted in the example of David, two complementary factors make rage more or less powerful and facilitate or reduce its generation, activation, and stabilization in the psyche. First are the young child's biogenetic dispositions; second are the experiences of excessive unpleasure. The child's inborn dispositions pertain to the neurohormonal, the biogenetic, and so on. In psychoanalytic structural terms this pertains to drive endowment and to primary ego dispositions such as stimulus-barrier incompetence, intolerance for unpleasure (frustration intolerance, especially in earliest childhood), and physiologic dysfunctions like difficulty in organizing sleep, processing stimuli, and feeding (Hartmann, [1939] 1958; Bergman and Escalona, 1949; Alpert, Neubauer, and Weil, 1956; Sander, Stechler, and Burns, 1979; Greenspan and Porges, 1984; Emde, 1989).

The second factor, experiences of excessive unpleasure, especially in early life but even later, are always intrapsychically self-object associated, whether caused directly by the libidinal object or by a nonlibidinal object factor that cannot be mitigated by the libidinal object's ministrations. In direct observation, the evidence recommends a distinction between two forms of the libidinal object's failures in mitigating excessive unpleasure experiencing. The more benign form is that whereby the object tries to mitigate excessive unpleasure by positively experienced libidinal means (empathy, thoughtfulness, tenderness, etc.) but fails to rid the child of unpleasure because its source cannot be stopped or abated. For example, an infant's teething or earache cannot be diminished even though the unpleasure experienced may be mitigated by the mother's nurturing or soothing ministrations. The more malignant forms of the libidinal object's failure in mitigating unpleasure experiencing are those whereby the object's efforts are of themselves excessive unpleasure-inducing (e.g., infant and child abuse), or the object makes insufficient effort to mitigate the excessive unpleasure experienced.

In early life, experiences of excessive unpleasure determine the development of hostile destructive structure formations not only by virtue of the generation and stabilization of hostile destructiveness itself, but also by the heightened sensitization of the ego to the unpleasure experience and the emergent use of defenses to cope with heightened levels of hostile destructiveness. The experience of excessive unpleasure is inconstant, not only from one individual to another, but even within the same individual. A given unpleasure-engendering stimulus will not invariably act in the same way or activate the same degree of unpleasure each time it is presented to the subject. Unpleasure cannot be predicted only by the quality or intensity of the stimulus that has the potential to be experienced as unpleasurable. It is codetermined by the child's experience and capacity to tolerate it. The child's ego-functional capacity creates variability from child to child and within the same child from day to day and even from hour to hour.

As I pointed out earlier, one of the principal means by which the unpleasure potential of a stimulus affects the self (ego) is by virtue of the *meaning* for the child of the particular stimulus at a particular time. From its specific meaning, each child will be more vulnerable to some kinds of unpleasure-producing events than to others, even among those that are predictably painful for every child. The meaning of an unpleasure-producing event is strongly influenced by the child's stage of development as well as by, as emphasized before, the quality of the child's relatedness to objects. What does the mother's walking out the door mean to the eight-month-old? The twenty-four-month-old? A seven-year old? To the twenty-four-month-old, does it mean that the mother is going to work and will be back before dinner and bedtime? Does it mean that she will never come back because "I was bad"? Does it mean, "She hates daddy and me and is throwing us away"?

The meaning of experience is codetermined by what the child perceives actual events to be and by the child's fantasies. Direct observations indicate that under two years of age, a child's fantasizing, while progressively operative from about six months of age, is not as large a determiner as is the perception of actual experiences. This is not to say that actuality cannot be distorted prior to age two. Nonetheless, by contrast, from the third year of life, fantasy rapidly begins to play a major part in psychic experience. In a remarkable confluence of the maturations of cognitive functioning (and with it the differentiation in capacity for fantasizing), the biologic substrate of sexuality, and self-object relatedness development (separation-individuation being well under way), the ground is being prepared in the child's psyche for the emerging Oedipus complex. In other words, during the first two years of life, the developmental unfolding of hostile destructiveness, and specifically of rage, is more power-fully determined at first by actual experiential events, whereas from about two years of age on, the emergent capacity for fantasy leads to a powerful intrapsy-chic determination of the balance between fantasy and actual events in the activation of excessive unpleasure, thereby becoming much more complex. In fact, in well-cared-for children of $2^1/_2$ years or older, fantasy may play the dominant part in the production of excessive unpleasure experience and in activating hostile destructiveness.

From early life, the mitigation of excessive unpleasure and hostile destruc-tiveness and of the latter's stabilization in the psyche is profoundly influenced by the quality of child rearing and of object relatedness, which especially affects the development of the ego and, eventually, the superego. The chal-lenge of rage to the ego is enormous. In the direct observation of young children, I have often seen the thrust toward expressing and discharging hostility, especially when heightened into rage, to be extremely difficult for the child to contain and mediate. I have reported on the emergence of the defenses children implement to cope with such experiences (see Parens, 1979a, 1989b). In many children, the control of mounting hostile destructive feelings into rage reactions and tantrums does seem not achievable until latency and even early adolescence. This is evident not only in the actual gradual emergence of the rage and its discharge, but also in the after-reactions the children show. The behavioral evidence of exhaustion, shame, remorse, the directing of rage against the self, and defense against continuing discharge (e.g., displacement onto other objects) are evidence that this is so.

Fundamental is the question, What increases or lessens the generation of rage? Decades of psychoanalytic work, clinical and observational, have led psychodynamic clinicians and researchers to the following conclusion: Taking biogenetic dispositions as well as resultant temperament variations into account, the poorer the emotional investment in the child, the poorer the caregiving and emotional availability, the less empathic (child aware) the rearing, the greater the chance that primitive high levels of hostile destructiveness and rage will be generated and stabilize intrapsychically. The more primitive and higher the levels of hostile destructiveness and rage, the greater their disruptive influence will be on development and the greater their contribution to conflict and maladaptation. In contrast, the more benign the levels of hostile destructiveness and rage, the more these will serve self-protective and goal-achieving adaptation and conscience formation.

The Development of Hostile Destructive Affects in Early Childhood

I will detail now some aspects of the unfolding of the hostile destructiveness spectrum of affects, from irritability and anger to hostility, hate, and rage—conceptualizations that evolve from direct observations and clinical psychoanalytic work.

As Spitz (1946, 1965) has emphasized, unpleasure experience becomes manifest from birth by behavioral evidence of irritability, crying, and so on. Whereas from birth to two months of age pleasure experience seems usually to manifest itself simply in the quieting of distress, the manifestation of unpleasure is directly evident even during the first weeks of life. It is assumed that unpleasure reactivity is primarily physiologically determined. I agree with Rochlin (1973) that rage is an affectophysiologic reaction capable of becoming activated from birth.

For the sake of understanding, exploration, and handling (parental and clinical), unpleasure-dependent hostile destructive affects during the first weeks of life may be characterized as going from mild irritability, with fussing and crying, to heightened irritability-demandingness, which can become more and more negatively valenced, to rage. These represent the earliest hostile destructive affects. The trend of hostile destructiveness is characterized by a peremptory inner pressure experienced as a need to act upon, assert oneself over, control, master, and break down unpleasure-inducing noxiae. The psychobiological influence of unpleasure is the decisive factor, which, by introducing its affective character into the aggressive drive, changes the aim of aggression, which then becomes to inflict pain or harm upon and to effect the hostile destruction of the object (including the self as object) (Parens, 1979a, 115).

In the first weeks of life and even beyond, negatively valenced affect that cannot be sufficiently organized and mediated by a primary adaptive mechanism (primary autonomous ego [Hartmann, (1939) 1958]) is manifest as irritability. In normal infants with average expectable biogenetic and central nervous system maturational dispositions, when unpleasure persists and intensifies, the observably better-organized reactivity (beyond irritability) may first elicit some fussiness, and then a defense against the unpleasure experience, as, for example, stimulus avoidance, including falling asleep, and if the unpleasure persists further, expressions of negatively valenced feeling manifest in crying. When the unpleasure persists still further, the intensity of crying mounts and a form of nonideational demandingness becomes perceptible (Parens, 1991). As unpleasure continues, the demandingness takes on a more negatively valenced affect empathically perceived by observers and parents as evidencing increasing urgency. Although I do not assume the infant's having a capacity for ideation, parents often experience the baby as being "angry." Further unpleasure persistence leads to a shift from negatively valenced irritability-demandingness to rage, again auditorily and visually discernible. The raging infant exhibits a total-body, "organismic" reaction (Spitz, 1965; Mahler, 1968).

The shift from fussiness to crying and then to negatively valenced demandingness and to rage is usually progressive, children varying from birth as to the rapidity with which they traverse this earliest affect spectrum. Inborn dispositions—whether conceptualized as drive-ego dispositions (Alpert, Neubauer, and Weil, 1956; Bergman and Escalona, 1949); thresholds and patterns of reactivity; variances in capacity to organize stimuli, perception and physiologic reactivity (Sander, Stechler, and Burns, 1979; Greenspan and Porges, 1984; Emde, 1989); or as variations in temperament (Thomas and Chess, 1977)—determine the character and quality of unpleasure experience, affective reactivity, expression of hostile destructive feelings, and the velocity with which the unpleasure affective spectrum is traversed. Some infants slowly and gradually progress from one state to the next and with good-enough caregiving seldom reach rage. Others seem to bypass intervening affective states altogether, going almost directly from mild unpleasure experience to rage reactions. In Prevention/Early Intervention Parent-Child Groups (Parens et al., 1974; Parens, 1988) and in infant therapy sessions (Fraiberg, 1980), we enjoin mothers to help their infants who are rapidly reactive to slow down the pace of their reactivity. Such infants are much more difficult to rear for most parents.

The period from about two to eight months of age stretches between two maturational shifts in central nervous system, physiologic, and emotional functioning, each suggestive of a progressive level of organization (Benjamin, 1961; Spitz, 1965; Mahler, 1965; Mahler, Pine, and Bergman, 1975; Emde, 1980; Greenspan, 1981; Parens, 1989b). Functional capacities (ego) begin to emerge that influence the development of hostile destructiveness and rage. Ample observational evidence has been found (Parens, 1979a) to document the beginnings of cognitive (sensorimotor) functioning (Piaget, [1937] 1963), the capacity to express a wish (Schur, 1966), causality, and intentionality (Hartmann, 1939).

Before about eight months of age, the psychic (ego) functioning prerequisites for the differentiation of unpleasure-induced irritability to rage feelings into anger, hostility, and hate have not yet sufficiently developed (see Parens, 1991). The hostile destructive affects of irritability, anger, hostility, hate, and rage are distinguishable by two parameters: first by the varying intensity of unpleasure-experience, and second in that irritability and anger do not reach the level of being experienced as excessive, whereas hostility, hate, and rage do. The experience of unpleasure becoming excessive is a subjective one, codetermined by the characteristics of the unpleasure-inducing event, the state of ego functioning (which is dependent on ego development), and the meaning of the event to the self. The most fluctuating of these determinants is the state of ego functioning, which, in fact, influences the meaning to the self of the event.

During the period from two to eight months of age, then, a number of functional capacities emerge that lead to an incremental differentiation in the experiencing of hostile destructiveness and rage (Parens, 1991). In addition, progressively, the hostile destructiveness affects become connected to increasingly organized primitive psychic content. A negatively valenced affect now contains or is associated with an idea or wish, even though a primitive one. For instance, Spitz (1946) tried to explain what he perceived might occur in children who suffer from anaclitic depression, which he found to begin from the middle of the first year of life. He, like Freud (1926), assumed from the evidence at hand that object loss was experienced by the six-to-eight-month-old child. Spitz, using the then-current model of aggression, assumed that undischarged rage was turned against the self; he proposed this to be the cause for the anaclitic depression and showed that it could be resolved by replacing the lost object. These conceptualizations infer the beginnings of ego functioning as an agency (also see Weil, 1976; Parens, 1991), including the capacities for the primitively differentiated recording of affective experience and the beginning organizing part these affects play in early life. The hostile destructive affects now become associated with ideas primitively representative of experiences that become internalized.

Psychoanalytic and developmental psychology literature (Piaget, 1954; Bell, 1969; Mahler, 1965, 1968; Mahler, Pine, and Bergman, 1975; Emde, 1980, 1989; Emde, Gaensbauer, and Harmon, 1976) suggests that from about eight months of age on self-object differentiations and cognitive functioning (concept formation) bring about a differentiation in hostile destructive affects such that children become capable of experiencing and expressing anger and hostility. These differentiations coincide with a second shift in psychic organization (Emde, 1980); with the entry into the practicing subphase of separation-individuation (Mahler, 1965); the second phase of psychosocial development (autonomy versus shame) (Erikson, 1959); the biological upsurge of aggression (Parens, 1979a); and the beginnings of ambivalence (Parens, 1979b; see also Greenspan, 1981; Sander, 1985; Stern, 1985). In addition, there is ample observational evidence (Parens, 1979a; McDevitt, 1983; Stechler and Halton, 1983) that from the last quarter of the first year, hostile destructive affects evolve along several parameters. First, infants of that age turn the discharge of hostile destructiveness outward with more motoric directedness and object specificity—including striking with arms and legs and biting—and with vocalizations that clearly communicate anger and hostility. But under average expectable conditions, where traumatization is not excessive, these behaviors tend also to be limited to the time of the event and can be reduced or resolved by removing the unpleasure-inducing stimulus or by competent, empathic caregiving.

From the age of eight months, developing unpleasure-activated negatively valenced affects, embedded in object relatedness from birth, becomes organized by two developments: (1) the structuring of the libidinal object, and (2) the emergence of a biologically determined, marked upsurge in aggression that complements central nervous system and locomotor systems maturations (Parens, 1979a). Even more specifically than before, experiences in relatedness to libidinal objects is all-determining of the generation of hostile destructiveness and its stabilization in the psyche. Clinical experience and direct observation (Rochlin, 1973; Kohut, 1977; Parens, 1979a; McDevitt, 1983; Stechler and Halton, 1983) show that a critical developmental line operating in the self and in object relatedness that pertains to the vicissitudes of hostile destructiveness is that of *ambivalence*. The evolving co-existence of love and hate feelings in relatedness is the experiential context in which the emergence and stabilization (structuring) of rage, hostile destructiveness, and hate toward self and others develops. I have proposed that owing to its importance to the infantile psyche, the valence of the emotional investment made in the symbiotic partner (libidinal object) during the symbiotic and separation-individuation phases becomes prototypic for and most influential in all subsequent object relations, as does the valence of the emotional investment made in the evolving self representation. Because of their earliest and all-important epigenetic status (in his last major work Freud [1940] noted that the earliest cathexes are indelible), these internal representations of the object and the self will spawn object relations modeled upon them. Because of this indelible and omnipresent influence, the hostile destructiveness invested in the earliest object and self representations becomes the fountainhead of hostility in the psyche (see also Kernberg, 1966; 1976). From this psychic structuralization, hostile destructiveness becomes part of repetitive, automatic, and patterned modes of functioning in intrapsychic dynamics and in object relations (Parens, 1979a, 116-117).

The evolving developmental line of ambivalence may be usefully clarified by exploring first the further evolution of the earliest hostile destructive feelings into hate, and second, the evolution of the two basic conflicts of ambivalence we have found to occur in every child we observed in our Early Child Development Program (Parens, 1979a, 1979b).

Progressively, differentiations of ego capacity for cognition, memory, ideation, and the synthesizing of inner pressures and internalization of experience, organize the cumulative experiences of excessive unpleasure and the negatively valenced affects they activate (McDevitt, 1983; Settlage et al., 1985; Stern, 1985; Parens et al., 1989) culminating at about sixteen to eighteen months in the capacity to experience hate.

Hate, like love, becomes possible from about the middle of the second year of life. It requires a capacity for affect sustainment (felt consciously or unconsciously) over a more or less extended period of time and is more stably experienced and enduring (McDevitt, 1983), less peremptory than hostility to immediate motor expression and action, and is associated with a more elaborate and complex object-related psychodynamic. Hate is more compelling than hostility toward internalization and influences the quality of intrapsychic experience more. It is the uniquely human, complex, negatively valenced affect that enters into the experience of ambivalence, intrapsychic self-experience and object relatedness, and into psychic structure formation, especially in the vicissitudes of self-esteem and superego formation.

By the end of the second year of life, the basic hostile destructiveness affects—irritability, anger, hostility, hate, and rage—are differentiated and experienced by the child in reaction to unpleasurable life events, fantasized or real. Because the development of ambivalence has a powerful influence on personality formation, I will outline a model of the development of ambivalence and the major early psychic development-inducing conflicts that ambivalence creates. I emphasize that although ambivalence produces an intrapsychic state of conflict (in essence the wish to destroy a loved object), in its benign form, that is, in the normal child, it brings about most salutary developments. For example, under optimal conditions of object-related experience, love for objects brings about the taming and mastery of hostile destructiveness and rage. Indeed, as is well known in psychoanalysis, during the Oedipus complex era, it also brings about the development of the superego proper in both boys and girls (Parens, 1990). In contrast, when ambivalence is too weighted with primitive and high levels of hostile destructiveness—rage and then hate—it may induce harsh primitive defenses such as projection and splitting and create significant intrapsychic, maladaptive, and object-related problems (Klein, [1939] 1960; Kernberg, 1966, 1976; Mahler, Pine, and Bergman, 1975).

On the Evolution of Early Childhood Conflicts of Ambivalence

In "Developmental Considerations of Ambivalence" (Parens, 1979b), I proposed that we should find evidence of intrapsychic developments evolving in children that are determined by feelings of ambivalence that organize into two basic conflicts. The first conflict of ambivalence occurs in the context of dyadic object-relatedness. Some of its determinants and precursors may be established in the psyche during the symbiosis. It seems to originate at the end of the first year during the differentiation-practicing subphases, and it gains a significant contribution from the rapprochement subphase when it becomes focused, organized, and preexisting ambivalence may be intensified or ameliorated (p. 388). The second conflict of ambivalence occurs in the context of first genital-phase, triadic object-relatedness. It both arises within the classical Oedipus complex and gives rise to its core intrapsychic conflict. It is largely determined by the then-current status of ambivalence in dyadic object relations and may in turn retrogressively reactivate and intensify dyadic object-related ambivalence (pp. 413–414).

The first conflict due to ambivalence has its beginnings in battles of wills that emerge beginning in the last quarter of the first year of life. It starts as an interpersonal conflict between primary caregiver and toddler and usually arises in limit setting instigated by the child's powerful thrust to autonomy and exploratory activity (e.g., a toddler's early efforts at crawling up the stairs or a two-year-old's exploring an electrical outlet). This is the conflict that in classical psychosexual theory has been ascribed to the anal phase. I have emphasized that although it is amply evident during the second half of the second year of life, the anal conflict has antecedents in the battles of wills that begin during the last quarter of the first year of life. I have proposed (1979b) that the experience of ambivalence may begin even during the last quarter of the first year, when negatively valenced affects, especially hostility and rage, become progressively and increasingly enduring. Of course, this beginning conflict (at first interpersonal but then intrapsychic) is influenced by the confluence of constitutional givens and the already-patterned thresholds of unpleasure experience, patterns of reactivity, and internalized hostile destructiveness determined by antecedent experiences (Weil, 1970; Emde, 1983).

The second basic conflict of ambivalence, that contained within the Oedipus complex, is well known to clinicians, amply evident in early childhood behavior (see Parens et al., 1976; Parens, 1989c), and constitutes the nucleus of the oedipal conflict, namely, the wish to destroy the beloved rival parent (Freud, 1913, 1926).

It is also well known to clinicians that analysis of the repressed components of those conflicts due to ambivalence is essential for their adequate resolution, which gives credence to the view that no analysis can be sufficient without analysis of the negatively valenced (hostile, hateful) transference.

The Endangering of Self and Others

The internalization of experience, gradual structure formation, and average expectable developments are substantially determined by the extent to which hostile destructiveness is generated and accumulates in the psyche. How well the ego can mediate experiences of excessive unpleasure and hostile destructiveness that have accumulated in the psyche and that are currently generated will determine how well the child will be able to organize affective experience, mediate hostility, hate, and rage, and adapt accordingly. Where the ego cannot mediate or contain an imposing excessive unpleasure experience, rage is likely to become manifest. The more excessive unpleasure and rage (especially tantrums) are experienced, the less likely it is that the ego will be able to organize the instigating experience, attend to experiences outside the domain of conflict, practice skills to master these, and so on. Clinical experience readily and amply reveals the constrictions and inhibitions that follow from the ego's being overwhelmed by the generation of primitive and high levels of hostile destructiveness.

Thirty-eight-month-old David showed amply that his tantrum was a complex, difficult experience for him (and his mother). It was evident that he was suffering inordinate distress (excessive unpleasure), the miserable affective state of a tantrum, and that he was powerfully pressured to discharge his rage feelings by emotional expression and by acts of hostility. I have described how he not only directed this emotional expression toward the beloved mother with whom he was now enraged, but that by inhibiting the rage toward this mother, he also *displaced* this mother-instigated rage in acts of hostility toward three other persons and that some of it was also directed toward himself. Psychoanalysts assume that if put in the mind and body of a sixteen-year-old or a thirty-year-old, such experiencing might motivate the near-injury of a non-instigating neighbor, sibling, or a benevolent helper, the storming and flailing at a beloved object and danger even to oneself.

We could infer the influence in David of his dispositions: his low threshold of irritability, low frustration tolerance, high-degree reactivity, high aggression endowment, difficulty in containing unpleasure affects—all suggestive of a constitutionally determined heightened vulnerability to rage and temper tantrums. Fortunately for David, he lives in a benevolent environment that promises, as he grows, that his capacities to mediate, control, and sublimate such outbursts will be fostered. What most supports this prediction is that the quality of his object attachments, although emotionally invested with substantial rage feelings now, were nonetheless heavily endowed with love feelings and that the objects were loving, concerned, and capable of responsible (if not always the most helpful), growth-promoting caregiving. Too many thirty-eight-month-olds with such dispositions—some harsher, some more benign—however, are reared under conditions that are growth-disturbing, that do not promise in these children the evolving capacity to mediate, control, and sublimate the hostile destructiveness and rage generated in them *by experience*, however benign or vulnerable their inborn dispositions may be. Direct longitudinal observations of children and their primary caregivers, mostly mothers, have opened to view the many minute interactional events that day by day mitigate or enlarge the experiencing of excessive unpleasure and the generation of hostile destructiveness in them (Parens, 1979a; Parens et al., 1986; Parens et al., 1989).

As has long been extensively detailed by an awe-inspiring list of clinical psychoanalytic researchers, whatever the model used, the differentiation of self and object (intrapsychic representation) is intimately interdependent and reciprocal from the outset. In addition to infant observers, the reconstructively generated hypotheses of Kohut (1971, 1977) have also contributed to this understanding. Whatever primitive hostile destructive affects are generated by experience, and especially rage, they pervade representations of the earliest internalizations of the self-object: Mahler proposes this to occur from symbiosis through the separation-individuation process; Kohut proposes these to be stably extant in the psyche throughout life. The emergent capacity for anger and hostility from about eight months of age enlarges the varying and discrete forms of unpleasure-derived affects that imbue the internalizing self-object experience (Kernberg, 1966, 1976) during the first eighteen months of life. From about sixteen months, the emergence of hate qualitatively determines self, object, and the relationship between them during the latter half of the separation-individuation phase, which lays down the intrapsychic matrix with which the child enters the Oedipus complex.

Where ambivalence during the separation-individuation process is especially weighted with high levels of rage and hate, defenses against its expression toward primary love objects become virtually obligatory and range from denial and splitting (Kernberg, 1966, 1976; Mahler, Pine, and Bergman, 1975; Socarides, 1988) to internalizations (turning hate against the self, hate-imbued identification, and identification with the aggressor), and eventually repression and guilt, and to externalizations (projection, projective identifications, and, commonly, displacement). Considering the consequences of these defenses leads not only to an awareness of the problems created in the self by denial, splitting, and internalization, but also of the problems created by externalizations in object relations. Not only does hate and rage attach to emotionally invested objects, they go beyond them. Observation suggests that the major externalizing defense employed by even fairly well-cared-for children is *displacement*. David directed the rage he experienced toward his mother onto three objects in rapid succession, the objects being more or less discriminately selected for this displacement. Should we not consider the possibility that such displacements, when fueled by a large load of internalized hate and rage, may later lead to scapegoating and bullying? Might such externalizations, when perpetuated, contribute to antisocial destructiveness and crime? Furthermore, might displacement and prohibitive rage toward needed libidinal objects, when perpetuated and combined with a stranger anxiety, play a part in prejudice and racial discrimination?

The clinical situation has taught us, and it is confirmed by direct observational research, that in modest doses, rage and hostile destructiveness serve adaptation; but in large doses, rage and temper tantrums are especially burdensome to and disruptive of the child's ongoing development and adaptive efforts. This is so in at least three ways: (1) in having a disorganizing effect on adaptive functioning itself, (2) in effecting defenses that may lead to severe pathological compromise formations and symptoms, and (3) in making oppressive demands for mediation, control, and disposition that rob the child of opportunities to meet other demands made on the ego for adaptive development—for example, developing skills in essentially nonconflictual sphere functioning. In addition, the oppressive influence of constant demands to cope with primitive, high levels of hostile destructiveness leads to harsh self and object representations, schematized (stabilized) in conflict, and leads to harsh superego formation, troubled self-esteem, narcissism, and more. In sum, the development of the self and the self's relations to objects are jeopardized by high levels of internalized hate and rage. We know only too well from the transference that excessive hostile destructiveness in early relationships becomes paradigmatic for later relationships.

REFERENCES

Alpert, A., Neubauer, P. B., and Weil, A. P. 1956. Unusual variations in drive endowment, in *The psychoanalytic study of the child*, vol. 11, 125–163.

Aring, C. 1973. Aggression and social synergy. *Amer. J. Psychiatry* 130:297–298.

Bell, S. M. V. 1969. *The relationship of infant-mother attachment to the development of the concept of object-permanence.* Ann Arbor, Mich.: University Microfilms.

Benjamin, J. 1961. Some developmental observations relating to the theory of anxiety. *J. Amer. Psychoanal. Assn.* 9:652–668.

Bergman, A., and Escalona, S. K. 1949. Unusual sensitivities in very young children, in *The psychoanalytic study of the child*, vol. 3/4, 333–352.

Berkowitz, L. 1969a. The frustration-aggression hypothesis revisited, in *Roots of aggression: A re-examination of the frustration-aggression hypothesis*, ed. L. Berkowitz, 1–28. New York: Atherton.

———. 1969b. Simple views of aggression. *American Scientist* 57:372–383.

Brazelton, T. B. 1981. The first four developmental stages in attachment of parent and infant. Presented at the Twelfth Margaret S. Mahler Symposium on Child Development. Philadelphia, Pa., 16 May.

DeWit, J., and Hartup, W. W. 1974. *Determinants and origins of aggression behavior.* The Hague: Montow.

Dollard, J., Doob, L. W., Miller, N. E., Mowner, O. H., and Sears, R. R. 1939. *Frustration and aggression.* New Haven: Yale University Press.

Emde, R. 1980. Toward a psychoanalytic theory of affect, chap. 1, The organizational model and its propositions, in *The course of life,* vol. 1, *Infancy and early childhood,* ed. S. I. Greenspan and G. H. Pollock, 63–83. Washington, D.C.: Government Printing Office.

———. 1983. The pre-representational self and its affective core, in *The psychoanalytic study of the child,* vol. 38, 165–192.

———. 1989. The infant's relationship experience: Developmental and affective aspects, in *Relationship disturbances in early childhood,* ed. A. J. Sameroff and R. N. Emde, 33–51. New York: Basic Books.

Emde, R., Gaensbauer, T., and Harmon, R. 1976. *Emotional expression in infancy: A biobehavioral study. Psychological Issues,* monograph 37. New York: International Universities Press.

Erikson, E. H. 1959. *Identity and the life cycle. Psychological Issues,* monograph 1. New York: International Universities Press.

Feshbach, S. 1970. Aggression, in *Carmichael's manual of child psychology,* vol. 2, ed. P. H. Mussen, 159–259. New York: Wiley.

Fraiberg, S. 1980. *Clinical studies in infant and mental health: The first year of life.* New York: Basic Books.

Freud, A. 1963. The concept of developmental lines, in *The psychoanalytic study of the child,* vol. 18, 245–265.

Freud, S. 1913. Totem and taboo. *S.E.* 13:1–162. London: Hogarth Press.

———. [1915] 1957. Instincts and their vicissitudes. *S.E.* 14:111–140. London: Hogarth Press.

———. 1920. Beyond the pleasure principle. *S.E.* 18:1–64.

———. 1926. Inhibitions, symptoms and anxiety. *S.E.* 20:77–174.

———. 1930. Civilization and its discontents. *S.E.* 21:59–145.

———. 1940. An outline of psychoanalysis. *S.E.* 23:141–207.

Ginsberg, B. E. 1982. Genetic factors in aggressive behavior. *Psychoanal. Inquiry* 2:53–75.

Greenspan, S. I. 1981. *Psychopathology and adaptation in infancy and early childhood.* New York: International Universities Press.

Greenspan, S. I., and Porges, S. W. 1984. Psychopathology in infancy and early childhood: Clinical perspectives on the organization of sensory and affective-thematic experience. *Child Development* 55:49–70.

Gunther, M. 1980. Aggression, self psychology, and the concept of health, in *Advances in self psychology,* ed. A. Goldberg. New York: International Universities Press.

Hamburg, D. A., and Trudeau, M. B., eds. 1981. *Biobehavioral aspects of aggression.* New York: Alan R. Liss.

Hartmann, H. [1939] 1958. *Ego psychology and the problem of adaptation.* New York: International Universities Press.

Jacobson, E. 1964. *The self and the object world.* New York: International Universities Press.

Kernberg, O. 1966. Structural derivatives of object relationships. *Int. J. Psycho-Anal.* 47:236–253.

———. 1976. *Object relations theory and clinical psychoanalysis.* New York: Aronson.

———. 1982. Self, ego, affects and drives. *J. Amer. Psychoanal. Assn.* 30:893–917.

Klein, M. [1939] 1960. *The psychoanalysis of children.* New York: Grove Press.

Kohut, H. 1971. *The analysis of the self.* New York: International Universities Press.

———. 1972. Thoughts on narcissism and narcissistic rage, in *The psychoanalytic study of the child,* vol. 27, 360–400.

———. 1977. *The restoration of the self.* New York: International Universities Press.

Lorenz, K. 1966. *On aggression.* New York: Harcourt, Brace and World.

Mahler, M. S. 1965. On the significance of the normal separation-individuation phase, in *Drives, affects, behavior,* vol. 2, ed. M. Schur, 161–169. New York: International Universities Press.

———. 1968. *On human symbiosis and the vicissitudes of individuation,* with M. Furer. New York: International Universities Press.

Mahler, M. S., Pine, F., and Bergman, A. 1975. *Symbiosis and individuation: Psychological birth of the child.* New York: Basic Books.

Marcovitz, E. 1973. Aggression in human adaptation. *Psychoanal. Q.* 42:226–233.

McDevitt, J. D. 1983. The emergence of hostile aggression and its defensive and adaptive modifications during the separation-individuation process. *J. Amer. Psychoanal. Assn.* 31:273–300.

Moyer, K. E. 1968. Kinds of aggression and their physiological basis. *Communications in behavioral biology,* part A, 2:65–87.

Parens, H. 1973. Aggression: A reconsideration. *J. Amer. Psychoanal. Assn.* 21:34–60.

———. 1979a. *The development of aggression in early childhood.* New York: Aronson.

———. 1979b. Developmental considerations of ambivalence, in *The psychoanalytic study of the child,* vol. 34, 385–420. New Haven: Yale University Press.

———. 1982. A response, in *Commentaries on Henri Parens' The development of aggression in early childhood. Psychoanal. Inquiry* 2:283–320.

———. 1984a. Toward a reformulation of the theory of aggression and its implications for primary prevention, in *Psychoanalysis: The vital issues,* vol. 1, ed. J. E. Gedo and G. H. Pollock. New York: International Universities Press.

———. 1987. Cruelty begins at home. *Child abuse and neglect* 11:331–338.

———. 1988. A psychoanalytic contribution toward rearing emotionally healthy children: Education for parenting, in *New concepts in psychoanalytic psychotherapy,* ed. J. M. Ross and W. A. Meyers. Washington, D.C.: American Psychiatric Press.

———. 1989a. Toward a reformulation of the psychoanalytic theory of aggression, in *The course of life.* vol. 2, *Early childhood,* ed. S. I. Greenspan and G. H. Pollock, 643–687. New York: International Universities Press.

———. 1989b. Toward an epigenesis of aggression in early childhood, in *The course of life,* vol. 2, *Early childhood,* ed. S. I. Greenspan and G. H. Pollock, 689–721. New York: International Universities Press.

———. 1990. On the girl's psychosexual development: Reconsiderations suggested from direct observation. *J. Amer. Psychoanal. Assn.* 38:743–772.

———. 1991. A view of the development of hostility in early life. *J. Amer. Psychoanal. Assn.* 39:75–108, supplement: *On affects,* ed. T. Shapiro and R. N. Emde.

Parens, H., Pollock, L., and Prall, R. 1974. *Film #3: Prevention/Early Intervention Mother-Child Groups.* Philadelphia: Audio-Visual Media, Eastern Pennsylvania Psychiatric Institute/MCP.

Parens, H., Pollock, L., Stern, J., and Kramer, S. 1976. On the girl's entry into the Oedipus complex. *J. Amer. Psychoanal. Assn.* 24:79–107.

Parens, H., Rowe, D., Singletary, W., Schramm, K., Barcan, D., and Skivone, L. 1986.

Toward preventing the development of excessive hostility in children: Advances in methodology. Presented at meetings of the American Psychoanalytic Assn., New York, 20 December.

Parens, H., Scattergood, E., Singletary, W., and Duff, A. 1987. *Aggression in our children: Coping with it constructively.* New York: Aronson.

Parens, H., Singletary, W., Skivone, L., and Jessar, G. 1989. Toward preventing the development of excessive hostility in children: Evolving methodology. [Available from H. Parens]

Patterson, G. R. 1982. *Coercive family process.* Eugene, Oreg.: Castalia Press.

Piaget, J. [1937] 1963. *La Construction du réel chez l'enfant.* Neuchatel: Delachaux et Niestle.

―――. 1954. *Les Relations entre l'affectivité et l'intelligence dans le development mental de l'enfant.* Paris: Centre de Documentation Universitaire.

Reis, D. J. 1973. The chemical coding of aggression in the brain. Manuscript for Colloquium on Aggression of the American Psychoanalytic Assn., New York, December. (See D. J. Reis, 1973, *Central neurotransmitters in aggression, Res. Publ. Assn. of Res. Nerv. Ment. Dis.)*

Rochlin, G. 1973. *Man's aggression: The defense of the self.* Boston: Gambit.

Sander, L. 1985. Toward a logic of organization in psychobiological development, in *Biologic response styles: Clinical implications,* ed. H. Klar and L. Siever, 20–35. Washington, D.C.: American Psychiatric Press.

Sander, L., Stechler, G., and Burns, P. 1979. Change in infant and caregiver variables over the first two months of life, in *Origins of the infant's social responsiveness,* ed. E. Thomas. Hillsdale, N.J.: Lawrence Erlbaum.

Schur, M. 1966. *The id and the regulatory principles of mental functioning.* New York: International Universities Press.

Scott, J. P. 1958. *Aggression.* Chicago: University of Chicago Press.

Settlage, C. F., Afterman, J., and Bemesderfer, S. 1985. The appeal cycle phenomenon in early mother-child interaction. Presented at meetings of the American Psychoanalytic Assn., New York, 20 December.

Socarides, C. W. 1988. *The preoedipal origin and psychoanalytic therapy of sexual perversions.* Madison, Conn.: International Universities Press.

Spitz, R. 1946. Anaclitic depression: An inquiry into the genesis of psychiatric conditions in early childhood, in *The psychoanalytic study of the child,* vol. 1, 53–74. New York: International Universities Press.

―――. 1965. *The first year of life.* New York: International Universities Press.

Stechler, G., and Halton, A. 1983. Assertion and aggression: Emergence during infancy. Paper presented at meetings of the American Psychoanalytic Assn., New York, 18 December.

Stern, D. 1985. *The interpersonal world of the infant.* New York: Basic Books.

Storr, A. 1968. *Human aggression.* New York: Atheneum.

―――. 1972. *Human destructiveness.* New York: Basic Books.

Thomas, A., and Chess, S. 1977. *Temperament and development.* New York: Brunner / Mazel.

Weil, A. 1970. The basic core. *Psychoanalytic study of the child,* vol. 25, 442–460.

―――. 1976. The first year: Metapsychological inferences of infant observations, in *Ego of child development,* 1–20.

8

The Development of
Anger and Rage

MICHAEL LEWIS

In this chapter I draw a distinction between anger and rage, both of which are natural emotions. Anger develops early and can be seen within the first few months of life. Rage, however, involves the self system and does not emerge until after the first year and a half of life. More important for my considerations, anger is the consequence of the frustration of a goal-directed action, while rage is the consequence of shame and is, therefore, a failure in the ability to maintain self-esteem. The important distinction between the origins of anger and rage is found in the role of shame in these emotions. As I have argued elsewhere (Lewis, 1991, 1992), the emergence of shame cannot take place until after the development of objective self-awareness or consciousness. Shame, therefore, does not make its emergence until sometime after the end of the second year of life. Because of the connection between shame and rage, I must consider four related topics: anger, self-consciousness, shame, and rage.

The Definition of Anger

To make sense of the concept of anger, it is necessary to appreciate that there are different kinds of anger—even though the various types are often lumped in a single category. With anger and will, the problem is evident in the topic of narcissism. Much has been written about narcissism (see Andrew Morrison's *Essential papers on narcissism*, 1986) that is relevant here. Narcissism can be defined as a description of certain human behaviors or as a behavioral disorder. As we know, Freud viewed narcissism in two ways: primary narcissism, which involves the initial libido investment of energy to the as yet undifferentiated ego, and secondary narcissism, which is a withdrawal of psychic energy

148

from objects back to the ego ([1914] 1957). In some sense, then, for Freud, primary narcissism is a normal phase, a position similar to Heinz Kohut's. Kohut (1972) argued that narcissism is not necessarily pathological but instead leads to object love, that is, love for another, at the beginning of life. In its more mature form, narcissism leads to other skills; for example, creativity, empathy, and humor. From another perspective, and the perspective that I take here, we can think of narcissism, at least the nonpathological type, as a will to power (Nietzsche, [1904] 1964; Rank, 1945), assertiveness (White, 1959), or even anger and intention (Lewis, 1990, 1991).

The difficulty in having at least two definitions of narcissism applies to the term *anger*. We need to distinguish the two emotions of anger and rage.[1] First I will consider anger; here I rely on Charles Darwin and others for the definition.

Darwin considered anger as an emotion that "habitually leads to action" (1872, 78). "Anger and joy are, from the first, exciting emotions, and they naturally lead, more especially the former, to energetic movements which react on the heart and thus again on the brain" (p. 79). For Darwin, the most important feature of anger was its action orientation, the attempt of the organism to overcome an obstacle. This feature of anger, which includes facial expression, remains central to Darwin's idea of the function of anger: "The excited brain gives strength to the muscles, and at the same time, energy to the will" (p. 239). For Darwin, then, the function of anger is clear; it is action oriented and facially expressive. Carroll Izard (1977) picks up on this feature: "Anger often results from physical or psychological restraint, or from *interference* with goal-oriented activity. . . . Readily mobilized energy tenses the muscles and provides a feeling of power, a sense of courage or confidence. . . . The emotion of anger should be distinguished from acts of aggression" (p. 87).

Notice that this definition of the emotion of anger is associated with restraint or interference with goal-oriented behavior and involves the muscles (or action) of the organism to overcome the cause of the emotion. Neither Darwin nor Izard distinguish between anger and rage, indeed they believe they differ only by degree. Here I will part company with their definition, since, for me anger, at least in the very young, is not a form of rage. Rage requires such elicitors as "personal insult . . . being taken advantage of, and being compelled to do something against one's wishes" (Izard, 1977, 330). These elicitors cannot be present in the very young since they assume a level of objective self-awareness or consciousness that is not present until later, somewhere around two years of age.

My definition of anger makes reference to a basic emotion whose function

---

1. The term *aggression* is often used, but aggression may or may not be accompanied by anger or rage. Aggression makes reference to action toward another or others, whereas anger and rage speak to emotions as located within the individual.

is to provide the organism with motivated capacities to overcome obstacles. Notice that in this definition there is no implication of the negative features that we usually attribute to this emotion. The form of anger that I address is the type most similar to the concept of will, efficacy, or even primary narcissism as discussed by others. It is simply the organism's attempt to overcome obstacles. The most important point in discussing the emergent property of anger is that its chief function is its association with action in the world. This action may take the form of behavior toward others or toward objects, but its primary function is its efficacy. It is, to use Nietzsche's phrase, the will to power, the will to action (1964).

Studies in the Origins of Anger

Until recently, angry expressions were thought to emerge in infants between four and six months of age. It is interesting to note in this regard that the emergence of expressions of anger seems to coincide with the emergence of the child's mental capacity to learn the relationship between cause and effect. That anger expressions emerge at the same time as the child's capacity to learn how to affect his or her environment again reinforces Darwin's idea of anger as part of the instrumental action to overcome barriers in the environment. The examination of anger in young children typically has been indexed by increased instrumental responding. For example, John Watson (1925), M. Sherman and I. Sherman (1925), and Sherman, Sherman, and Charles Flory (1936) reported an increased avoidance in defensive behavior elicited by arm and leg restraint. Infants younger than six months originally responded to restraint by increased tension, breath holding, and by increased movement of the arms and hands. Robert Sears and Pauline Sears (1940) and D. Marquis (1943), who examined frustration during interrupted feeding periods, also reported that blocking the feeding activity resulted in immediate reaction characterized by increased defensive activity and crying.

These early reports collectively suggest that inducing frustration by restraining an infant's movement or by interrupting feeding behavior elicits increased motor activity and the occurrence of negative vocalizations. One of the limitations of this earlier research, however, was that an assessment of specific emotions by looking at the face was not attempted. The limitation was due in part to the lack of discriminative measures of negative emotion and to the prevailing theory that emotional behavior was relatively undifferentiated early in life (Bridges, 1932). Technological developments and the refinement of facial expression coding systems have allowed researchers to assess and differentiate infant emotional behavior, yet only a limited amount of data related to emotions associated with the blockage of an action in infancy have been reported.

Anger expressions in response to a frustrating event have been examined in four- to six-month-olds (Stenberg, 1982; Stenberg, Campos, and Emde,

1983). In four-month-old infants, they occurred when arm movements were restrained and in seven-month-olds when a teething biscuit was withdrawn from the baby's grasp. In addition, Craig Stenberg, Joseph Campos, and Robert Emde (1983) reported that infants expressed more anger when mothers, rather than strangers, removed the biscuit and that repetition of the task increased the amount of anger expressed by the infant. These studies demonstrate that eliciting situations that block instrumental actions, even in young infants, reliably elicits anger expressions.

The onset of anger between four and six months of age has been theoretically linked to the development of means-end ability. Means-end ability refers to the infant's understanding of the relationship between his or her own activity and a desired object or goal. This understanding is thought to develop over the first two years of life, from simple body-centered actions to more flexible and insightful goal-directed behavior toward objects or goals (Piaget, 1952). Anger is the emotional response typically associated with the blockage of activity toward an expected goal (Plutchik, 1980; Stein and Jewitt, 1986) and should be related to young infants' emerging means-end knowledge. Thus, for example, Izard, Elizabeth Hembree, and Robin Huebner (1987) observed a response of general distress to pain in infants of up to seven months of age. Thereafter, anger, rather than a pain response, was predominant. Stenberg (1982) and colleagues (Stenberg, Campos, and Emde, 1983) likewise reported anger to frustration at four to seven months. In general, anger seems more likely to occur after infants have attained some understanding of the means-end relationship. For anger to occur, it may be necessary that the organism be able to associate the blockage of the goal with the source of the failure to obtain that goal. It makes little adaptive sense to express emotional responses related to overcoming a blockage to a goal without being able to recognize a means related to that goal.

Thus, certainly by four months of age and after the emotional response of anger, including facial expression and motor action, is likely to be the case. This anger response is an adaptive response to overcoming an obstacle to a goal. Any time an organism can learn a relationship between an action and an outcome, when that action is blocked, an angry response may be expected. An angry response should be related not only to the general ability of children to establish means-end relationships—something that Jean Piaget (1952) has argued does not occur until after four months of age—but should occur in an organism *when the infant has learned a response to a desired goal that can be interrupted.* In the following discussion, I will describe the results of a study conducted in the laboratory to test this hypothesis. The experimental paradigm of the study was intended to examine whether very young infants could learn a simple task and what would happen when, once they learned the task, the rules changed. Because this study has been carefully described elsewhere (see Alessandri, Sullivan, and Lewis, 1990; Lewis, Alessandri, and Sullivan, 1990), I will describe only its main features here.

Since the learning consisted of pulling a string to obtain a reward, observation of motor action constituted the criteria of learning. In addition, the faces of the infants were continuously monitored to measure emotional expression. A simple operant-conditioning task was used. A string connected to a Velcro wrist cuff activated a microswitch. A pulling movement of the string triggered a brief presentation of a colored slide of an infant's smiling face, which was accompanied by a recording of children's voices singing the "Sesame Street" theme song. Arm-pulling responses were recorded and each child was videotaped.

Each session included a two-minute baseline during which we were able to demonstrate the ongoing rate of arm movement, as well as that of facial expression. Infants then received a learning phase of contingent stimulation in which the audiovisual stimulus was activated by each arm pull. All infants learned the task within the first three minutes of the learning period. When learning was achieved, a two-minute extinction phase occurred, followed by a second three-minute learning phase. During the extinction phase, no event was presented following each arm pull. Thus, the child's learned response no longer resulted in the desired outcome. Rates of arm pulling throughout the sessions were computed, as were facial movements, using a coding system known as the Maximally Discriminative Facial Movement Coding System (MAX) (Izard, 1979).

At each age—two, four, six, and eight months—infants were assigned to a treatment and yoked control condition. The treatment infant's arm pull resulted in the event occurring, while the control subjects received the same amount of the event as did the treatment subjects, although it was not related to their arm-pull behavior. For them, there was no possibility of associating a cause and effect. The data for the study are presented in figures 8-1, 8-2, and 8-3.

The arm-pull data for each age group show that the pattern is the same; the only thing that differs is the amount of arm pulling. Notice that the control subjects show no change from their baseline; that is, since their arm pull did not result in any outcome, their arm-pull rates remained the same as those during the baseline phase. This pattern was not so for the treatment subjects. Infants who were able to cause the event to continue significantly increased their arm-pull behavior. Of particular interest was the response of the treatment subjects once the association between arm pull and event ceased to work, that is, during the extinction period. When the arm pull no longer caused the event, arm-pulling behavior significantly increased rather than declined over the period of disassociation. In fact, during the extinction phase, there was a 154 percent increase in arm pulling over the learning phase and a 376 percent increase over the base. Once the extinction phase was over, the infants returned to the rate of arm pulling they had shown during the first learning phase. All of these differences are highly significant.

I will now discuss two of the many facial expressions that were scored.

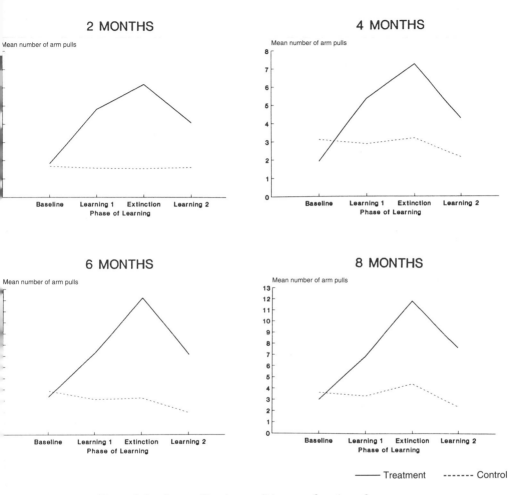

Figure 8-1   Arm pulling by condition as a function of age

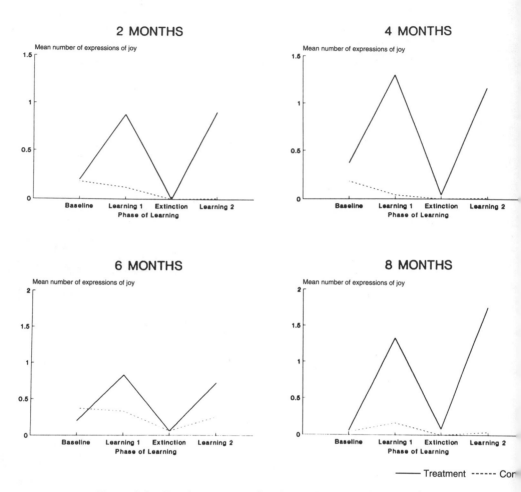

Figure 8-2   Facial expression of joy by condition as a function of age

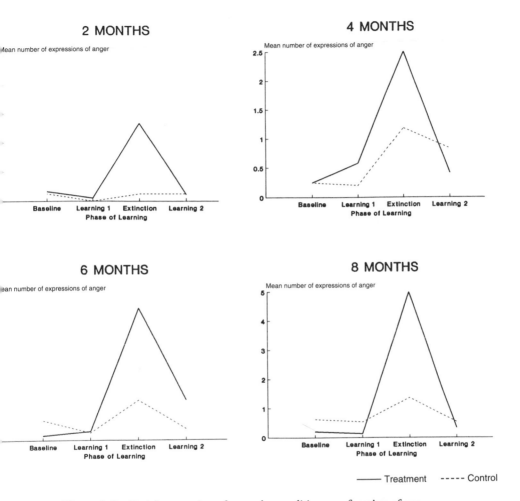

Figure 8-3 Facial expression of anger by condition as a function of age

Expressions of joy followed what had been reported in earlier work (Lewis, Sullivan, and Michalson, 1984). There was little joy during the base phase, and no change for the control subjects. The subjects who learned showed increases in joy during the initial learning phase, a complete absence during extinction, and renewed joy once the second learning phase returned. Looking at figure 3, we find that anger expressions followed a reverse pattern. There was little anger during the base or initial learning phase; anger increased markedly once the association between action and outcome had been broken and declined as rapidly once the second learning or control phase had begun.

There were no age effects. Even the eight-*week*-old infants showed the same anger pattern to the blockage of an instrumental act as did the eight-*month*-olds. The only difference was that the younger infants showed less of every emotion and less of arm pulling than did the older subjects. Thus, although age affects the amount of behavior expressed, it does not affect its pattern. The original design of the experiment had called for a second extinction period and a third learning period, but too few subjects were able to finish all seven parts. The 40 percent of the subjects who did complete all phases showed an increase in arm pull and anger and a decrease in joy during the second extinction period, and an increase in joy and a decrease in anger and arm pull once the association was restored. There was a high correlation between arm-pull rate during extinction and the number of angry faces.

I will summarize the results of these observations. In order to determine how children in the first year of life learn and what they do when what they have learned changes, a situation was created whereby an arm pull resulted in some unusual event. I say unusual since, from the perspective of the scientist there is no reason to believe that the child, before manipulation, had ever experienced an association between an arm pull and the appearance of pictures and sounds. Certainly, although it is possible that children in cribs learn that moving their arms produces some effect, such as the shaking of a mobile above them, pictures and sounds are unlikely.

Regardless of whether or not it was an unusual association, the children demonstrated that they could learn, and learn quickly, that the movement of the arm would increase the occurrence of the event. All infants, regardless of age, learned this association. Moreover, as they learned the necessary response, their faces showed interest as well as joy and surprise. Because the connection or association was made for them through an electronic-mechanical contraption, whether or not they wished to learn this response cannot be determined. Once attached to the mechanism, however, they did appear interested and happy when they made it work. Since they could stop their arm pulling if they so desired, it can be argued that its continuation reflected a desire to do so.

Having learned this association between arm pull and event, the infant can cause the event to stop suddenly. The arm pull no longer results in this event, the infant's joy disappears, he or she may become angry or may show fear and sadness as well. What occurs next is interesting: The response that leads to the event does not work and so the infants increase the response level and at the same time appear angry. Moreover, the increased effort to produce the effect and the angry face are related to the disassociation between action and outcome because *as soon as* the association is restored the anger disappears, frequency in arm pull declines, and the joy response returns. These children, even the eight-week-olds, appear to be angry when they do not get what they expect to get. Moreover, like angry adults who bang the pay telephone when they lose their quarter, the increased action disappears once the learned association returns.

Elsewhere (see Lewis, 1991) I have argued that this response reflects the intention of the child to obtain a desired outcome. The association between intention, blockage of a goal, and anger can be allowed because an environmental situation has been created where the child has been able to learn a particular association between its action and a desired goal. The blockage of that goal results in anger. Anger is characterized by an increase in instrumental response learned to achieve a desired outcome as well as by facial expression. To demonstrate that there is a strong connection between the learned response and the expression of anger, children's limb movement was observed throughout the study. The activity of each of the child's arms was measured and showed that although initially movement in both was present during the learning of the association, only the arm-hand pulling of the string increased in activity. The movement of hand not pulling decreased. Perhaps more important, when the arm-pull rate increased as the angry face appeared, it did so *only* in the arm associated with the learned response. The movement of arm not associated with the arm pulling did not increase. The response to the disassociation, even in eight-week-olds, was not a generalized activation but a highly specific response to a learned association.

These data, then, make clear that anger can be shown even in infants as young as eight weeks. Moreover, if my argument is correct, anger, both in terms of facial expression and physical action, is associated with an attempt to overcome the blockage of a response known to result in a desired goal. This response of anger is not seen as maladaptive, nor should this response be described as a negative event. Clearly, the infant wishes to reinstate the outcome that it found pleasurable. As a response to the loss of the goal, an affective motivational state occurs that is likely to aid in its reinstatement. By defining anger in this way, it is assumed that this form of the expression of anger does not represent a maladaptive or antisocial action.

Individual Differences

Not all infants show an angry facial expression when a disassociation between their action and a learned outcome appears. For example, in these studies approximately 20 percent of the children observed did not show an angry face, nor were there increases in the rate of arm pulling during the disassociation or extinction period; that is, not all children show the angry motivational system associated with reinstating a desired outcome. The most common facial response observed during the period was one of sadness. The majority of the 20 percent of the children during the extinction period showed a sad expression rather than an angry one. When a sad expression was shown, the children did not show an increase in arm pulling.

Figures 8-4 and 8-5 show the data of two typical children. Subject A shows the typical response, that described for the majority of subjects. The arm-pull rate increased significantly during the extinction period, as did expressions of anger, and expressions of joy decreased. In subject B, a different pattern emerges. Although subject B learns as well as subject A—they both achieve the learning criteria within three minutes—subject B's response to the disassociation is quite different. Instead of anger, the predominant response is sadness, and rather than increasing the arm-pulling rate, it declines. In fact, when control is reestablished, this subject is unable to marshal its resources to act in a fashion similar to what was shown earlier. Here, then, is an example of the utility of the anger expression in allowing the subject to maintain a desired goal. It is therefore extremely difficult to characterize the anger expression shown by the majority of the subjects by the more common use of the term anger. A reconsideration of our use of the term as well as its origins is in order.

Anger versus Rage

A central thesis of this chapter is that anger is first seen in relation to action aimed at overcoming barriers to goal-directed behavior or to the goal itself.

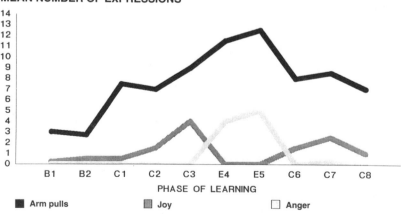

Figure 8-4   Subject A Responses

MEAN NUMBER OF EXPRESSIONS

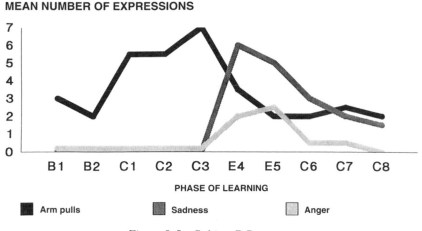

Figure 8-5   Subject B Responses

Rage, however, is a distinctly different emotion, one that does not exist at the beginning of life and one that requires the development of a self system.

As seen in the above study, the anger response consists of a particular neuromusculature facial expression and bodily activity designed to overcome the source of frustration. The connection between frustration and anger has long been recognized (see Berkowitz, 1989). Anger, on the one hand, is a natural and normal occurrence in all organisms, including infants, in their daily attempts to overcome barriers to desired goals. Some have likened it to will (Nietzsche, [1904] 1964), some to efficacy (White, 1959), and others to power (Rank, 1945). Rage, on the other hand, is less related to overcoming an obstacle and more related to an attack on the self; it is a response to an injury to the self. As such, it is more intense, less focused, and longer lasting. Kohut (1977) is helpful here with his discussion of narcissistic rage—although in a sense, this phrase may be redundant, all rage being narcissistic. When we think of an enraged person, we think of something having to do with a serious intense wounding or injury to the person's feelings. Such an analysis almost immediately leads us to consider rage as a response to shame (Lewis, 1992).

Such a conceptualization has recently been presented by Suzanne Retzinger (1987) in studies of the shame-rage spiral. Retzinger has drawn a distinction that she calls "shame-rage versus the rage response." From our perspective, she is making a distinction between rage and anger, although she calls one normal rage and the other rage-shame-rage. Even so, her analysis is helpful in distinguishing between anger and rage. According to Retzinger, normal rage—what I call anger—is different from rage in nine ways.

Anger is a simple bodily response, whereas rage is a process. This process involves moving from shame to rage in an alternative, spiral fashion: that is, shame leads to rage, which leads to more shame, which leads to more rage.

Implied in her analysis is that rage, having to do with shame, has to do with narcissistic injury. It is a process that requires elaborate cognitive capacity, whereas anger is a simple bodily response.

In anger one feels justified, whereas in rage one feels powerless.

Injury is recognized in anger, but in rage the injury is denied.

Anger is conscious, whereas rage, based on shame substitution, is pushed from awareness. Here, Retzinger is making the point that rage is the consequence of a set of emotions, shame being the prototype, whereas anger is not the consequence of a set of emotions but a consequence of the interference with the instrumental response.

Although anger may be easily resolved, rage, created by shame, sets up a feeling trap in which shame leads to rage, which in turn leads to shame, and so on.

Anger is not displaced, whereas rage is.

Anger focuses on actual cause, whereas rage is a generalized response.

Anger is an individual phenomenon, rage is a social phenomenon.

Anger results in few negative consequences, rage results in many.

It is clear that anger is a restricted, focused response, while rage is not; anger has a specific object, while rage tends to be diffused, both in terms of its occurrence and in terms of its object. Finally, anger appears bounded, that is, there is a way to resolve it, whereas rage itself may be unbounded.

Temper Tantrums: Rage or Disrupted Anger?

In this analysis, the distinction between anger and rage I have drawn rests on the specificity of the emotion relative to goals and to the activities to reach those goals, and on the relationship to the emotion of shame. Before considering this distinction, it is important to discuss a commonly observed phenomenon that occurs in young infants. Consider the example of a child who at nine months of age is blocked from obtaining a desired goal. The child becomes upset and throws what is commonly called a *temper tantrum*. Does not this temper tantrum constitute a rage response? It certainly appears to satisfy the requirements of intense anger in that it is unfocused and diffuse: it is not directed toward a specific target or person, and it appears ineffective in obtaining a desired goal. I have argued that these are critical features in defining anger, and it would seem that the child's response would satisfy the definition of rage. We should have no problem with this analysis if, in fact, it were reasonable to think of a nine-month-old child as capable of being shamed. Thus, we might say that the child is angry when it cannot locate and carry out a response for a desired goal and is enraged when humiliated or shamed.

The difficulty, however, arises in attributing shame to a nine-month-old child. The self-conscious evaluative emotions, including pride, shame, and guilt, do not occur until a child is capable of consciousness (what Duval and

Wicklund, 1972, have called *objective self-awareness*) and is able to evaluate its behavior in terms of standards or goals (Lewis, 1990; Lewis et al., 1989). When consciousness or objective self-awareness emerges and the child is capable of evaluating its goals, then the child is able to experience shame. I have defined shame as the evaluation of the whole self as failing to realize or maintain some important standard, goal, or rule. Phenomenologically, the failure to maintain such standards results in a wish to die, hide, or disappear. Another way to think about the feeling of shame is that it is the result of a disastrous decline in self-esteem.

The problem here is that children do not acquire consciousness or the ability to compare their own behavior to standards until they are at least eighteen to twenty-four months old (Heckhausen, 1984; Lewis et al., 1989). If this analysis is correct, a child is unlikely to be shamed prior to this age. Thus, temper tantrums cannot be the same as rage; that is, they cannot be under the control of the shame-rage axis as described by others (Lewis, 1971). We are confronted with the problem of explaining the occurrence of temper tantrums in children before the emergence of shame. Nevertheless, what is clear is that temper tantrums and anger responses appear to be different in the young child, even though both are seen in early life. If we wish to maintain that rage in adults is elicited by a humiliated self, whereas anger is elicited by instrumentality toward a blocked and frustrated goal, we need to consider the issue of development.

The Adult Forms of Anger and Rage

The distinction has been drawn between anger and rage; and it has been demonstrated experimentally that anger can be elicited in the human infant as young as eight weeks as long as the child has learned a particular response leading to a desired outcome and that particular outcome has become blocked. I have also discussed clinically based evidence that children show early temper tantrums—or what appear to be ragelike responses. We need now to consider how and in what way infants' manifestation of these emotions bears any resemblance to their adult form.

The Development of Anger

Consider first anger. It seems reasonable that the initial material of the action connection that I have called anger exists in human infants as a basic mechanism or structure, something I will call a *primitive*. This anger primitive, useful in aiding organisms to overcome obstacles, can be and is captured for other uses. In particular, the primary emotion and its regulation, through the socialization process, becomes tied to a large class of action devised to allow the organism to obtain its goals. The direct connection between the blockage of an action toward a goal and anger, through socialization, becomes disassociated. The energy and affect of anger are captured and used to motivate an organism toward any goal structure. Thus, if I wish to possess the property of another, I can cognitively construct a propositional system that allows me to argue that the other's possession of the object, which I want, is blocking my goal; I therefore can connect that proposition with the anger system. In this way, the primitive anger response is captured by the environment and is used to motivate the adult to action around any goal, whether or not it is blocked. This can apply to our feelings about people, objects, social structures, and organizations, such as religions and nations. It is simply a developmental process whereby there is a disassociation between the direct expression of anger and a blocked goal.

The Development of Rage

Adult rage grows out of another primitive. The rage primitive seen as temper tantrums is anger plus disassociated behavior. This early rage occurs through the elicitation of anger that cannot be satisfied by any instrumental response capable of overcoming an obstacle. The incomplete anger processes deteriorate and are no longer associated with specific behaviors constructed to recover the blocked goal; it is as if there were a short circuit in the anger mechanism. The specific focus deteriorates because no specific response is possible or because the intensity of the anger response is sufficiently great to disrupt the self-organization of the infant. The breakdown of this organized, goal-directed response—something we see as temper tantrums—can come about because of the blockage of all possible avenues toward obtaining the goal. The ability to tolerate and maintain an organized response in the face of strong emotions is likely to vary among individuals. Temperamental differences in infants in regard to stress have been shown (Worobey and Lewis, 1989). For some infants, overstimulation, regardless of the nature of the emotion, leads to a disorganization of their behavioral patterns. For these children, the elicitation of anger, as in the blockage of an instrumental response, leads to disorganized anger or to temper tantrums. Individuals differ in this disorganized anger response as a function of having environments that prevent an instrumental response from occurring (we might think of these environments as highly restrictive in nature), or in possessing certain types of temperaments that are likely to facilitate disorganized behavior.

The temper tantrum response we see in infancy is likely to represent a distortion of the anger response; not so for the rage response seen later in life, which is a consequence of being humiliated and shamed. It is not an angry response, for it does not seek to overcome an obstacle to a desired goal. Rather, it seeks to destroy the object causing the shame and humiliation. An example of a shame situation that involves a parent and a child and that is probably a prelude to child abuse is the following:

Recently I was in a department store and was watching a mother with a young child, a boy of about five years. The mother wanted to shop, and the child was crawling around under some garments. She told the child to stop, but he continued to play. She then grabbed him and picked him up, at which point he began to cry loudly. His loud cries attracted other people's gaze. She looked around and saw another woman looking at her disapprovingly. She appeared to be shamed by her child's loud crying. To get him to quiet, she hit him. This only made him cry more, which drew more attention to her. She hit him again to get him to stop. He only cried more. She was about to hit the child again when a saleswoman came over and gave the child a lollipop to quiet him.

What happened here? The woman appeared enraged. I believe this was a typical shame-rage spiral as has been described (Scheff, 1987). The child's behavior of crying in public after being stopped from crawling on the floor (anger in the child) made the woman angry. She hit him in anger. His cries and her behavior were seen by others, which shamed the mother. Her shame led to rage and her hitting the child even more, which, in turn, led to more crying and more shame, itself leading to rage. This progression or spiral is likely to be the cause of many forms of violence. Although this is not the child abuse we read about in the newspapers, it does have the same structure as more serious cases. How different is this from another similar scenario?

The caregiver attempts to quiet a distressed baby. The baby does not quiet readily because of its particular characteristics; for example, it is premature. The caregiver's attempt at mothering does not seem to work. The consequence is that the caregiver feels shame over her [his] failure to soothe the child. Shame turns to rage. Because the source of the shame is the child and its crying, the caregiver strikes out and smacks it. The child, of course, does not quiet.

The caregiver's punishment precipitates increased shame, which leads to further rage. This spiral affect of shame-rage-shame results in child abuse. Jackson Reid (1986), in studying the punishment patterns of abusing and nonabusing parents, found that the punishing bouts of different groups varied in length. Abusing parents' abusive chain was three times as long as an abusive chain of a nonabusing parent, indicating that once abusing parents start to punish, they have trouble stopping. Their shame-rage spiral may be out of control. Because of the spiraling effect, what is often a simple punishment of the child (anger) becomes, in effect, child abuse.

Even in the case of murder, we can see the difference between the rage caused by shame and that caused by anger. A police detective told me something interesting about murders: forensic experts can give the police some idea as to the likely identity of a murderer by examining the extent and nature of the physical injury that led to the person's death. Homicides come in two types. There are those whereby the victim is killed in a rather simple and direct fashion: shot, stabbed, or strangled. More brutal murders involve a multitude of wounds and destructive forces: a victim is shot ten times, stabbed repeatedly, or murdered by a combination of shooting, stabbing, and mutilation. These brutal murders are quite different than those from a single wound.

Although murders are likely to be caused by someone the person knows, complex murders are likely to be caused by someone the victim knows well, usually a family member. I asked the detective why this should be the case. His response was essentially the following: In every murder there is anger, and perhaps even rage—although there are some murders that are done for financial gain in which there may be no rage (such as in someone being paid to murder another person). In simple murders, the injury to the person is sufficient to kill him or her. In brutal murders, someone is, in effect, murdered ten times over. These murders are likely to be murders of rage. Murders of rage are most likely to be caused by someone who knows the victim.

I have puzzled over the police detective's statement for quite some time, and it seems to me that the shame-rage spiral fits the phenomenon. The detective is correct: brutal murders are likely to be caused by someone the person knows well because it is likely that the cause was the shame-rage of the murderer. The victim, either knowingly or not, shames the murderer, who becomes enraged over the shame and commits multiple violence against the victim.

In another example of the shame-rage, as opposed to anger, scenario, the matter has to do with rage, not against individuals but against property. In a walk through any large American city, the great amount of violence against property is evident: telephones ripped out of walls, buildings scarred with paint and graffiti, monuments and statues destroyed. All of these signs are witness to a destructive element on the part of a segment of the citizenry against the superstructure of the society in which they live. While such action against the structures of cities can be found in the countries of Asia or Europe, it clearly seems to be more extensive in the United States. How are we to understand this violence against property? Might it not be the case that the poor, the black—the disenfranchised—are continuously shamed? The shame-rage spiral would seem to apply to much of the antisocial action we see around us.

In the 20 August 1989 *New York Times Magazine*, there is a story by Anthony Walton, "Willie Horton and Me." Walton is a writer and filmmaker: successful, black, middle class, and professional. He related how one night a temporary doorman at his Greenwich Village high-rise had refused to let him pass into the building because he was black. The doorman assumed that a black man could not live in such a building. He also described waiting thirty minutes for a taxi and realizing that no taxi driver was going to stop and pick him up because he was a black man. Walton went on: "I am recognizing my veil of double consciousness, my American self and my black self. I must battle like all humans to see myself. I must also battle because I am black to see myself as others see me." It seems to me that what this black man is telling us is that even as a middle-class and successful human being, he is and continues to be humiliated and shamed because of the color of his skin. The realization of this successful human being that he is humiliated and shamed because he is black leads him increasingly toward a dissatisfaction, which leads him "to despise the white dragon, instead of the white dragon of racism." (Notice the term *despise*.) Further on, the article talked about how his best friends probably would not understand why he "was ready to start World War III over perceived slights in an American Express office." It seems to me that we are reading from the pen of an articulate, sensitive human being a cry for the need to recognize how white society treats blacks, and how the shame inflicted upon even the best of blacks must be faced and owned up to because that humiliation and shame carries with it the potential for rage and violence.

Various studies indicate that psychological attacks on the self—insult, humiliation, and threats—make aggressive reactions probable. Threats to the self-concept lead to aggression (Averill, 1982; Barron, 1977). What we have here, then, are clear examples of how rage is associated with attacks on the self and therefore is related to shame. Moreover, and perhaps even more important, we see the distinction between shame-rage and anger.

Anger is the initial and primary emotion. It is not species-specific but exists in all organisms. It occurs when a goal is interfered with and when organisms wish to overcome the obstacle to that goal. Anger, at least as a primary emotion, is designed to provide the motivation, including internal affective state and behaviors, to overcome the obstacle. This primitive pattern, through socialization processes, still in need of specification, becomes the anger form that we witness in adult action. As suggested, the immediate association between the blockage of a goal and instrumental action is disassociated in the adult form of anger, and anger can be used over thoughts or cognitive elaborations that require the motivating force of the anger affect. Darwin said in this regard, "A physician once suggested to me as a proof of the exciting nature of anger, that a man, when excessively jaded, will sometimes invent imaginary offenses and put himself into a passion, unconsciously for the sake of reinvigorating himself" (1872, 78–79).

Rage, on the other hand, has a somewhat different developmental course. The rage or temper tantrums in infancy and early childhood are most likely incomplete or disorganized forms of anger. Rage that we see in children over the age of two and in adults, however, is likely to be associated with the emotion of shame. Rage is a response to humiliation or shame, a threat to the self-esteem and well-being of the individual. In this regard, it is interesting that suicides are often the expression of rage against the self, given the self shamed by the self (see Lansky, 1988). Unlike anger, it does not have a direct and clear goal, except to destroy the shaming agent.

The distinction I have made between anger and rage comes from a developmental perspective: it is quite clear that anger, as we measure it in the eight-week-old infant, cannot either in form or function be the same response that we see in older children or adults. Without a careful analysis, we are likely to commit a serious error when we do not separate these terms. The existence of anger in the very young infant indicates that this is a primitive affect whose chief function is its organized, motivating power to help organisms overcome barriers to desired goals. It is only later that this emotion becomes elaborated to become anger in the adult form; that is, anger that is still useful in obtaining desired goals but no longer an automatic and organized response to overcome a specific blockage to a goal. Finally, disorganized anger, which we may call temper tantrums in early infancy, is prototypic of the rage that humans feel when their self-esteem is injured. By making these distinctions and by careful articulation through differential language of the difference between anger as an instrumental action, anger as an antisocial action, and anger as the consequence of shame, we may go a long way in understanding not only the developmental sequence but also the routes of psychopathology.

REFERENCES

Alessandri, S., Sullivan, M. W., and Lewis, M. 1990. Violation of expectancy and frustration in early infancy. *Developmental Psychology* 26(5).

Averill, J. R. 1982. *Anger and aggression: An essay on emotion.* New York: Springer-Verlag.

Barron, R. A. 1977. *Human aggression.* New York: Plenum.

Berkowitz, L. 1989. Frustration-aggression hypothesis: Examination and reformulation. *Psychological Bulletin* 106:59–73.

Bridges, K. L. 1932. Emotional development in early infancy. *Child Development* 3:324–341.

Darwin, C. R. 1872. *The expression of the emotions in man and animals.* Chicago: University of Illinois Press.

Duval, S., and Wicklund, R. A. 1972. *A theory of objective self awareness.* New York: Academic Press.

Freud, S. [1914] 1957. *On narcissism: An introduction.* S.E. 14:67–102. London: Hogarth Press.

Heckhausen, H. 1984. Emergent achievement behavior: Some early developments, in *The development of achievement motivation,* ed. J. Nicholls, 1–32. Greenwich, Conn.: JAI Press.

Izard, C. E. 1977. *Human emotions.* New York: Plenum Press.

———. 1979. The Maximally Discriminative Facial Movement Coding System (MAX). Newark: University of Delaware, Instructional Resources Center.

Izard, C. E., Hembree, E. A., and Huebner, R. R. 1987. Infants' emotion expressions to acute pain: Developmental change and stability of individual differences. *Developmental Psychology* 23(1): 105–113.

Kohut, H. 1972. Thoughts on narcissism and narcissistic rage, in *Psychoanalytic Study of the child,* vol. 27, 360–399.

Lansky, M. R. 1988. Shame and the problem of suicide: A family system's perspective. Presented at the symposium "Suicide and the Family," Los Angeles Suicide Prevention/Family Service for Los Angeles, 5 November 1988.

Lewis, H. B. 1971. *Shame and guilt in neurosis.* New York: International Universities Press.

Lewis, M. 1990. Social knowledge and social behavior. *Merrill-Palmer Quarterly* 36(1): 93–116. (Special issue)

————. 1991. The development of intentionality and the role of consciousness. *Psychological Inquiry* 1(3): 231–247.

————. 1992. *Shame: The exposed self.* New York: Free Press.

————. In press. Self-conscious emotions and the development of self, in *Journal of the American Psychoanalytic Association* supplement, *New Perspectives on Affect and Emotion in Psychoanalysis,* ed. T. Shapiro and R. Emde. (Monograph)

Lewis, M., Alessandri, S., and Sullivan, M. W. 1990. Expectancy, loss of control and anger in young infants. *Developmental Psychology* 25(5).

Lewis, M., and Michalson, L. 1983. *Children's emotions and moods.* New York: Plenum Press.

Lewis, M., Sullivan, M. W., and Michalson, L. 1984. The cognitive emotional fugue, in *Emotions, cognition, and behavior,* ed. J. Kagan, C. E. Izard, and R. B. Zajonc, 264–288. London: Cambridge University Press.

Lewis, M., Sullivan, M. W., Stanger, C., and Weiss, M. 1989. Self-development and self-conscious emotions. *Child Development* 60:146–156.

Marquis, D. 1943. A study of frustration in newborn infants. *Journal of Experimental Psychology* 23:123–138.

Morrison, A. P. 1989. *Shame, the underside of narcissism.* Hillsdale, N.J.: Analytic Press.

————., ed. 1986. *Essential papers on narcissism.* New York: New York University Press.

Nietzsche, F. [1904] 1964. *Will to power.* New York: Russell & Russell.

Piaget, J. 1952. *The origins of intelligence in children.* New York: International Universities Press.

Plutchik, R. 1980. A general psychoevolutionary theory of emotion, in *Emotion: Theory, research, and experience,* ed. R. Plutchik and H. Kellerman, vol. 1, 3–33. New York: Academic Press.

Rank, O. 1945. *Will therapy and truth and reality.* New York: Knopf.

Reid, J. B. 1986. Sexual interaction patterns in families of abused and nonabused children, in *Altruism and aggression,* ed. C. Zahn-Waxler, E. M. Cummings, and R. Iannotti, 238–255. Cambridge: Cambridge University Press.

Retzinger, S. M. 1987. Resentment of laughter: Video studies of the shame-rage spiral, in *The role of shame in symptom formation,* ed. H. B. Lewis, 151–181. Hillsdale, N.J.: Erlbaum.

Scheff, T. J. 1987. The shame-rage spiral: A case study of an interminable quarrel, in *The role of shame in symptom formation,* ed. H. B. Lewis, 109–150. Hillsdale, N.J.: Erlbaum.

Sears, R., and Sears, P. 1940. Minor studies of aggression, V: Strength of frustration-reaction as a function of strength of drive. *Journal of Psychology* 9:297–300.

Sherman, M., and Sherman, I. C. 1925. Sensorimotor responses in infants. *Journal of Comparative Psychology* 5:53–68.

Sherman, M., Sherman, I. C., and Flory, C. D. 1936. Infant behavior. *Comparative Psychology Monographs* 12:1–107.

Stein, N. L., and Jewitt, J. J. 1986. A conceptual analysis of the meaning of negative emotions: Implications for a theory of development, in *Measuring emotions in infants and children,* vol. 2, ed. C. E. Izard and P. B. Read. New York: Cambridge University Press.

Stenberg, C. R. 1982. *The development of anger facial expressions in infancy.* Ph.D. diss., University of Denver, Colorado.

Stenberg, C. R., Campos, J. J., and Emde, R. N. 1983. The facial expression of anger in seven-month-old infants. *Child Development* 54:178–184.

Walton, A. 1989. Willie Horton and me. *New York Times Magazine,* 20 August.

Watson, J. B. 1925. Experimental studies on the growth of the emotions. *Pediatric Seminars* 32:328–348.

White, R. W. 1959. Motivation reconsidered: The concept of competence. *Psychological Review* 66:297–323.

Worobey, J., and Lewis, M. 1989. Individual differences in the reactivity of young infants. *Developmental Psychology* 25(4): 663–667.

III

Origins and Sources

The integration of knowledge and perspective from fields outside clinical psychoanalysis into psychoanalytic theory requires rigorous attention to the compatibility of observational data and conceptual language. Venturing into *Origins and Sources,* we leave the realms of psychoanalytic and developmental psychology and enter the worlds of anthropology, ethology, and neurobiology. We are asking, Are all humans aggressive and dangerous? Is violence an intrinsic part of societal life? Or are there societies in which violence and power have no place? If we look at other primates, can we find in their behavior clearer evidence of an aggressive instinct to confirm drive theories? And finally, are our brains rageful and dangerously aggressive and violent?

In "Do We Need Enemies? The Origins and Consequences of Rage," Melvin Konner draws on observational data from human and animal societies to address the question of whether we are by nature violent. Competition and frustration, he concludes, are intrinsic features of communal life, both human and animal. Aggressive displays of violence follow from frustration and threat. In all societies, acts of violence are more evident in males than females. Fear, Konner suggests, particularly fear of the stranger, is a universal experience, for individuals and groups. It is the collective desire to reduce this fear that leads human and animal societies to form social structures to which the individual cedes power in the hope of ensuring protection and safety. Ironically, our human dynamic capacity for internal representations of real and symbolic danger creates the adaptive and maladaptive potential for constant and highly influential fears and more compelling needs for safety. In lower primates, such instinctually imprinted fears are manifest as episodic phenomena. When a society is frustrated in its attempt to reduce fear, organized social violence, such as war, results. It is man's nature, in Konner's view, to be competitive, frustrated, afraid, violent, and in search of protection from danger and fear.

One of the popular misconceptions about primate behavior is that primates are less inhibited or restrained than humans, closer to the primitive instincts. Leonard Rosenblum, in "Human Aggression: A Perspective drawn from Nonhuman Primates," cautions against reductionistic, misleading, and simplistic interpretations of primate behavior, particularly in terms of their relevance to human behavior. For example, Rosenblum recognizes the linkage among sexuality, dominance, and aggression, readily observable in primates. Sexual rights, however, are a component of social hierarchy and power relations. Indeed, if one looks at variations in food and survival conditions, as Rosenblum does, struggles for power and dominance have surprising influences on sexual and social relations.

Studies of brain structure and function, notably those in which areas of the brain are stimulated to produce anger and rage attacks, have been considered by psychoanalysts and developmentalists alike as revealing the underlying "hard-wiring" of our affect systems, particularly rage. In "Aggression: A Neuropsychiatric Perspective," Fred Ovsiew and Stuart Yudofsky challenge such assumptions with studies of discrete brain centers thought to be related to expressions of rage and violence and studies of rage attacks in patients with epilepsy and other brain injuries. The authors suggest caution in conceptual leaps from such brain observational data to abstract constructs like inherent aggressive drive.

9

Do We Need Enemies?
The Origins and
Consequences of Rage

MELVIN J. KONNER, M.D.

Rage is the name we give to the emotion that sometimes underlies the behaviors we describe as aggressive, although the emotion and the behavior can exist independently. In characterizing such behaviors and emotions and their causes, it is generally useful to begin descriptively. To get an idea of the magnitude of the problem, consider the following pattern of behavior. Many species in the cat family exhibit a sequence of predatory behaviors that is as close to constituting an instinctive coordination of motor-action patterns as mammals are likely to get. It includes lying in wait, crouching, stalking, pouncing, seizing between the paws, and directing a "killing bite" at the nape of the neck of the prey, where it will do mortal damage to the brain stem. A cat with no experience of prey will not do this properly at first, but with a few repeated opportunities, especially under conditions of playful excitement, the sequence "clicks"; it does so in a tiny fraction of the time required for cats to learn comparably complex sequences that do not draw on phylogenetic preparation (Leyhausen, 1979).

Consider the more unusual human act of violence in which a man who has been rejected by a woman assaults that woman in a mood of rage and kills her.

I thank Nicholas Blurton Jones, Josiah Bunting, Irven DeVore, David Edwards, Irenaus Eibl-Eibesfeldt, Martin Etter, René Girard, Julian Gomez, James Gustafson, Robert Hamerton-Kelly, Marvin Harris, Bruce Knauft, Richard Lee, Robert Paul, Paul Pavel, Jonathan Schell, Marjorie Shostak, Stefan Stein, Lionel Tiger, Robert Trivers, and John Whiting for essential conversations, access to unpublished materials, and other valued assistance. Some of the ideas in this chapter were developed in 1986-87 at the Center for Advanced Study in the Behavioral Sciences, with the partial support of the Harry Frank Guggenheim Foundation. Earlier versions were presented at the Stanford Physicians for Social Responsibility conference in the fall of 1983 and the series "What Is an Enemy? Views of War and Peace," at Stanford University in the spring of 1986.

The gulf between the action of the cat and the violent human action, which is of interest to psychoanalysts and others in the human sciences, is great and the list of differences long. First, the hunting behavior described is normal for all wild cats, while the human action is rare and abnormal. Second, the cat behavior necessarily involves the motor-action sequence described with little variation, while the specific motor-action sequence in the human case of homicide is largely incidental. Third, the cat's attack is directed at another species, while the human act (like all violent acts of real interest to the human sciences) is directed at conspecifics—members of the same species. Fourth, the cat behavior serves the obvious adaptive purpose of getting food while the human behavior—if it is functional in any sense at all—is certainly much more obscurely so and perhaps is a case of function gone awry; in any event it has nothing to do with food. Finally, the cat sequence is carried out in a spirit of playful excitement, even in a subdued mood, while men who attack their lovers often do so in a mood of intense rage.

Nevertheless, behavioral scientists, sometimes with important and confusing consequences, classify such very distinct sequences of behavior under the general rubric of *aggression* because they both have the effect, in some sense intended, of inflicting damage upon other creatures. The category of "aggressive behavior in animals" includes at least the following: serious fights that can inflict real damage; play fights, or rough-and-tumble play, that generally cannot; dominance hierarchies that eventually result from a settling out of winners and losers into a temporarily stable social pattern; threats of violent action, which can begin fights, play a role in them, or prevent them; and predation.

Threat, attack, and fighting can serve a wide range of adaptive functions: competition between individuals for mates, food, and other scarce resources; play and exercise; enforcement of sexual intercourse and defense against such enforcement; defense of the young; elimination of the young, either one's own or those of others, for purposes related to the reduction of competition; competition between groups for territory and other scarce resources; exploitation of prey species for the purpose of obtaining food; and action against members of another species, one's own species, and even one's own family, for purposes of self-defense. To these must be added an unknown quotient of functionless aggression that surely must emerge, the inevitable misfirings of so complex a system of hurtful acts.

Some distinctions of kind must now be made. Playful fighting, or perhaps more properly rough-and-tumble play, is a universal characteristic of the mutual behavior of young mammals and also occurs among many mammalian adults. It is not violent, it is usually not damaging, and it involves different behaviors of threat, attack, defense, and especially expression from those involved in real fighting. Nevertheless, it can sometimes gradually progress into real fighting, provide exercise for real fighting, and help to establish the dominance hierarchy that will regulate real fighting.

Predatory aggression involves members of another species rather than one's own, is usually done in a playful mood or a mood of skilled challenge, and is motivated by hunger rather than anger or competitiveness. It does inflict mortal damage using at least some of the same motor actions and fighting apparatus that the predator may use against conspecifics. Nevertheless, the common notion that predation is a type of angry or rageful behavior— expressed, for example, in the old theory that human aggressiveness is based on hunting during human evolution—is far off the mark. It is in herbivorous species such as the English red deer or the Uganda kob antelope that some of the most intense, violent competition occurs between males over females, while maternal aggression in defense of the young occurs in herbivorous and carnivorous mammals alike (Wilson, 1975; Trivers, 1985).

To complicate matters further (or perhaps to help explain some of the complexities), rage and fighting behavior can be dissociated in experimental animals in the laboratory using appropriate and different brain lesions. Cats may have real rage, as shown by expressive signals under sympathetic nervous system control—widening of the eyes, growling and hissing, arching of the back, and erection of the fur—which appears as a prelude to attack; but after an appropriate brain lesion, they will have only "sham rage," the same expressive signs never followed by attack. Cats may kill their prey with all expressive signs, following stimulation of one part of the midbrain, but stimulation of another midbrain location produces only a quiet-biting attack, the unemotional killing characteristic of cat predation in the wild (Flynn et al., 1970; Fuchs et al., 1980).

The Causes of Aggressive Behavior

The various forms of aggressive behavior and their emotional concomitants, if any, may have varying levels of unlearned and learned components. Every such behavior, in every species without exception, has some of both. In some, however, genetically determined fixed-action patterns and releasing mechanisms play a powerful role, in others little or none, with innate factors reduced to some characteristics of motive and mood. Adapting for present purposes a scheme originally put forward by the Dutch ethologist Niko Tinbergen (1963), we may say that to ask the question, What causes aggressive—or indeed any—behavior? is really to ask a series of questions. An attempt to provide an answer will be greatly aided if we are aware of the various questions involved in advance and indeed organize our explorations accordingly. The series of questions is not that engendered by our usage of the word *aggressive* to denote certain categorically different behaviors, but rather by the word *cause* and the various things we can mean by it.

First we mean, What events in the individual's environment immediately or recently preceded the behavior and seem to have precipitated it? These are called by ethologists *releasing stimuli,* and they may be learned or unlearned.

Second, we are asking about fast-acting physiological causation: the neural circuitry and associated neurotransmitters whose activation preceding or concurrent with the behavioral output produced it. Third, slower-acting physiological determinants within the organism, such as hormone levels or disease processes, must be considered. Fourth, environmental events of fairly recent vintage, such as training or observation—though not the immediate precipitating factors—may have had a strong influence on the behavior by altering the organism's response tendencies, just as hormones and disease do. Fifth, we want to know the events of gene coding and embryonic development—really a sort of remote physiology of the behavior, which tells us something about the raw materials of the organism—in relation to the particular behavior. Sixth, we are interested in environmental causation of a remote sort: "sleeper effects" that may arise from experience, nutrition, or insults in early life, including life before birth or hatching. Seventh, Why did the organism do that? can mean, What adaptive function does it serve? To a pre-Darwinian such as Goethe, this might have meant, Why did God give it that behavior? But to us it means, What were the forces of natural selection that favored it, given the environment inhabited by the creature and its recent ancestors? Eighth and last, we want to know the phylogenetic history of the animal. The wings of flies come from the thorax; of birds, from forelimbs; of bats, from fingers; and of humans, from technology. In each case the same adaptive function is served: flight, which in various ways enhances survival. But these very different creatures must solve this problem in very different ways, each consistent with its own, unique phylogenetic history. That history directs and constrains the animal in its evolutionary response to the adaptive problem posed by the environment.

In this framework, and only in this framework, is it possible to give more than a partial account of the causation of behavior, including aggressive behavior. It would be misleading, perhaps even dangerous, to suggest that behavioral biology can provide a satisfactory explanation for human violence. Indeed, it is doubtful whether any amount of research in behavioral biology will make possible the prediction or control of individual or collective acts of violence. Such research should, however, produce a more comprehensive understanding of anger and violence in general—an understanding of the sort that could lead to the better prediction, management, and prevention of conflict of a more ubiquitous sort, from marital fights to child abuse and international warfare. To approach the comprehensive explanation of human conflicts, we must first proceed to a much more detailed kind of analysis, one that carries us from the physiological laboratory through the field setting of the natural historian to the annals of human history. These components will give at least an outline of what will one day be as nearly as possible a complete explanation of violent and other conflict-related behavior, drawing on all of the eight categories of causes—from the immediate precipitating cause, through the physiological mediators, to the phylogeny. In the process we will have found a method for explaining behavior that is more balanced and eclectic than any that has been previously devised: an outline for the understanding not only of rage and conflict, but all human emotional behavior.

What is new here—new in the sense of being only just over a century old— is the concept of the human organism as the product of phylogeny, an eons-long formative process energized by genetic mutation and guided, at least partly, by Darwinian natural selection. One need only think of the number of national leaders today who do not accept this model to appreciate how little it influences conventional thinking about violent crime, ethnic conflict, or war. This, to a biologically inclined anthropologist, is like trying to put a space module on Mars with a team of engineers who follow Aristotelian models of weight and motion, rejecting the contributions of Galileo and Newton. The likelihood that these conventional politicians—applying the same models that have been in place for millennia—will achieve their stated goal of bringing violence under control, is not great.

A Model of Violent Conflict

To the extent that what follows is of use, it is because it summarizes some now well-accepted principles of evolutionary biology and biological anthropology. The model is not deterministic but merely biologically "aware." It consists of eight propositions, drawing upon but not precisely parallel to the eight levels of explanation outlined earlier.

First, every living creature exists in a natural state of conflict with every other creature in its environment, no matter how apparently closely allied. This does not mean that the alliances are fake, merely that the conflict is not incidental; that is, it is not like the friction between surfaces of moving bodies best modeled as frictionlessly ideal, but rather like the repulsion of similarly charged bodies attracted to each other by, say, gravitation. The conflict is as intrinsic as the alliance (Williams, 1966; Trivers, 1985; Huntingford and Turner, 1987).

Underlying this view is the notion that an organism—a person—is in an important sense only a gene's way of making another gene (Dawkins, 1989). Since the gene cannot but be blind to any higher purpose the organism proposes, it must guide its lumbering protoplasmic vehicle in cooperative or conflictful modes more or less as its past successes dictate. Those genes that have not guided their carriers successfully—success that inevitably includes success in conflict—are not around now to do any guiding at all.

The second proposition has to do with external mechanisms: the triggers of conflict. It is a general characteristic of vertebrate species that certain social signals—the position of a tail, a facial expression, a grunt—can increase the likelihood of an act of aggression on the part of an individual that perceives them. Two individuals posturing at each other, whether with antlers or with words, encourage each others' nervous systems in the propensity for aggression, and this seems to happen with a certain amount of automaticity (Wilson, 1975; Huntingford and Turner, 1987; Alcock, 1989).

It used to be said, by Konrad Lorenz (1966) for example, that animals exhibiting such displays are usually bluffing, and that natural mechanisms for the prevention of violence come into play as automatically as the triggers. A wolf, for example, bares its throat to its enemy, and this act turns off the enemy's anger. Humans and ants, according to this theory, are among a very few species actually capable of homicide. In the human case, the failure of the control mechanisms—especially in war— was attributable to the distance at which our weapons work. This cultural innovation enabled us to escape the controls that operate when adversaries square off face to face.

Unfortunately, this admirable viewpoint has fallen under a steady barrage of inconvenient facts. It was pointed out by E. O. Wilson (1975), among others, that if a group of baboons on the African savanna had the same homicide rate as the nastier sections of, say, Dallas, a field observer would have to watch them continuously for hundreds of years before seeing a single actual homicide. Sure enough, as the number of person-years of field research have mounted, killings have been demonstrated in one free-ranging animal species after another (Hausfater and Hrdy, 1984; Huntingford and Turner, 1987). Under natural circumstances, then, controls on violence usually work, but not infrequently they fail.

This is true of humans as much as it is of other species (Daly and Wilson, 1988; Knauft, 1987; Edgerton, 1992). Claims for the nonviolence of certain primitive societies are subject to the same kind of methodological criticism as are parallel claims relating to animals. The Kung San, hunter-gatherers of northwestern Botswana, made famous in a book *The Harmless People* (Thomas, [1959] 1990) and known for their effective control of conflict without officially designated authority, were shown by Richard Lee (1979) to have a homicide rate like that of American cities. The motives involved—usually sexual jealousy or revenge—are familiar. The Samoans depicted by Margaret Mead (1928) as nonviolent and devoid of adolescent "storm and stress" were shown by others (e.g., Freeman 1983) to have more in common with our society in these respects than had been documented by Mead, including a typical surge of male crime in adolescence. The Semai of Malaysia were also known for their nonviolence and for methods of child rearing designed to discourage all forms of aggression. In the context of training for counterinsurgency against the Communist rebellion of the 1950s, they became (by their own description as well as that of others) exceptionally vicious and bloodthirsty killers (Dentan, 1968; Paul, 1978).

These are not the most but the least violent of societies. People such as the Yanomamo (Chagnon, 1968, 1988), the Ilongot (Rosaldo, 1980, 1989), the Sioux Indians (Hassrick, 1964), the Zulu (Walter, 1969), the Dani of highland New Guinea (Heider, 1979), and the Germans under the Third Reich (Shirer, 1960; Hilberg, 1973) help to demonstrate what people are capable of when violence is encouraged rather than *dis*couraged. The differences among human societies in the rate and type of violent behavior are significant not just statistically but philosophically, and these differences are attributable to historical circumstances and to culture. But the concept of an essentially nonviolent people produced by a nonviolent society can now be laid to rest as a myth.

The third proposition describes an internal triggering mechanism, the principle of nonspecific, frustration-induced aggression (Dollard et al., 1939; Berkowitz, 1969, 1981). Complex organisms—the point is best made for mammals—appear to be designed to react to frustration with anger. For example, in one experiment, two rats are placed on an electrified grid. They have no bones to pick with each other. Yet, when shocked, they fight. Unable to see the real enemy—the removed, arbitrary, godlike experimenter—they seem to blame each other for an extrinsic pain that they can neither interpret nor control (Ulrich and Azrin, 1962; Blanchard and Blanchard, 1977).

Although there are many straightforward examples of frustration-induced aggression in humans, none is more poignant than a variety of headhunting among the Ilongot of the Philippines, analyzed by Rosaldo (1980, 1989). Young men hunt heads in the heat of teenage sexual passion, attempting to validate their manhood; as indicated below, this is a cross-culturally widespread form and context of aggression (Daly and Wilson, 1988). More interesting is the less passionate form taken by headhunting in older men who have suffered losses. In an impressive chapter called "Grief and a Headhunter's Rage," Rosaldo (1989) convincingly argues that grief produces an emotional state that for these men quietly smolders until it results in a culturally sanctioned action seen and felt as cleansing: the taking of a head from an enemy.

Increasingly, the physiological bases of aggressive motivation are being understood, both in animals and humans (Moyer, 1987; Tardiff, 1988). Motivation in general, however, appears to be partly nonspecific. Arousal has long been suspected to be general, on purely phenomenological grounds; it has some common features, irrespective of motivation. Specifically, though, experiments with rats have shown that stimulation of the lateral hypothalamus—a part of the brain clearly involved in motivated behavior—will produce a variety of patterns of action depending on the context (Valenstein, Cox, and Kakolewski, 1968, 1970; Mittleman and Valenstein, 1984). It may be food hoarding, retrieval of pups, or nest building, but it will be somewhat agitated and full of apparent determination. The suggestion is that the brain cannot quite tell from internal cues exactly what it is that it wants. Frustrations may thus be frequently misinterpreted, and any resulting aggression misplaced—anger, as it were, looking for an outlet.

The fourth proposition is that of sex-specificity: In every known human society and at all ages studied, males exhibit more aggression than females. This does not mean that a female is always gentle or incapable of violence; this imagined creature, to use Sarah Hrdy's (1981) phrase, is "the woman that never evolved." Yet whatever measure is used, the tendency to do bodily harm—playfully or seriously, spontaneously or with malice aforethought, individually or in groups—is more common in boys and men than it is in girls and women (Mead, 1949; Maccoby and Jacklin, 1974; Goldstein and Segall, 1982; Whiting and Edwards, 1973, 1988); the basis for this difference is partly physiological (Konner, 1982, chap. 6; Meyer-Bahlburg and Ehrhardt, 1982; Hines, 1984).

Despite this constancy, societies differ in overall amount of violent behavior and also in the magnitude of the sex difference (Whiting and Edwards, 1973, 1988). John Whiting and Beatrice Whiting (1975) made the interesting discovery that societies with a high level of husband-wife intimacy—as measured by eating and sleeping together and by the husband's involvement with the children—have a lower likelihood of male violence. Many traditionally martial cultures practiced female infanticide, producing a markedly skewed sex ratio in childhood, only to balance the sexes again through male deaths in conflict (Divale and Harris, 1976). To achieve an effective fighting unit, many societies appear to have to separate males from females, housing the boys and men in an all-male world. In an extreme version of this phenomenon, bellicose societies of highland New Guinea place adolescent boys in the men's collective house, deliberately removing them from feminine influence. Here they are trained and prepared for war and other forms of deliberate organized violence, which will claim as many as 25 percent of their lives (Meggitt, 1977; see also Heider, 1970; Koch, 1974). As Lionel Tiger (1985) pointed out in his study of men in groups, men kept together and apart from women experience something special, something that is frequently not quite nice.

Both the evolutionary and the organismal biology of this sex difference have begun to become clear. As shown by Robert Trivers (1972, 1985), following a suggestion of Darwin, the sex that invests more in the production of offspring—in birds and mammals, almost always the females—will exercise firm mate choice among the members of the other sex. These in turn—usually males—will compete with each other for females, and winners and losers will differ greatly in reproductive success. The more such competition occurs, the more the sexes will diverge with evolution, both in physique and behavior, including violence.

Thus, in addition to the purposes of aggression that the two sexes may share—competition for resources, protection of the young, and so on—there is a further purpose in which males exceed females: aggressive competition for access to the opposite sex. This helps to account for the fact that males exceed females in aggressive behavior in the majority of species of higher vertebrates, just as in human cultures (Daly and Wilson, 1988).

The mechanism is complex and cannot be treated at length here, but it appears to involve androgens in at least two separate ways (Meyer-Bahlburg and Ehrhardt, 1982; Hines, 1984). First, testosterone has had a permissive or facilitative effect on aggression in many studies. This partially explains not

only the disproportionate amount of violence in males but also the disproportionate amount in young adult males, who have relatively high testosterone
levels. Second, and more interesting, is the phenomenon that has come to be
known as fetal androgenization of the brain. Circulating androgens, especially
testosterone, during late prenatal life, appear to alter the structure and function of certain regions of the hypothalamus in several mammal species. These
alterations account in part for the sex difference in aggressive behavior in
those species. Clinical evidence in humans suggests something similar.

Despite these effects, it is beyond dispute that cultural, learned influences
help to determine both the overall likelihood of aggression and the extent of
the sex difference. These include modeling, imitation, identification, rein-
forcement schedules, verbal instruction, cultural symbols, and so on (Bandura, 1973; Feshbach and Fraczek, 1979; Center for Research on Aggression,
1983). What is argued here is that some part of the difference is attributable to
irreducible biological factors, these being part of the phylogenetic endowment
of the organism.

As for the evolutionary destiny of males to compete over females, our
paradigmatic war in Western civilization is the Greek adventure in Troy, and
that is said to have started as a conflict between two men over a woman.
Needless to say, this was not the whole story, and there cannot have been many
wars in which such a competition was really central. Even the martial events of
the *Iliad* cannot be reduced to the paradigm of two male lizards challenging
each other over a female. Yet there is a not insignificant similarity between
these disparate situations.

Which brings us to the fifth proposition: Groups in conflict are collections
of individuals who feel that they have more to gain than to lose by fighting
(Clausewitz, 1940; Waltz, 1959; Otterbein, 1970; Blainey, 1973). Consider
the foot soldier in the army of Menelaus. As a subject of the wronged husband,
he stands to become a target of misplaced rage if he refuses to follow his
leader. Going to war, he runs the risk of being maimed or killed; in view of the
usual risks of life, this may not be excessive. He also stands to gain the material
and sexual spoils of war, together with other rewards at home (Rosaldo, 1980;
Tiger, 1985; Betzig, 1986).

This is the evolutionary risk-benefit analysis that leads to and helps to
explain the subtler psychological gains. The soldier gets to turn his back on the
thousand frustrations of home life and to teach his family a lesson about how
much they need him; to commit for a time to a purpose that seems pure and
clear; to experience the unique excitement of martial adventure and the rewards of masculine company in a dangerous situation; to express and assuage
deep-seated frustrations and griefs; and to achieve the enduring satisfaction of
having faced and triumphed over fear and of having been willing to risk his
life—a piece of self-knowledge that may be a lasting source of strength.

Others in the military hierarchy, including those at the top, have purposes of
their own, some more compelling than those of the foot soldier. How these

purposes are mutually articulated to produce the oxymoron *organized violence* is at the heart of the difference between individual and group conflict. The difference is not trivial. Some of the same human societies for whom I would debunk what I call the myth of the absence of violence *have* in fact been free of organized violence. This is because they lack organization, not because they lack the propensity for violence (Bohannon, 1967; Fried, 1967; Johnson and Earle, 1987).

Nor is their freedom from organized violence because they lack a parallel propensity for hostility toward identified enemies. Kung hunter-gatherers were contemptuous of people of slightly different racial type and even of neighboring Kung, whom they readily identified as inferior (Shostak, 1981). Throughout Africa, and indeed throughout the world, similar contempt is directed at those who are culturally or racially different, in a nested hierarchy of tribal animosities. In a very large proportion of cases, political controversy conceals tribal conflict that is much older and more deeply felt. Underlying the current political rivalry in Zimbabwe, for example, is the old tribal rift between Ndebele and Shona. In Uganda, too, the real struggles are old ones among the Baganda, Acholi, and Langi, who have been enemies for many generations.

This process, which Erik Erikson called pseudospeciation, did not, of course, evolve only in Africa. The Greeks had their barbarians, the Jews their Gentiles, the Christians their heathen. Ilongot headhunters feud murderously and enduringly with close neighbors. Traditional highland New Guinea is a patchwork of crisscrossing homicidal enmities. Even the Kung refer to themselves as "the real people," and to others as strangers. Violent tribal standoffs are occurring now throughout the world: Bosnians, Serbs, and Croats in the former Yugoslavia; Azerbaijanis and Armenians in the former Soviet Georgia; Sikh, Moslem, and Hindu in India; Sunni and Shi'a Moslem in the Middle East; Catholics and Protestants in Ireland. Sometimes ethnicity and religion are superimposed in these conflicts, but there is no world population that is free of such dichotomies. As the anthropologist E. E. Evans-Pritchard wrote in a classic work on the Nuer, Nilotic cattle-herders of the Sudan, "either a man is a kinsman . . . or he is a person to whom you have no reciprocal obligations and whom you treat as a potential enemy" (Evans-Pritchard, 1940). Something similar can be said about human beings throughout the world, at all levels of societal complexity.

There is now some possibility that a rudiment of this process is observable in nonhuman primates. Jane Goodall (1986) and others, in ongoing studies of wild chimpanzees in the Gombe Stream Reserve, have observed intergroup violence that appears to have an almost organized quality. Bands of roving males from a group in the north of the reserve have repeatedly ambushed isolated males from an adjacent group to the south, savagely attacking and killing them. In some cases, this has involved an incursion into the territory of the adjacent group to locate a victim. After a series of such killings, the target group was effectively decimated, and the original northern group became adjacent to yet a third group farther south, whereupon new hostilities emerged.

This is an incipient level of organized violence similar to that observed in many simple human societies (Knauft, 1987; Johnson and Earle, 1987). Societies become more complex as their population density increases, with such features as social stratification, division of labor, and taxation playing an increasing role. Military and religious hierarchies, always allied and sometimes overlapping in structure and function, form the core of these societies, which continue to grow by conquest. The Nuer, with their clear concept of who is an enemy and with certain advances in military recruitment, became an effective organization for predatory expansion at the expense of their Dinka neighbors, despite having a relatively simple level of social order (Sahlins, 1961; Kelly, 1985).

With the advent of true religious and military hierarchies, this pattern becomes much more clear: The hierarchical society involved in predatory expansion comes increasingly to resemble a state rather than a tribe. At this point we have the level of social organization exhibited by the antagonists in the Trojan War, and from there it is anthropologically a small step—mainly technological—to the vastly more dangerous antagonisms of modern states—the nationalism that Toynbee (1972) called a new wine in the old bottle of tribalism.

This ubiquitous tendency to dichotomize the social world brings us to the sixth proposition: The human mind has a tendency to categorize by twos, and this dualistic tendency of thought applies to social as well as nonsocial objects (Levi-Strauss, 1963; Douglas, 1966; Maybury-Lewis and Almagor, 1989). Night and day, human and animal, good and evil, male and female, right and left—these are but a few of the dichotomies that have been not merely recognized (a seemingly obvious and necessary step) but positively institutionalized in a wide range of human cultures. What is perceptually in fact a weak dichotomy, or even a continuum, is exaggerated by mental processes that make it seem to be two irreconcilable principles divided by an insurmountable gulf.

Why this happens is not clear. It has been suggested that it has something to do with the well-known lateralization of the human cerebral cortex, but this seems finally to be more an analogy than an explanation. More likely, it has something to do with an intolerance for subtleties and for what psychologists call cognitive dissonance (Festinger, 1957). In phonetics, the quintessential dichotomization becomes the very basis of meaning. In purely physical terms, there may be a continuum between p and b, but we must make up our minds whether a given sound is one or the other in order to have a language that works (Jakobson, 1968).

Something similar may be true in other realms of cognition. In many situations for much of our evolution it must have been desirable to make decisions quickly, and what could be simpler than an algorithm with two choices? Confronted with a stimulus, we have first to classify it as familiar or strange and then to decide between approach and avoidance. Discrimination, a positive thing in matters of taste, becomes ironically unfortunate, even evil, in social classification. Yet such dichotomies as we and they, kin and nonkin, real people versus barbarians or strangers are virtually human universals.

The seventh proposition describes the emotional valence of the cognitive dichotomies: Fear is a fundamental characteristic of nervous systems, and fear of the strange in particular is an extension of that basic characteristic. A variety of studies—from those of the effects of novelty on infants to those of the effects of stimulation of the brain in cats—have suggested the existence of a continuum from attention through arousal to fear. Low-level stimulation of the brain nucleus known as the amygdala can produce alertness, while more intense stimulation in the same place can produce fear (Ursin and Kaada, 1960). Human studies have shown that novelty, depending on the circumstances, can produce either attention or fear in infants.

The suggestion is that our basic relationship to the world—some level of attentiveness to every new stimulus that appears, with the hope of reacting appropriately once we have understood it—is on a physiological continuum with a potentially lifesaving flight from danger. In the case of infants, the latter part of the first year of life is characterized by new discriminations in the social world. While younger infants respond positively to practically everyone, many begin at around seven or eight months to respond warily or fearfully to strangers. The mechanism probably involves an initial assessment—I know this person, I don't know this one—in which the face is compared with stored images in the infant's brain. The discrepancy, if there is one, is reported—possibly from the hippocampus to the hypothalamus—sometimes resulting in the emotion of fear.

In infants who can walk or crawl, the behavioral concomitant of this emotion may be flight, in particular a flight to a protective figure, such as the mother (Bowlby, 1969; Lewis and Rosenblum, 1974). The tendency to flee to a protector is almost as fundamental as the tendency to fear, and it is likely that just as our everyday interactions with the world involve a certain amount of at least mild fear, so all of us much of the time probably experience a slight desire to flee to some sort of protector. If in adults the infant's discriminating fear of strangers has been transformed into something more like contempt (Girard, 1977), then the flight to a protector has become something more like obedience, conformity, chauvinism, idolatry, or loyalty.

This brings us to the eighth and final proposition. Individuals fairly readily submerge their capacity for independent action to the purposes of a collective will or higher authority, or both. The ubiquitous mild fear or anxiety that most of us feel—exacerbated by the ambiguity we experience as the natural complexity of the world impinges on the simplicity of our minds—is most easily dealt with if we do not have in addition to take responsibility for our actions.

We can reduce this sense of responsibility, and the anxiety associated with it, by one of three means: following a set of rules; participating in a group that is acting in unison; or following a leader. Of these, the most benign is probably following rules: these have durability, and over time are responsive to what might be called collective thoughtfulness rather than mere collective will. They also are tested by time and when necessary can be judiciously changed. Of course, to the extent that they invite us to suspend judgment, they may in many specific cases be inflexibly and inappropriately applied.

Considerably more ominous in its negative capability is mass or mob psychology. Charles Mackay ([1841] 1980) in *Extraordinary Popular Delusions and the Madness of Crowds*, first published in the mid–nineteenth century, describes this phenomenon well:

> In reading the history of nations, we find that whole communities suddenly fix their minds upon one object, and go mad in its pursuit; that millions of people become simultaneously impressed with one delusion, and run after it, till their attention is caught by some new folly more captivating than the first. We see one nation suddenly seized, from its highest to its lowest members, with a fierce desire of military glory; another as suddenly becoming crazed upon a religious scruple; and neither of them recovering its senses until it has shed rivers of blood and sowed a harvest of groans and tears, to be reaped by its posterity. . . . Men, it has been well said, think in herds; it will be seen that they go mad in herds, while they only recover their senses slowly, and one by one.

The variety of phenomena that Mackay takes up in this treatise is in itself instructive: lynch mobs and witch-hunts; reckless investment schemes such as the South Sea Bubble and the Tulip mania; fads, pilgrimages, revolutions, and wars; all these and more are grist for an analytic mill that concerns itself with the muting or abandonment of individual will. Only the mass hysteria that involves enemies is of ultimate concern to us here, but we need to consider first the possibility that people are by nature susceptible to behavioral or psychological contagion.

According to this model, the notion that one should buy a piece of property in the South Seas, or eat in a certain restaurant, or go to a certain holy place, or wear a miniskirt or a bustle, can spread through a population and take hold of each successive individual for no very good reason except that it has already taken hold of so many others. Perhaps the fear of ostracism or merely of being left behind takes precedence over rational disadvantages. But something more fundamental—something like the fear that what is different must be dangerous—may be operating. What has been called the herding instinct cannot, strictly speaking, be applied to human groups. We are not, by our original nature, herd animals, but participants in small groups with complex social dynamics. In fact, our particular herdlike behavior may be best understood as a result of population densities that violate the small-group dynamics we are comfortable with by nature.

Be that as it may, behavioral contagion often has as its purpose the identification and destruction of enemies. This process, which I will call contagious enmity, has two major forms. The first identifies internal enemies who are relatively weak, isolates them, and destroys them. Obvious examples are lynch mobs, witch-hunts, inquisitions, and genocide. The enemies are different, confusing, evil, and dangerous; their very existence gravely threatens the spiritual and physical life of the larger group. Their elimination becomes a ritual of purification and is seen as an absolute good (Girard, 1977; Hamerton-Kelly, 1987).

The second form identifies external enemies. These are treated in a manner parallel to that of internal ones but are generally more capable of defending themselves both rhetorically and physically. The concept of holy war is intimately related to sacrificial traditions in primitive and ancient societies because of widespread human attitudes toward the sacredness of bloodshed (Girard, 1977; Hamerton-Kelly, 1987). Ilongot headhunting represents an interesting intermediate stage, since though directed at enemies, "it involves the taking of a human life with a view toward cleansing the participants of the contaminating burdens of their own lives" (Rosaldo, 1980, 140). Through a process that Girard has called *mimesis*, the juxtaposed collective emotions of two groups experiencing reciprocally contagious enmities eventually justify each other: that is, what may begin as an irrational fear may end as a rational one as each side contemplates the growing fear and hatred in the other.

A very large and very dense human group is still not a herd and may not even be a mob, strictly speaking, if it has a leader. Freud's monograph ([1921] 1949) *Group Psychology and the Analysis of the Ego* ("group psychology" being a questionable translation of the German word *Massenpsychologie*) makes this distinction. Mass psychology, according to Freud's formulation, does not operate as a thing-in-itself but only and fundamentally in relation to a leader. He describes vividly the characteristics of groups:

> The lack of independence and initiative in their members, the similarity in the reactions of all of them . . . the weakness of intellectual ability, the lack of emotional restraint, the inclination to exceed every limit in the expression of emotion and to work it off completely in the form of action . . . [pp. 81–82]
>
> . . . We are reminded of how many of these phenomena of dependence are part of the normal constitution of human society, of how little originality and personal courage are to be found in it, of how much every individual is ruled by those attitudes of the group mind which exhibit themselves in such forms as racial characteristics, class prejudices, public opinion, etc. [p. 82]

Freud's interpretation of group or mass psychology is that it is not merely analogous with but identical to hypnosis: "Hypnosis is not a good object for comparison with a group formation, because it is truer to say that it is identical with it. Out of the complicated fabric of the group it isolates one element for us—the behavior of the individual to the leader" (p. 78). He later emphasizes that the power of suggestion is exercised not only by the leader but mutually by group members. Thus, the flight to a protector—what Erich Fromm ([1941] 1965) called the escape from freedom—is a flight to leader and group alike. Freud's two main examples are not mobs but armies and churches, both of which have the we-they distinction as their essence. Groups and leaders hypnotize their followers (Asch, 1951), sometimes in isolation but often in relation to an enemy.

Among the most important and surely the most disturbing behavioral science research ever conducted is that of Milgram (1974) on obedience to authority. Naive subjects were ordered to give electric shocks to a person they thought was another subject but was really a confederate of the experimenter. Most people gave what they believed were very dangerous shocks simply because they were ordered to do so by an authoritative figure.

> What is the limit of such obedience? At many points we attempted to establish a boundary. Cries from the victim were inserted; they were not good enough. The victim claimed heart trouble; subjects still shocked him on command. The victim pleaded to be let free, and his answers no longer registered on the signal box; subjects continued to shock him. (p. 188)

Adding the encouragement of peers to the orders of the experimenter made the obedience even more reflexive. "And what is it we have seen?" Milgram asks.

> Not aggression, for there is no anger, vindictiveness, or hatred in those who shocked the victim. Men do become angry; they do act hatefully and explode in rage against others. But not here. Something far more dangerous is revealed: the capacity for man to abandon his humanity, indeed, the inevitability that he does so, as he merges his unique personality into larger institutional structures.
>
> This is a fatal flaw nature has designed into us, and which in the long run gives our species only a modest chance for survival. (p. 188)

Freud the psychoanalyst and Milgram the social psychologist both speak freely of the way nature or evolution has designed us, and both assessments are consistent with current views in biological anthropology.

An anthropological model of human enmity has been presented. It holds

1. that competition between individual organisms is an intrinsic feature of animal life
2. that individual violence, sometimes including homicide, is a general characteristic of animal evolution and is also found in all human societies

3. that frustration, including nonspecific frustration, predisposes a mammal to aggression
4. that males are more disposed to violence than females, partly for biological reasons
5. that groups in conflict are collections of individuals who feel that they have more to gain than to lose by fighting
6. that there is a strong, general, dualistic tendency in human thought that exaggerates natural differences, including those in the social world
7. that fear, like nonspecific frustration, is a fundamental characteristic of nervous systems, and fear of the strange in particular is its most common manifestation
8. that individuals readily submerge their independent wills to the will of a collective or an authoritative leader, a mechanism for the reduction of fear.

Freud conceived his mass-psychology monograph in the wake of World War I, Milgram his obedience experiments in the aftermath of World War II. After World War I, it was presumed that the worst had happened, but of course the worst had not happened yet. Today, in the wake of the cold war, as nuclear weapons are acquired by more and more nations, large and small—we have ample reason to fear that what may come will be the worst of all (Pilat, 1992).

Still, even in Milgram's discouraging study there was evidence of individual resistance. Perhaps the most touching story was that of Gretchen Brandt, a thirty-one-year-old medical technician who had grown to adulthood in Nazi Germany and was exposed as a girl to Hitler's propaganda. Simply, courteously, decisively, she refused to continue with the experiment. She later explained, "Perhaps we have seen too much pain." We also have the remarkable example of Natan Sharansky (1988), who after countless acts of defiance, on the verge of his release from prison, threw himself in the snow to avoid parting with his book of Psalms. Charles Mackay wrote over a century ago, people go mad in herds, but they only recover their senses slowly and one by one.

Incidentally, the Judeo-Christian tradition would not be surprised at the viewpoint presented here, which couches in scientific language—on the basis of new evidence, to be sure—some hypotheses about human nature and human weakness that are approximately as old as the hills. The same tradition advises us that we should recognize our baser passions, including aggressive ones; that we should strive mightily to subdue those passions; that we should try to love our neighbors as ourselves; and that we should not follow a multitude to do evil. Where all these *shoulds* come from is a question in itself, but their widespread existence in religious systems supports the hypothesis of a violent tendency in human nature. As pointed out by Elaine Pagels (chap. 12, "The Rage of Angels," this volume), the same traditions provide opportunities for sanctioned or sacred violence that gives periodic expression to those same tendencies.

As Albert Einstein wrote in a famous letter to Freud suggesting an exchange of observations on the course of war, "How is it that these devices succeed so well in rousing men to such wild enthusiasm, even to sacrifice their lives? Only one answer is possible. Because man has within him a lust for hatred and destruction. In normal times this passion exists in a latent state, it emerges only in unusual circumstances; but it is a comparatively easy task to call it into play and raise it to the power of a collective psychosis." I would dissent from this observation only in reference to the purported "lust for hatred and destruction." Such a lust may exist under certain circumstances, but a far more general and easily evoked human emotional state is the above-described anger resulting from frustration, fear, and grief.

Instead, Freud expressed "entire agreement" with Einstein on this point. The two differed, however, on at least one important point: Freud claimed that "whatever fosters the growth of culture works at the same time against war." Einstein remained skeptical of any such civilizing power. An anthropologist must side unequivocally with Einstein. What we call civilization arose in ecological circumstances in which militaristic tribal groups like the Nuer were able to operate as organizations for predatory expansion. Through a combination of military force and supportive religious ideology, they were able to pacify large regions; these in turn provided centralized resources for further expansion, up to the point of confrontation with another similar power. These are Erikson's pseudospecies, and the monotonous pattern of their emergence throughout the world constitutes an enduring threat to human survival. This pattern has changed little, if at all, in the thousands of years leading to the nuclear age. We flatter ourselves that we are in control of the process, but human weakness looms large in the recent risk of war (Gracken, 1983; Dyson, 1984; Jervis, Lebow, and Stein, 1985; Ford, 1986). A study of the culture and language of defense intellectuals strongly suggests that fundamental motivational patterns continue to operate (Cohn, 1987).

As for the question, Do we need enemies?—put to a well-known advocate of the abolition of nuclear weapons, he answered in his thoughtful way, "We certainly seem to like to have them." We say that we need food, sex, love, and entertainment; we need peace of mind, water, exercise, and sleep. We never say that we need enemies, or even that we like to have them. If we could just make that concession, achieve that bit of self-knowledge, then we might have taken the first step toward a world in which, if we could not embrace our enemies, we could at least, perhaps, leave them alone.

REFERENCES

Alcock, J. 1989. *Animal behavior: An evolutionary approach.* 4th ed. Sunderland, Mass.: Sinauer Associates.

Asch, S. E. 1951. Effects of group pressure upon the modification and distortion of judgements, in *Groups, leadership and men*, ed. H. Guetzkow, 177–190. Pittsburgh: Carnegie Press.

Bandura, A. 1973. *Aggression: A social learning analysis.* Englewood Cliffs, N.J.: Prentice-Hall.

Berkowitz, L. 1969. *The roots of aggression: A reexamination of the frustration-aggression hypothesis.* New York: Atherton.

———. 1981. On the difference between internal and external reactions to legitimate and illegitimate frustrations: A demonstration. *Aggressive Behavior* 7:83–96.

Betzig, L. L. 1986. *Despotism and differential reproduction: A Darwinian view of history.* New York: Aldine.

Blainey, G. 1973. *The causes of war.* New York: Free Press.

Blanchard, R. J., and Blanchard, D. C. 1977. Aggressive behavior in the rat. *Behavioral Biology* 21:197–224.

Bohannon, P., ed. 1967. *Law and warfare: Studies in the anthropology of conflict.* New York: Natural History.

Bowlby, J. 1969. *Attachment and loss*, vol. 1, *Attachment*, 327–330. London: Hogarth.

Brain, P. F., and Benton, D., eds. 1981. *The biology of aggression.* Alphen aan den Rijn, The Netherlands: Sijthoff and Noordhoff.

Cannon, W. B. 1932. *The wisdom of the body.* New York: Norton.

Center for Research on Aggression. 1983. *Prevention and control of aggression.* New York: Pergamon.

Chagnon, N. 1968. *Yanomamo: The fierce people.* New York: Holt, Rinehart, and Winston.

———. 1988. Life histories, blood revenge, and warfare in a tribal population. *Science* 239:985–992.

Clausewitz, C. V. 1940. *On war*, ed. F. N. Maude. 3 vols. London.

Cohn, C. 1987. Sex and death in the rational world of defense intellectuals. *Signs* 12:687–718.

Daly, M., and Wilson, M. 1988. *Homicide.* New York: Aldine de Gruyter.

Dawkins, R. 1989. *The selfish gene.* 2d ed. New York: Oxford University Press.

Dentan, R. K. 1968. *The Semai: A non-violent people of Malaysia.* New York: Holt, Rinehart, and Winston.

Divale, W., and Harris, M. 1976. Population, warfare, and the male supremacist complex. *American Anthropologist* 78:521–538.

Dollard, J., Doob, L. W., Miller, N. E., Mowrer, O. H., and Sears, R. R. 1939. *Frustration and aggression.* New Haven: Yale University Press.

Douglas, M. 1966. *Purity and danger: An analysis of concepts of pollution and taboo.* London: Routledge & Kegan Paul.

Dyson, F. 1984. *Weapons and hope.* New York: Harper and Row.

Edgerton, R. B. 1992. *Sick societies: Challenging the myth of primitive harmony.* New York: Free Press.

Eibl-Eibesfeldt, I. 1979. *The biology of peace and war.* London: Thames and Hudson.

Einstein, A. [1932] 1963. Why war? Letter to Sigmund Freud, in *Einstein on peace*, ed. O. Nathan and H. Nordan. London.

Evans-Pritchard, E. E. 1940. *The Nuer: A description of the modes of livelihood and political institutions of a Nilotic people.* New York: Oxford University Press.

Feshbach, S., and Fraczek, A., eds. 1979. *Aggression and behavior change: Biological and social processes.* New York: Praeger.

Festinger, L. 1957. *A theory of cognitive dissonance.* Evanston, Ill.: Row, Peterson.

Flynn, J., Venegas, H., Foote, W., and Edwards, S. 1970. Neural mechanisms involved in a cat's attack on a rat, in *The neural control of behavior,* ed. R. F. Whalen, M. Thompson, M. Verzeano, and N. Weinberger. New York: Academic.

Ford, D. 1986. *The button.* New York: Simon and Schuster.

Freeman, D. 1983. *Margaret Mead and Samoa: The making and unmaking of an anthropological myth.* Cambridge: Harvard University Press.

Freud, S. 1932. *Why war? Letter to Albert Einstein,* in *Standard Edition of the Complete Psychological Works of Sigmund Freud.* London: Hogarth.

———. 1949. *Group psychology and the analysis of the ego.* London: Hogarth.

Fried, M. H. 1967. *The evolution of political society.* New York: Random House.

Fromm, E. [1941] 1965. *Escape from freedom.* New York: Avon.

Fuchs, S. A. G., Dalsass, M., Siegel, H. E., and Siegel, A. 1980. The neural pathways mediating quiet-biting attack behavior from the hypothalamus in the cat: A functional autoradiographic study. *Aggressive Behavior* 7:51–67.

Girard, R. 1977. *Violence and the sacred,* trans. P. Gregory. Baltimore: Johns Hopkins University Press. (*La violence et le sacre,* Paris: Bernard Grasset, 1972.)

Goldstein, A., and Segall, M., eds. 1982. *Aggression in global perspective.* New York: Pergamon.

Goodall, J. 1986. *The chimpanzees of Gombe: Patterns of behavior,* chaps. 12, 17. Cambridge: Harvard University Press.

Gracken, P. 1983. *The command and control of nuclear forces.* New Haven: Yale University Press.

Gray, J. A. 1971. *The psychology of fear and stress.* New York: McGraw-Hill.

———. 1982. *The neuropsychology of anxiety.* New York: Oxford.

Hamerton-Kelly, R. G. 1987. *Violent origins: Walter Burkett, Rene Girard, and Jonathan Z. Smith on ritual killing and cultural formation.* Stanford: Stanford University Press.

Hassrick, R. 1964. *The Sioux: Life and customs of a warrior society.* Norman, Okla.: University of Oklahoma Press.

Hausfater, G., and Hrdy, S. B., eds. 1984. *Infanticide: Comparative and evolutionary perspectives.* New York: Aldine.

Heider, K. 1970. *The Dugum Dani: A Papuan culture in the highlands of west New Guinea.* Chicago: Aldine.

Hilberg, R. 1973. *The destruction of the European Jews.* New York: Franklin Watts.

Hines, M. 1984. Prenatal gonadal hormones and sex differences in human behavior. *Psychological Bulletin* 92(1):56.

Hrdy, S. 1981. *The woman that never evolved.* Cambridge: Harvard University Press.

Huntingford, F. A., and Turner, A. K. 1987. *Animal conflict.* New York: Chapman and Hall.

Jakobson, R. 1968. *Child language, aphasia, and phonological universals.* The Hague: Mouton.

Jervis, R., Lebow, R. N., and Stein, J. G. 1985. *Psychology and deterrence.* Baltimore: Johns Hopkins University Press.

Johnson, A. W., and Earle, T. 1987. *The evolution of human societies: From foraging group to agrarian state.* Stanford: Stanford University Press.

Keegan, J. 1976. *The face of battle.* New York: Viking.

Kelly, R. C. 1985. *The Nuer conquest: The structure and development of an expansionist system.* Ann Arbor: University of Michigan Press.

Knauft, B. 1987. Reconsidering violence in simple human societies, with commentary and author's reply. *Cultural Anthropology* 28:457–500.

Koch, K.-F. 1974. *War and peace in Jalémó: The management of conflict in highland New Guinea.* Cambridge, Mass.: Harvard University Press.

Konner, M. 1982. *The tangled wing.* New York: Holt, Rinehart, and Winston.

Lee, R. B. 1979. *The !Kung San.* New York: Cambridge University Press.

Levi-Strauss, C. 1963. *Structural anthropology.* New York: Basic Books.

Lewis, M., and Rosenblum, L., eds. 1974. *The origins of fear.* New York: Wiley.

Leyhausen, P. 1979. *Cat behavior: The predatory and social behavior of domestic and wild cats.* New York: Garland STPM.

Lorenz, K. 1966. *On aggression.* New York: Harcourt, Brace & World. (*Das sogennante böse: Zur naturgeschichte der aggression,* Borotha-Schoeler Verlag, Wien, 1963.)

Maccoby, E., and Jacklin, C. 1974. *Psychology of sex differences.* Stanford, Calif.: Stanford University Press.

Mackay, C. [1841] 1980. *Extraordinary popular delusions and the madness of crowds.* New York: Harmony Books.

Maybury-Lewis, D., and Almagor, U., eds. 1989. *The attraction of opposites: Thought and society in the dualistic mode.* Ann Arbor: University of Michigan Press.

Mead, M. 1928. *Coming of age in Samoa.* New York: William Morrow.

———. 1949. *Male and female.* New York: William Morrow.

Meggitt, M. 1977. *Blood is their argument: Warfare among the Mae Enga tribesmen of the New Guinea highlands.* Palo Alto: Mayfield.

Meyer-Bahlburg, H. F. L., and Ehrhardt, A. 1982. Prenatal sex hormones and human aggression: A review, and new data on progestogen effects. *Aggressive Behavior* 8:39–62.

Milgram, S. 1974. *Obedience to authority: An experimental view.* New York: Harper and Row.

Mittleman, G., and Valenstein, E. S. 1984. Ingestive behavior evoked by hypothalamic stimulation and schedule-induced polydipsia are related. *Science* 224:415–417.

Moffitt, T. E., and Mednick, S. A., eds. 1988. *Biological contributions to crime causation.* Boston: Martinus Nijhoff.

Moyer, K. E. 1987. *Violence and aggression: A physiological perspective.* New York: Paragon.

Otterbein, K. F. 1970. *The evolution of war.* New Haven: Yale University Press.

Paul, R. A. 1978. Instinctive aggression in man: The Semai case. *Journal of Psychological Anthropology* 1:65–79.

Pincus, J. H., and Tucker, G. J. 1985. *Behavioral neurology.* 3d ed. New York: Oxford University Press.

Pilat, J. F. 1992. Iraq and the future of nonproliferation: The roles of inspections and treaties. *Science* 255:1224–1229.

Rosaldo, R. 1980. *Ilongot headhunting, 1873–1974: A study in society and history.* Stanford: Stanford University Press.

———. 1989. Grief and a headhunter's rage, in *Culture and truth: The remaking of social analysis,* 1–21. Boston: Beacon.

Sahlins, M. D. 1961. The segmentary lineage: An organization of predatory expansion. *American Anthropologist* 63:322–345.

Sharansky, N. 1988. *Fear no evil.* New York: Random House.

Shirer, William L. 1960. *The rise and fall of the Third Reich: A history of Nazi Germany.* New York: Simon and Schuster.

Shostak, N. 1981. *Nisa: The life and words of a !Kung woman.* Cambridge: Harvard University Press.

Svare, B. B., ed. 1983. *Hormones and aggressive behavior.* New York: Plenum.

Tardiff, K., ed. 1988. *The violent patient. Psychiatric Clinics of North America* 11 (4): 499–698.

Thomas, E. M. [1959] 1990. *The harmless people.* 2d ed. New York: Vintage.

Tiger, L. 1979. *Optimism: The biology of hope.* New York: Simon and Schuster.

———. [1969] 1985. *Men in groups.* 2d ed. New York: Random House.

Tinbergen, N. 1963. On the aims and methods of ethology. *Zeitschrift für Tierpsychologie* 20:410–433.

Toynbee, A. 1972. *A study of history.* New York: Oxford University Press.

Trivers, R. L. 1972. Parental investment and sexual selection, in *Sexual selection and the descent of man,* ed. B. Campbell. Chicago: Aldine.

———. 1985. *Social evolution.* Menlo Park, N.J.: Benjamin Cummings.

Ulrich, R. R., and Azrin, N. H. 1962. Reflexive fighting in response to aversive stimulation. *Journal of the Experimental Analysis of Behavior* 5:511–520.

Ursin, H., and Kaada, B. R. 1960. Functional localization with the amygdaloid complex in the cat. *Electroencephalography and Clinical Neurology* 121–120.

Valenstein, E. S., Cox, V. C., and Kakolewski, J. W. 1968. Modification of motivated behavior elicited by electrical stimulation of the hypothalamus. *Science* 159:1119–1121.

———. 1970. Reexamination of the role of the hypothalamus in motivation. *Psychological Review* 77:16–31.

Walter, E. V. 1969. *Terror and resistance.* New York: Oxford University Press.

Waltz, K. N. 1959. *Man, the state, and war: A theoretical analysis.* New York: Columbia University Press.

Whiting, B. B., and Edwards, C. P. 1973. A cross-cultural analysis of sex differences in the behavior of children aged 3–11. *Journal of Social Psychology* 91:171–188.

———. 1988. *Children of different worlds: The formation of social behavior.* Cambridge: Harvard University Press.

Whiting, J. M. W., and Whiting, B. B. 1975. Aloofness and intimacy of husbands and wives: A cross-cultural study. *Ethos* 3:183–207.

Williams, G. C. 1966. *Adaptation and natural selection: A critique of some current evolutionary thought.* Princeton, N.J.: Princeton University Press.

Wilson, E. O. 1975. *Sociobiology: The new synthesis.* Cambridge: Harvard University Press.

10

Human Aggression:
A Perspective drawn from
Nonhuman Primates

LEONARD A. ROSENBLUM

Few aspects of human behavior display the intensity, emotional consequences, or societal significance seemingly inherent in expressions of sexuality and aggression. Aspects of the complex linkage of these two domains to one another and to the structure of the societies within which they are expressed, seen through a primatologist's eyes, will be the focus of this chapter. Given the current limits to our abilities to disentangle the sex-status–stress-aggression matrix at the contemporary human level, it is of value to consider some of the likely evolutionary anlagen of these features in terms of their expression in contemporary animal forms bearing a close affinity to *Homo sapiens*.

Based on dubious beliefs of the ubiquity of the sexual drives and perhaps as a reflection of the presumptively constricted sexuality of many western cultures, we are prone to making assumptions of less constrained sexuality in individuals of societies different from our own. The less like our own such societies are (that is, the more "exotic"), the more likely we are to make false assumptions about the sexual "freedom" of its members. We expect that forces held in check in our own culture may run rampant in those less "civilized." Discussing the release of our usual restraint of "the beastly and savage part" of us during sleep, Plato, in *The Republic,* goes on to say, "There is nothing it will not venture to undertake as being released from all shame and reason. It does not shrink from attempting to lie with a mother in fancy or with anyone else, man, god, or brute. . . . There exists in every one of us, even in some most reputed and respectable, a terrible, fierce and lawless brood of desires." Whatever linkages we theorize to exist between this repressed brood of desires and the incubation of aggressive impulses, they will depend, therefore, on the validity of our assumptions regarding the nature of human sexuality.

Whatever the culturally embedded myths of less inhibited sexuality in what

194

are considered "primitive" or "more natural" cultures or societies, these are at times carried even further when we speculate about the sexuality of other species. Animals, while holding identifiable similarities to us in some ways, seem less likely to be shackled by the constraints we assume to be operating to prevent the unbridled expression of our own sexuality. Two thousand years ago, the Roman philosopher Seneca suggested that "if sensuality were happiness, beasts were happier than men." Ironically, beliefs regarding the sex drives of animals, erroneous though they may be, have reinforced our notions of the unrelenting significance of sexual drives at the human level.

Constrained Sexuality in Nonhuman Primates

In changing names and applying the same story to our species, there is the risk that the story itself may well be wrong, that is, our hypothesized edifice of human sexuality may have little evolutionary foundation. Certainly for nonhuman primates the evidence fails to support the myth (or is it a wish?) that, unlike ourselves, the "beasts" are free to permit the unhindered rush of Eros throughout their lives. Quite to the contrary, an examination of the expression of sexuality within those forms sharing with us the most recent common ancestry, that is, the nonhuman primates, indicates that under so-called normal, or "natural," conditions, sexual behavior is often, although not always, circumscribed.

With the impetus and constraints derived relatively directly from the neurobiological and hormonal variations in individual subjects (e.g., Steklis et al., 1983; Michael, Wilson, and Plant, 1973; Michael et al., 1978; Coe and Rosenblum, 1978), there are additional limits to the behavioral expression of sexuality that have characteristic chronological, temporal, and social characteristics. Early observations carried out under conditions in which subjects were severely physically restricted and population density was extreme, suggested to initial observers that sexual and aggressive patterns may be the central themes of all primate life throughout the year (Zuckerman, 1932). We now know that such features, at least in the species under study, were distortions of natural circumstances and uncharacteristic of what actually occurs in the wild or within captive settings more sensitively attuned to a species' social and physical characteristics (Wallen, 1989). To be sure, in some species—even those in which females at least normally demonstrate rather restricted annual or monthly periods of active sexuality—females may show situation-dependent receptivity at any time that disrupted social relations seem to warrant. In brief, based on studies of a large number of species throughout the primate order, we now recognize that for most species, for most of the year, overt sexuality is virtually absent in most primate groups (e.g., Lindburg, 1987; Coe and Rosenblum, 1978; Herndon et al., 1981; Gordon and Bernstein, 1973; Lancaster and Lee, 1965). Moreover, even during the limited annual period within which sexual expression and conceptions do occur and for those species showing less seasonally restricted breeding, on most days most males and most females remain noninteractive sexually.

Seasonal Variations in Sexual Activity

First, it is abundantly clear that for many of the primates that have been studied systematically, sexual activity is largely restricted to at most three to four months of the year. Asexuality, testicular regression in males and amenorrhea or anestrus (often the by-product of prolonged lactation) in females, typifies the remainder of the year. Several factors are hypothesized to have played important roles in influencing the evolution of these patterns. One such factor is the seasonal changes in available food sources. Relatively abundant nutrients are necessary to underwrite (particularly the last phases of) the prolonged pregnancy of primates and primate mothers' substantial postpartum investment in their young entailed in lactation and nursing. Normally entering into breeding (i.e., overt sexual behavior) during annual periods of diminishing light-dark ratios (Lancaster and Lee, 1965), after approximately a half year of gestation (longer in the apes, shorter in the more primitive forms), late pregnancy and births occur as light ratios and plant and insect availability increase. At another level, temporally restricted breeding activity may also have been significant in evolution in ensuring various aspects of primate social development through the presence of a mixed-sex, same-age peer group during each infant's early months and years of life. In addition, there may be a reduction in predatory behavior toward infants because of the presence of large peer groups (Goldfoot et al., 1984; Boinski, 1983). Although it is certain that many factors coalesced in generating this periodic rather than continuous sexuality, socially coordinated, time-limited breeding and a similarly limited birth season have evolved as characteristic of most of the primate order.

Male-Female Dominance and Sexual Activity

Once the appropriate time of year comes around, who then acts as the primary participants in sexual activity in the group? Both maturational and social factors control the access of males and females to one another. To gain a general understanding of the operation of these factors, primary attention here will be focused on the Macaca genus, the most widely dispersed and adaptive group of primates other than man. To do this, we must first step outside the clearly sexual domain and consider the general social significance of patterns that are embedded within the sexual interactions of our subjects. In its most complete form, the heterosexual mounting of these species involves the male clasping the calves of the female while she assumes a quadrupedal position, with her rump oriented toward the male and somewhat elevated. The male, clasping her hips with his hands, achieves intromission upon mounting. Depending on the species of macaque, anywhere from one to six to eight of these mounts, each with intromission and thrusting, will be necessary to produce male ejaculation, thus terminating that phase of their sexual interaction. The range within this general pattern is considerable (Nadler and Rosenblum, 1973; Chevalier-Skolnikoff, 1975). In some species (the bonnet macaque, for example), a single mount, lasting perhaps ten to fifteen seconds and involving perhaps fifteen to twenty thrusts, is sufficient to produce ejaculation; in another (the stumptail macaque), a single mount may last as long as five minutes, with the male thrusting perhaps one hundred times in that period, with the pair even sitting, ventrodorsally, while coupled.

In spite of the undoubted role of sexual motivation and the importance of the reproductive sequelae involved in the appearance of these patterns at times, virtually identical male mounting patterns as well as the female rump-presentation component can be seen in both males and females with partners of either sex fulfilling the alternate role. In such instances there is substantial evidence that these presentations and mounting behaviors constitute an expression of subordination and dominance, respectively, between the two partners (Akers and Conway, 1979; Hanby, 1974; Kaufman and Rosenblum, 1966). Thus, the dominant partner, regardless of sex, does the mounting and the subordinate partner, regardless of sex, does the presenting, or at least receives the mounting. Although anal intromission between males has been reported (Erwin and Maple, 1976), even in female mounting pelvic thrusting by the mounter is often seen. Perhaps most striking is the fact that, at times, clearly dominant males may attempt to elicit social interaction with a clear subordinate (who might otherwise be too fearful to approach) by presenting to them and inducing the clearly subordinate partner to make a brief mount. Similarly, in one species that we have studied extensively (the bonnet macaque), two males of approximately equal status may, on occasion, simultaneously present to each other, move backward, touch rumps, and reach back to touch the testes of the other. Because these varied forms of dominance mounting occur throughout the year, that is, during periods when the subjects are not ovulating and active spermatogenesis is not occurring, we are forced to consider the social or interpersonal meaning of a mount even when conception is its actual or potential consequence. It is my view that regardless of the sex of the partners, the sexual motivations involved, or the reproductive outcome of the encounter, *mounting always represents a statement of one animal's dominance over the other.* In that sense, the establishment of relative status must precede the expression of the sexual drive between any male-female pair. I am not suggesting that there is a complete absence of sexual motivation in these behaviors, but rather that sexuality is *not necessarily* the primary motivation, nor are sexually significant features of the partner the effective stimuli mediating these seemingly sexually patterns.

Maturational Status, Dominance, and Sexual Expression

The significance of the dominance issue is reflected in the developmental progression of sexual behavior in these animals. Sexual components are initially seen to be embedded within early play behavior during the first several months of life; one can even occasionally see infant males thrusting against the ventrum of their mother. Moreover, with normal opportunities for both iso-sexual and heterosexual social experience, by the end of the first year of life (i.e., about two to three years before puberty), male and female patterns rapidly differentiate as males gradually acquire the "double-footclasp" dorsal mounting pattern and females transform initial "freezing" patterns into an oriented and elevated rump-presentation posture. A variety of evidence indicates that early distortions in social experience can markedly and enduringly deform the normal sexual pattern, particularly in males (Missakian, 1969; Goldfoot et al., 1984). Deficient early experience may produce males who, even as adults, will either not respond to sexually receptive or proceptive females, or will become sexually aroused in the females' presence but will either begin masturbation or will attempt to mount partially or from the side or head end (see also Rosen-blum and Smiley, 1984). Females seem less susceptible to the pathological sexual effects of early rearing deficits, although other aspects of their re-productive behavior, in particular their initial maternal responsivity, may be considerably affected (Suomi, 1978).

If we bring a sexually receptive female bonnet macaque, for example, to a single adult male, even though they are strangers to one another, the larger, more aggressive male will instantly assume the dominant position and mount-ing will occur within the first ten seconds. If, however, that same female is provided to a two-year-old male, one clearly no match for the larger adult female, the male will act as if he has no interest in the female whatsoever. Nonetheless, that same prepubertal young male, offered a young receptive female his own size, quickly establishes his dominance and engages in vig-orous and prodigious sexual interaction with her, mounting and reaching orgasm a number of times within a relatively brief test session. Males of intermediate age and size, roughly equal in size to the adult female, will show intermediate forms of response: fighting vigorously with the female in an attempt to establish a fragile dominance that will permit at least some degree of overt sexual behavior to be expressed during the testing. These intermedi-ate males (as is true of the full-size adults) readily mount the young, less dominant females (Rosenblum and Nadler, 1971).

When observing infants growing up in complex social groups, at times we see an interesting variant on this basic theme, which may on the surface appear to contradict the assertions made above. In social groups of bonnet macaques, it is not unusual to see a relatively young male, perhaps one to two years of age, succeed in mounting a fully adult female. How can it be that the male is dominant over a clearly larger female—a female he would surely avoid if tested with her alone? The answer lies in the fact that it is not the young male who is dominant, but it is the mother of the male who is dominant over the other female, and it is this transferred dominance to her son that permits him to mount the lower-status female. There are, incidentally, reports in several species of a relative lack of mounting between females and their adult sons, even when the latter has assumed a ranking in the group that might ordinarily permit sexual behavior with any of the troop's females (Sade, 1968; Bixler, 1981). Although it may be the sustained attachment bond of the male to its mother that inhibits sexual expression, it seems more likely that regardless of how the male's general social status may have increased, neither the male nor his mother is about to take any of this "dominance nonsense" too seriously when it comes to their own relationship.

Sexual Segregation: An Alternative Model of Social Structure

Yet another alternative primate social system provides relatively delimited sexual interaction between male and female members of the group. In a small South American primate, the squirrel monkey, some types maintain a social structure that is "sexually-segregated," that is, while remaining within a "sphere of potential interaction" in one another's vicinity, each sex maintains rather distinct isosexual subgroupings (Coe and Rosenblum, 1974). Even during the annual period of active mating, males will only briefly separate from the male cluster to pursue (court) a female who is in a sexually receptive state (females of this species have a relatively short, seven- to eight-day, cycle during the breeding season and are only receptive for about a day during this weekly interval). Following completion of the sexual encounter, the male rapidly returns to his male cohort. This segregated pattern emerges in the developing young of this species by the time of puberty (about two to three years) through the mediation of the already-segregated adult groupings (Rosenblum and Coe, 1977). The male subgroups are attractive to, and are more willing to accept the proximity of, young males, while a parallel pattern moves the young females into the adult female subgroup. Contrary to what we might naively expect, segregation in this species actually seems to depend significantly on the presence of the gonadal hormones, solidifying developmentally at around the time of puberty and breaking down to varying degrees following gonadectomy in adults (Bromley, 1978). It is interesting that in the squirrel monkey, the females, in spite of their somewhat smaller size, are somewhat dominant as a subgroup over the males, the latter often evacuating a desirable area when the female group approaches. It is possible that the uncertainties of male status vis-à-vis the female may enhance the segregation pattern and further minimize the total level of male-female sexual encounters.

Male-Male Dominance and Sexual Access to Females

Returning now to the general case, as illustrated by our macaque data, once the time of year is right and the males and females are unambiguous about their relative status, the status of the males among themselves also plays a significant part in determining who will and who will not be sexually active at any given time. Certainly, in a situation in which the direct competition of two or more males can occur, the appearance of sexually receptive female partners generally results in two clear patterns (Coe and Rosenblum, 1984). First, if the males have otherwise been relatively compatible and friendly in the absence of females, tension between the males will immediately increase and overt fighting may ensue. This aggression may well occur even if the more subordinate male is not directly challenging the status or access of the more dominant male since his mere presence when competition for females is possible can be sufficient to heighten aggressive reactions. With respect to the females, the response of the males is generally clear and unequivocal. Assuming the males have been together long enough to have established their relative status, only the more dominant male will even approach the waiting female.

This priority of access to females is one of the hallmarks of male status in primate groups and can be reliably demonstrated under a variety of conditions both in captivity and in wild troops. Something of a paradox exists, however, in that the biological significance of this dominant-male priority is unclear. We have long assumed that their more frequent mounting and freer access to females meant that more dominant males would have significantly more gene representation in the progeny of the group. Now that multiple-marker genetic analysis is possible—allowing a definite determination of paternity—the few extended studies performed with primate groups have failed to demonstrate a consistently higher level of reproductive success in the more dominant males of the group (Smith et al., 1984; Smith and Smith, 1988), but higher-ranking females in some settings may have higher reproductive success rates (Smith, 1981; Dunbar and Dunbar, 1977; Fedigan, 1983).

Cyclic Changes in Female Sexual Initiation and Receptivity

There is one final element in the chain of conditions that determines whether sexual behavior will or will not be expressed. The sexual status of the female can also figure significantly in this determination. In "Primate Origins of Human Sexuality," Hrdy (1977) summarizes the available data on female cyclicity: "In populations as different as a college community in Connecticut, a Kung San gathering and hunting group in the Kalahari desert, and a sample of American lesbians (a group presumably uncomplicated by any male involvement), researchers report a peak in sexual activity at midcycle. This midcycle peak was sometimes also accompanied by a second, minor peak just prior to menstruation; interestingly, this resembles that reported for rhesus macaques" (p. 110). Depending on the species, female primates play varying roles in sexual interactions. In some species, females may stimulate male behavior through their appearance (e.g., in baboons, Girolami and Bielert, 1987) or indirectly through some aspect of their behavior—for example, by simply receptively responding to male approaches by presentation and acceptance of mounting (Coe and Rosenblum, 1984). Alternatively, in other species, females may play a more directly initiating role, actively approaching the male and soliciting his mounting behavior through facial, manual, or postural presentation gestures. One sees all of these female sexual variants within the Macaca genus itself (Nadler and Rosenblum, 1969, 1973). Similarly, the females of some species develop large perineal swelling, a change in color, or perhaps pheromonal changes, which signal at a distance a female's sexual and reproductive readiness. In other species, females show little or no external changes in appearance to signal the onset of receptivity. Where physical changes do occur, males will be seen checking the status of the female at intervals through close visual or olfactory inspection. In general, however, regardless of the role of either male or female, sexual behavior under normal circumstances does not appear at equal frequency throughout the length of the females' reproductive cycle (usually such cycles are approximately monthly during the breeding season). Indeed, in most cases the periods of nonsexuality far exceed those in which the female initiates or is readily involved in sexual behavior (e.g., Michael, 1972; Pomerantz and Goy, 1983; Coe, 1976). Frank Beach, a pioneer in comparative research on sexuality, is often quoted as saying, "No human female is constantly receptive," and "any male who entertains this illusion must be a very old man with a short memory or a very young man due for bitter disappointment" (cited in Hrdy, 1988). Ronald D. Nadler, the world's leading authority on great ape sexual behavior, has indicated that as a general rule of thumb and in keeping with the crucial interrelationship between status and sexual expression, to the extent that the male primate is in control of sexual access, copulations will occur during a relatively greater part of the female's cycle; insofar as the female has control, sexuality will be more restricted to the periovulatory period (Nadler, 1986). In his seminal work with the orangutan, for example, Nadler (1988) was able to demonstrate that under conditions of restrained egress within large laboratory pens, if the female was brought to the male's pen, they would copulate during almost every day of the month, often after vigorous (albeit nondestructive) attacks by the male. However, when Nadler arranged the situation so that the female controlled access between the partners (by placing the potential partners in two adjoining rooms connected by a door too small for the male to pass through but possible for the much smaller orang female to cross), the female readily moved to the male and indeed even initiated copulations during the few days a month surrounding the period of her ovulation. As might be expected, such encounters initiated by the female were devoid of male aggressivity.

Thus we see that within a variety of settings and certainly under the conditions in which the primate order evolved and generally lives today, for both males and females for most of the year (and even during periods of maximal reproductive activity), sexual motivation and its free expression are more notable by their absence than by their sustained presence in primate life. Based on the overall diversity of primate breeding systems, factors relating to the "concealed" ovulation of human females, and the relatively small testicular size of the human male, it "seems unlikely that our ancestors lived in nuclear families with one male bonded for life with one female." "The strongest likelihood is that our ancestors lived in either one-male polygynous breeding units or else they pursued some mixed strategy" (Hrdy, 1988, 125). Such patterns, though flexibly responsive to changing social conditions that permit more temporally diverse sexual expression when "needed," were generally characterized by relatively restricted periods of sexual expression.

An Experimental Model of Inhibited Male Sexual Expression

Several years ago, I attempted to explore this capacity for sustained asexuality or sexual inhibition in a unique experimental situation (Rosenblum, Sunderland, and Chipkin, 1983). A series of sexually mature and competent bonnet macaque males was provided with hormonally receptive females. Following preliminary tests, each female had a custom-designed tampon inserted in her vagina just before her presentation to a male. Normally the mounting of such a female occurs within seconds of her entrance to the test area. Over a series of ten to fifteen trials in which the males were unable to enter the female on repeated tries, they showed tremendous increases in their latency to approach and in their attempts to mount the female. Some males stopped attempting to mount altogether. During these limited trials, the males were generally still aroused by the presence of the female (as indicated by prolonged periods of erection), but they either showed agitated locomotive behavior or other idiosyncratic affective patterns, or they began masturbating during the trials. Even though these adult males were clearly dominant over their female partners and could easily have injured them, despite evidence of the males' frustration, they never bit or slashed these females or injured them in any way. There was evidence of decreasing testosterone levels in these males after several weeks of this inhibitory experience, and follow-up examinations six months to one year later showed considerable maintenance of the inhibited sexual response to these and even to new female partners. Following a period of prolonged, sustained exposure to a continuously sexually receptive female (given long-acting estrogens), several males recovered, while others still showed the effects of their frustrating experience and continued to show inhibition toward now "open" female partners.

Hierarchical Relations and Environmental Demand

Although the interrelationship of social status, aggressivity, and sexuality is an important behavioral factor, most of the life of a nonhuman primate is relatively devoid of overt sexuality. Where then does the arduously structured social-status hierarchy gain its raison d'être for all the rest of the time? Theoretical perspectives and empirical data on the evolution and contemporaneous functioning of primates (as well as all other forms of animal life) under natural conditions and experimental work in the laboratory provide at least a partial answer to this question. We now believe that the need for individual group members to find a means of economically extracting necessary resources from the environment may be the primary sustained impetus to the establishment of hierarchically ordered relationships and the use of aggressive behaviors to establish and maintain those hierarchies over time (Rosenblum and Paully, 1984). It is assumed that, in general, it is vital for animals to maximize the balance between cost and benefits in their extraction of needed resources (i.e., the so-called cost-benefit ratio). Data from the field and experimental testing in the laboratory indicate that more dominant animals may gain access to the most easily obtained and nutritious of available food. The more dominant animal may, for example, feed from the lower branches of a tree, while more subordinate animals may be forced to climb to higher or outer branches to obtain the same or less beneficial food (Altmann, 1980). Thus the costs of extracting nutrients for the subordinate animal can be considerably greater than for the more dominant subject. Similarly, in experimental settings, the more dominant animal eats first and is less likely to be disturbed in its systematic foraging efforts.

Meal Patterns and Positive Social Referencing

An example of the effort of animals to enact strategically efficient patterns of foraging is Collier's pioneering work on the topic (Collier and Rovee-Collier, 1980). When monkeys are forced to engage in extended search behavior to obtain food (in this case, using an operant feeding paradigm), the subjects will systematically increase the size of meals taken once food is found and will decrease the total number of meals each day accordingly (Paully, 1984). By this means, primates (and all other types of animals that Collier and his group have tested) maximize their foraging efficiency by reducing the cost of repetitive search bouts. In Paully's (1984) primate study of bonnet macaques, when she compared the performance of subjects when alone and while in social groups, there were dramatic changes in each subject's foraging pattern. In the group setting, some subjects increased while others decreased the number of pellets extracted each day from a foraging apparatus. Indeed, in the rather gregarious bonnet macaques used in this research, when search costs were high, there was some "altruism" displayed, as some animals produced much more food than they themselves could eat and others produced none at all, subsisting on the food that others produced. In a sense, in this case, the group as a whole functioned strategically to minimize total group searching and brought the group's overall effort toward a more optimal foraging strategy. The positive, affiliative aspects of social interaction seem to be key in shaping the foraging behaviors of some animals. Clearly, animals will sacrifice the efficiency of foraging somewhat in order to be close to another partner—whether that partner be a sibling, an animal's mother, its infant, or whether the other animal is part of a bonded heterosexual pair (Andrews and Rosenblum, 1988).

Nonetheless, in spite of the generally overlooked importance of the affiliative social referencing that can occur when foraging takes place, it is clear that the more selfish achievement of efficient foraging is a positive correlate of high status in the group. As is true for sexual outlets, the more dominant animal holds greater priority of access to desirable nutrient resources and should achieve more optimal cost-benefit ratios than more subordinate subjects. More subordinate subjects are more constrained, must yield access to others, and necessarily, by reason of their lower status, find it difficult to proceed with their sustenance activities efficiently (Dittus, 1977). Thus the nature of a subject's feeding ecology and the costs of access to and acquisition of resources have been seen to shape the size and behavioral properties of the social groups of primates (Pyke, Pulliam, and Charnov, 1977). When food is abundant and distributed so that each subject's acquisition of it is relatively easy (that is, effective) and efficient individual strategies can be accomplished with minimal interindividual competition, aggressive hierarchical behaviors may be minimal. Nonetheless, the hidden hierarchical structure of the group can become immediately manifest when the nature of the environmental demands for survival change adversely (Hrdy, 1977).

Moreover, in addition to the contemporaneous impact of various environmental demands on the mature, independently foraging members of the group, when mothers of young infants are affected by these demands, the developing infants may be subject to pressures that may permanently alter their response to subsequent life events.

Rearing within Environments Differing in Environmental Demands

Our studies of the effects of environmental demand on primate aggressivity and hierarchical behavior began with a simple study of social interactions in a group of bonnet macaques exposed to either easy or more difficult foraging demands for a limited time each day. When available food was buried within large gravel pools, in addition to increases in overt aggression (largely directed at chasing lower status animals away from the foraging areas), there were clear-cut differences in the order and time spent foraging; the more dominant members of the group started and finished their foraging activities first, and the lower status subjects got the leftovers. When the same volume of food was simply placed on the top of the gravel pools, aggression was minimal and the hierarchical distinctions were far less clear. In this latter instance, all subjects foraged more freely in the presence of various other members of the troop, and each achieved its foraging goals much more rapidly (Plimpton, Swartz, and Rosenblum, 1981).

The Adverse Developmental Effects of Unpredictable Environments

My work on this topic over the last decade has made a number of basic principles clear. Comparisons of bonnet macaque social groups containing a number of mother-infant dyads were made across three types of foraging environments: either a continuously easy setting (low foraging demand, LFD), a continuously difficult setting (high foraging demand, HFD), or an environment in which the foraging demand varied from easy to difficult and back again across two-week intervals (variable foraging demand, VFD) (Rosenblum and Sunderland, 1981; Rosenblum and Paully, 1984; Andrews and Rosenblum, 1988). When groups were established and maintained on LFD, overt hierarchical behavior (i.e., threats, physical attacks, and avoidance or submissive gestures) in these relatively gregarious and placid animals was quite low after the first several days following group formation and remained low through the succeeding months. When demand was consistently high (HFD), there was an initial period of several weeks in which hierarchical patterns were much in evidence, but as the animals adjusted their foraging patterns to the difficulty that confronted them each day, hierarchical behavior diminished to levels similar to those seen in the LFD groups. Thus, in both the LFD and HFD groups, when the study concluded four months after group formation, both groups were at virtually negligible levels of aggressive, hierarchical patterns. In the case of the VFD groups, however, just the opposite proved to be the case. Hierarchical behavior began low and rapidly increased as the foraging requirements flip-flopped each fortnight. Thus at the end of the study, hierarchical behavior was at higher levels than ever seen in otherwise stable groups of this species. Typical of the hierarchical patterns in these animals, little destructive aggression took place that required medical treatment but rather took the form of threats, chases, and physical displacement of one animal by another, as well as heightened levels of avoidance, facial gestures of fear, and submission by the lower status animals. These differences in aggressive hierarchical behaviors were not due to a differential lack of food in the various groups—adequate amounts of food were always available for all groups—but to the work necessary to extract the food, which differed across conditions. As was true for LFD and HFD conditions, the VFD mothers maintained their normal body weights, while their infants grew at normal rates throughout the experiment. My hypothesis is that it was the psychological difficulties in establishing a stable strategy for foraging in the VFD setting that accounted for the increasing aggressivity in the interactions within the group. It is clear that in the absence of environmental stability, primates have difficulty approaching optimal foraging strategies. As Martin (1975) has pointed out: "Environmental stability was probably a key factor in primate evolution; the loss of such stability could be a key factor in primate extinction" (p. 57).

Of further significance, mothers not only became more aggressive toward one another under VFD conditions, but the level of tension in the group, coupled with increasing levels of maternal distraction and rejection of infants, resulted in less independent infants who were more hesitant to leave their mothers; when they did leave, it was for shorter intervals as they got older, instead of the normal, reverse pattern. Moreover, these VFD infants showed the highest levels of behavioral disturbance during development ever seen by the researchers. Indeed, several of the VFD infants began to show clear evidence of behavioral depression during periods when their mothers, though visually present, were psychologically unavailable to them because of their preoccupation with foraging and adult social interactions (Lewis and Goldberg, 1969). Such depressive patterns have never been seen in any infants in the physical presence of their mothers and has only rarely been seen in bonnet macaque infants fully separated from their mothers (Rosenblum, 1984; Rosenblum and Paully, 1987). More generally these depressive patterns have been observed in rhesus and pigtail macaques beginning twenty-four to thirty-six hours after maternal loss. In these latter species, infants typically form very intensive and selective attachments to their protective mothers and have relatively limited affiliative interactions with nonkin during early life. It is theorized that it is the disruption of this intense attachment, with little or no opportunity for other supportive attachments in the group, and a lack of nurturance from others during the separation that results in the typical separation-depression pattern seen in many youngsters in these species. In bonnet macaques, on the other hand, as a by-product of the very gregarious adult contact and proximity patterns seen under nondemanding environmental circumstances, infants generally establish close affiliative relationships with a number of other females of the group (and at times with the adult male), usually passing through complete maternal separations with only temporary affective disturbance and virtually never showing the depression syndrome. This is in keeping with much of the human separation data in which the importance of other social support for the bereft youngster is important. Regarding humans, Feinman and Lewis (1984) noted, for example, that "infants who are extensively socially connected appear to be less vulnerable when one primary caregiver is absent. . . . Children who have multiple caregivers may, indeed, be less dependent on any one particular person for their physical and emotional needs" (p. 27).

Social Support and Adaptive Maternal Behavior

The security of a supportive social group may be as important to the establishment and maintenance of nurturient maternal behavior in nonhuman primates as it is in humans. Nadler (1980) has provided an excellent comparative example of the role of species-relevant social contexts for maternal behavior in the great apes. Both orangutans and chimpanzees have been successful in rearing their infants born in captivity. Gorilla mothers, however, had been notoriously less successful under these conditions. After a review of the world's literature on gorilla births, Nadler noted that mothers who successfully reared their young were generally living in social settings, whereas those who abused or neglected their offspring were generally socially isolated. Nadler's review of the field literature indicated that orangutans, in fact, constitute one of the few primate species that rears its young and prefers to live in social isolation. Moreover, although chimpanzees do live in social groups, mothers maintain no permanent associations with other, unrelated adult members of the community, and the dyad is involved in little social interaction with others during the early postnatal period.

Gorillas, in contrast, live in relatively stable harem groups and rear their infants in the presence of a group of close associates with whom they frequently interact. These data led Nadler to conclude "that congenial companionship facilitates the maternal behavior of captive gorillas, whereas social isolation contributes to neglect and abuse of the offspring" (p. 117). Nadler's subsequent experience at the Yerkes Primate Center has borne out this conclusion. Data of this type have led primatologists (including Nadler, 1984; Plimpton and Rosenblum, 1983) to suggest that the disruption of species-characteristic social settings in humans may also impede or distort maternal patterns, particularly in vulnerable individuals whose pathological potential may emerge within the challenge imposed by maternity.

Manifest Developmental Symptoms and Latent Vulnerability

An additional principle has emerged from studies of the various elements of environmental demand. When the overall demand on mothers (foraging requirements, size and complexity of the physical setting, and size and composition of the social group) is somewhat difficult but is amenable to patterns of strategic response within the capacities of the animals involved, then manifest symptoms of disturbances in the development of the infants may be minimal. Thus, when a constant high demand is placed on subjects (HFD), even when living within a relatively large social group and pen, as indicated earlier, after a while the mothers adjust effectively and the infants appear normal in development. Indeed, they may actually appear to be developing somewhat more independently than their LFD counterparts. Similarly, even the VFD regimen— when imposed within a small group maintained in a simple, small pen— permits mothers to adjust reasonably well; in such circumstances, their infants develop few manifest symptoms of distress. This situation is in sharp contrast to that described in which larger social groups were maintained in a large complex environment within which manifest disturbance was observed in the development of the young.

When appropriately challenged, however, the seemingly normal infants raised in the relatively limited-demand settings show considerably more vulnerability to subsequent stress than do the infants raised under conditions that permitted the mothers to be generally attentive to their infants' changing needs. Thus, HFD infants, seemingly independent in the presence of their mothers, show far more marked and sustained depression following separation from their mothers than do LFD infants. Similarly, the infants raised in the more simplified VFD environment, who superficially looked similar to those from a simplified LFD environment during development, show markedly more dependent behaviors and far greater disturbance when confronted with a novel setting (Andrews and Rosenblum, 1990). Thus, the maternal adjustments made within environments whose total level of demand is relatively low do not produce manifest symptomatology in their young during rearing but generate latent affective problems that are evinced only when the infant or the dyad is exposed to a relevant challenge.

Consider, then, some of the possible consequences of the interrelation of stress, status, and sexuality in primate societies. When environmental conditions are increasingly difficult, there is a heightening of the functional significance of the dominance hierarchy, with attendant increases in more overt aggressive behaviors. Kinship groups become more selectively responsive to one another and more rejecting of those outside the consanguinal unit. Infants, developing within the tense social conditions of difficult environmental demand and faced with a less supportive mother but fewer available and uncontested nutrients in the extradyadic niche, are relatively more dependent on the mother as they mature. They are, in addition, more likely to respond stressfully to any perturbations in their habitat. These vulnerable infants, moreover, seem less able themselves as a consequence to develop adaptive strategic responses to new and more difficult challenges presented by the environments they subsequently confront. If such is the case, these individuals may well be prone to heightened hierarchical and aggressive behaviors in the groups in which they will become adult members. It is hypothesized that such repetitive, cyclic patterns can ultimately result in a diminution of breeding, partly because the more sustained dependence of the young may inhibit rebreeding by mothers; heightened levels of tension, aggression, and kin selection may result in reduced conceptions or sustained pregnancies within the group. If these sequelae do unfold, the population of the group may gradually fall, with resultant reductions in the imbalance between available resources and the population forced to live on them. As this negative feedback loop winds down and populations come more into line with available resources, hierarchical factors will become less salient; mothers will become more relaxed and supportive of their young; infants will develop earlier and more confident independence and be better able to cope with new challenges; mothers will return to rebreed more regularly; sexual and related interactions across kinship lines will increase; and the population will cease to fall. Whether we seek to understand humans or our closest relatives in the animal kingdom; whether our interests lie in the origins of sex, anger, fear, or rage, in assertion or passivity, or approach or withdrawal—while acknowledging the compelling role of genetics and the internal milieu—we can never fully sever the intricate matrix of connections between the organism and the physical and social environment within which it developed and in relation to which it now attempts to function.

REFERENCES

Akers, J. S., and Conway, C. H. 1979. Female homosexual behavior in *Macaca mulatta. Archives of Sexual Behavior* 8:63–80.

Altmann, J. 1980. *Baboon mothers and infants.* Cambridge: Harvard University Press.

Andrews, M. W., and Rosenblum, L. A. 1988. Relationship between foraging and affiliative social referencing in primates, in *The ecology and behavior of food-enhanced primate groups,* ed. J. E. Fa and C. H. Southwick, 247–268. New York: Alan R. Liss.

———. 1990. Attachment in monkey infants raised in variable- and low-demand environments. *Child Development* 62:686–693.

Bixler, R. H. 1981. Primate mother-son "incest." *Psychological Reports* 48:531–536.

Boinski, S. 1983. Squirrel monkey group structure dynamics: Interaction of foraging behavior and reproductive synchrony. *Behavioral Ecology and Sociobiology* 21:13–21.

Bromley, L. 1978. Hormonal determinants of sexual segregation in squirrel monkeys. Ph.D. diss., State University of New York, Downstate Medical Center.

Chevalier-Skolnikoff, S. 1975. Heterosexual copulatory patterns in stumptail macaques (*Macaca arctoides*) and in other macaque species. *Archives of Sexual Behavior* 4:199–220.

Coe, C. 1976. Factors influencing male socio-sexual behavior in the bonnet macaque (*Macaca radiata*). Ph.D. diss., State University of New York, Downstate Medical Center.

Coe, C. L., and Rosenblum, L. A. 1974. Sexual segregation and its ontogeny in squirrel monkey social structure. *Journal of Human Evolution* 3:551–561.

———. 1978. Annual reproductive strategy of the squirrel monkey (*Saimiri sciureus*). *Folia Primatologica* 29:19–42.

———. 1984. Male dominance in the bonnet macaque: A malleable relationship, in *Social cohesion,* ed. P. Barchas and S. P. Mendoza, 31–64. Westport, Conn.: Greenwood Press.

Collier, G. H., and Rovee-Collier, C. K. 1980. A comparative analysis of optimal foraging behavior: Laboratory simulations, in *Foraging behavior: Ecological, ethological, and psychological approaches,* ed. A. C. Kamil and T. Sargent. New York: Garland Press.

Dittus, W. P. J. 1977. The social regulation of population density and age-sex distribution in the toque monkey. *Behavior* 63:281–322.

Dunbar, R. I. M., and Dunbar, E. P. 1977. Dominance and reproductive success among female gelada baboons. *Nature* 266:351–352.

Erwin, J., and Maple, T. 1976. Ambisexual behavior with male-male anal penetration in male rhesus monkeys. *Archives of Sexual Behavior* 5:9–14.

Fedigan, L. M. 1983. Dominance and reproduction success in primates. *Yearbook of Physical Anthropology* 26:91–129.

Feinman, S., and Lewis, M. 1984. Is there social life beyond the dyad? A social-psychological view of social connection in infancy, in *Beyond the dyad,* ed. M. Lewis, 13–41. New York: Plenum Press.

Girolami, L., and Bielert, C. 1987. Female perineal swelling and its effects on male sexual arousal: An apparent sexual releaser in the chacma baboon (*Papio ursinus*). *Internal Journal of Primatology* 8:651–661.

Goldfoot, D. A., Wallen, K., Neff, D. A., McBrair, M. C., and Goy, R. W. 1984. Social influences on the display of sexually dimorphic behavior in rhesus monkeys: Isosexual rearing. *Archives of Sexual Behavior* 13:195–412.

Gordon, T. P., and Bernstein, I. S. 1973. Seasonal variation in sexual behavior of all-male rhesus troops. *American Journal of Physical Anthropology* 38:221–226.

Hanby, J. P. 1974. Male-male mounting in Japanese monkeys (*Macaca fuscata*). *Animal Behaviour* 22:836–849.

Herndon, J. G., Perachio, A. A., Turner, J. J., and Collins, D. C. 1981. Fluctuations in testosterone levels of male rhesus monkeys during copulatory activity. *Physiology and Behavior* 26:525–528.

Hrdy, S. B. 1977. *The Langurs of Abu*. Cambridge: Harvard University Press.

Kaufman, I. C., and Rosenblum, L. A. 1966. A behavioral taxonomy for macaques: Based on longitudinal observation of family groups in the laboratory. *Primates* 7(2): 205–258.

Lancaster, J. B., and Lee, R. B. 1965. The annual reproductive cycle in monkeys and apes, in *Primate behavior*, ed. I. DeVore, 486–513. New York: Holt, Rinehart, and Winston.

Lewis, M., and Goldberg, S. 1969. Perceptual-cognitive development in infancy: A generalized expectancy model as a function of mother-infant interaction. *Merrill-Palmer Quarterly* 15:81–100.

Lindburg, D. G. 1987. Seasonality of reproduction in primates, in *Comparative primate biology*, vol. 2B, *Behavior, cognition and motivation*, ed. G. Mitchell and J. Erwin, 167–218. New York: Alan R. Liss.

Martin, B. 1975. Parent-child relations, in *Review of child development research*, vol. 4. Chicago: University of Chicago Press.

Michael, R. P. 1972. Determinants of primate reproductive behaviour. *Acta Endocrinologica* 166:322–363 (supplement).

Michael, R. P., Richter, M. C., Cain, J. A., Zumpe, D., and Bonsall, R. W. 1978. Artificial menstrual cycles, behaviour and the role of androgens in female rhesus monkeys. *Nature* 275:439–440.

Michael, R. P., Wilson, M., and Plant, T. M. 1973. Sexual behaviour of male primates and the role of testosterone, in *Comparative ecology and behaviour of primates*, ed. R. P. Michael and J. H. Crook, 234–313. London: Academic Press.

Missakian, E. A. 1969. Reproductive behavior of socially deprived male rhesus monkeys (*Macaca mulatta*). *Journal of Comparative and Physiological Psychology* 69:403–407.

Nadler, R. D. 1980. Child abuse: Evidence from nonhuman primates. *Developmental Psychobiology* 13(5): 507–512.

———. 1986. Great ape sexual behaviour: Human implication, in *Proceedings of Seventh World Congress of Sexology*, ed. P. Kothari, 45–49. Bombay: Valkil.

———. 1988. Sexual aggression in the great apes, in *Human sexual aggression: Current perspectives*, vol. 528, ed. R. A. Prentky and V. L. Quinsey, 154–162. New York: Annals, New York Academy of Science.

Nadler, R. D., and Rosenblum, L. A. 1969. Sexual behavior of male bonnet monkeys in the laboratory. *Brain, behavior, evolution* 2:482–497.

————. 1973. Sexual behavior during successive ejaculations in bonnet and pigtail macaques. *American Journal of Physical Anthropology* 38:217–220.

Paully, G. A. 1984. Feeding strategies in individual and group living bonnet macaques. Ph.D. diss., State University of New York, Downstate Medical Center.

Plimpton, E., and Rosenblum, L. A. 1983. The ecological context of infant maltreatment in primates, in *Child abuse: The non-human primate data,* ed. M. Reite, 103–117. New York: Alan R. Liss.

Pomerantz, S. M., and Goy, R. W. 1983. Proceptive behavior of female rhesus monkeys during tests with tethered males. *Hormones and Behavior* 17:237–248.

Pyke, G. H., Pulliam, H. R., and Charnov, E. L. 1977. Optimal foraging: A selective review of theory and tests. *Quarterly Review of Biology* 52:137–154.

Rosenblum, L. A. 1984. Monkey responses to separation and loss, in *Bereavement: Reactions, consequences and care,* ed. F. Solomon and M. Green, 179–198. Washington, D.C.: National Academy Press.

Rosenblum, L. A., and Coe, C. 1977. Sexual segregation in squirrel monkeys, in *Socialization in primates,* ed. G. Poirier and S. Chevalier-Skolnikoff, 479–500. New York: Aldine.

Rosenblum, L. A., and Nadler, R. D. 1971. Ontogeny of male sexual behavior in bonnet macaques, in *Influence of hormones on the nervous system,* ed. D. Ford, 388–400. Basel: Karger.

Rosenblum, L. A., and Paully, G. 1984. The effects of varying environmental demands on maternal and infant behavior. *Journal of Child Development* 55:305–314.

————. 1987. Depression in nonhuman primates. *Psychiatric Clinics of North America* 10(3): 437–447.

Rosenblum, L. A., and Smiley, J. 1984. Therapeutic effects of an imposed foraging task in disturbed monkeys. *Journal of Child Psychology and Psychiatry* 25:485–497.

Rosenblum, L. A., and Sunderland, G. 1981. Feeding ecology and mother-infant relations, in *Parenting: Its causes and consequences,* ed. L. W. Hoffman, R. Gandelman, and H. R. Schiffman, 75–110. Hillsdale, N.J.: Lawrence Erlbaum.

Rosenblum, L. A., Sunderland, G., and Chipkin, S. 1983. Sexual frustrations and male performance: A monkey model for male sexual dysfunction, in *Challenges in sexual science,* ed. M. Davis, 109–127. Lake Mills, Iowa: Graphic.

Sade, D. S. 1968. Inhibition of son-mother mating among free-ranging rhesus monkeys, in *Science and psychoanalysis,* vol. 12, *Animal and human,* ed. J. H. Masserman, 18–38. New York: Grune & Stratton.

Smith, D. G. 1981. Birth timing and social rank of adult male rhesus monkeys (*Macaca mulatta*). *Journal of Medical Primatology* 10:279–283.

Smith, D. G., Small, M. F., Ahlfors, C. E., Lorey, F. W., Stern, B. R., and Rolfs, B. K. 1984. Paternity exclusion analysis and its applications to studies of nonhuman primates. *Advances in Veterinary Science and Comparative Medicine* 28:1–24.

Smith, D. G., and Smith, S. 1988. Parental rank and reproductive success of natal rhesus males. *Animal Behavior* 36:554–562.

Steklis, H. D., Linn, G. S., Howard, S. M., Kling, A., and Tiger, L. 1983. Progesterone and socio-sexual behavior in stumptailed macaques (*Macaca arctoides*): Hormonal and socio-environmental interactions, in *Hormones, drugs and social behavior in primates,* ed. H. D. Steklis and A. S. Kling, 107–134. New York: SP Medical and Scientific Books.

Suomi, S. J. 1978. Maternal behavior by socially incompetent monkeys: Neglect and abuse of offspring. *Journal of Pediatric Psychology* 3(1): 28–34.

Wallen, K. 1989. Nonfertile mating in rhesus monkeys: Sexual aggression or miscommunication. *Primate Report* 23:23–34.

Zuckerman, S. 1932. *The social life of monkeys and apes.* London: Routledge and Kegan Paul.

11

Aggression:
A Neuropsychiatric Perspective

FRED OVSIEW, M.D., and STUART YUDOFSKY, M.D.

In the novel *The Terminal Man* (1972), physician and author Michael Crichton focused the attention a best-seller commands on the idea that epileptic or surgical brain lesions can induce violence. Even a more sober scientific review of the data must conclude that aggressive behavior, ranging from mild irritability to serial murder, can have brain disease as a crucial determinant. In what follows, we review the mechanisms by which the brain organizes aggression, whether pathological or normal; offer illustrations of the clinical presentation of the aggressive behavior disorders related to brain disease; and speculate on the integration of neuroscientific findings on aggression with psychoanalytic theory.

By way of introduction, we must clarify that it is by no means our view that certain patients have "organic" disorders producing aggression whereas others have purely "psychological" disturbances. As our clinical examples will show, a variety of determinants must be considered to arrive at a comprehensive understanding of aggressive behavior. All of us are products of genetic predispositions, of nongenetic constitutional proclivities and aversions, of motives and compromises determined by our interpersonal and somatic experience. No study could be more complex than the attempt to untangle the contributions of each to a final behavioral outcome. Despite the uncertainty about whether, in the final analysis, the human brain can grasp the complexity of the human brain, for practical clinical purposes, we do quite well in the assessment and management of many aggressive disorders, and the scientific database upon which we can draw is growing rapidly.

Assumptions

Before focusing on regional brain function and dysfunction, we must advance several assumptions underlying our conceptualizations. We have considered that affective states—particularly anger—and the set of behaviors called aggression share certain brain mechanisms. Although in general the notion that anger is related to aggressive behavior is hardly controversial, our assumption requires certain annotations. First, as we will discuss below, hostile or destructive behavior does not necessarily arise from anger or rageful emotional states. Fear, pain, and other emotional states, subserved by distinct brain systems, may underlie aggression. Although the behaviors arising from these states may not be easily distinguishable, the emotional underpinnings may be biologically differentiated. How the activity of these differing brain systems plays out in overt *behavior* is a difficult issue; how it is manifest in human *experience* is even more complex. Second, the issue of evidence for affective states in animals must be considered. Only observable behavior is available for inference. In fact, similar considerations pertain to studies of children: some would argue that short of psychoanalytic data, all observational evidence is mere social psychology. For heuristic and clinical purposes, we accept that anger and aggression are linked. Our assumption is that, in general, affects and drives are related. Although this relationship has been the subject of much recent theoretical exploration, its full consideration is beyond the focus of this chapter.

Neurobiology of Aggression: Lessons from the Laboratory

Pitfalls of Localization Theories

It is not surprising that the study of aggression has occasioned much recent scientific interest. In 1984 in the United States, there were 18,692 murders, 685,349 aggravated assaults, 84,233 rapes, and uncounted unkind acts or harsh words among friends and family members (Dietz, 1987). In the extreme, human aggression has the potential to render scientific debate on any issue null and void through the use of nuclear weapons. A neurobiologic approach to the understanding of this issue is only one valid avenue. Far from replacing other, psychosocial viewpoints, the neurobiologic vantage is intrinsically psychosocial. The student of neurobiologic literature must consider the psychosocial setting of the organism under study.

An example of the caution necessary is the Klüver-Bucy syndrome. In 1937, Heinrick Klüver and Paul Bucy reported the results of bilateral resection of the temporal lobes of monkeys (Klüver and Bucy, 1937; Poeck, 1985). A number of drastic behavioral changes resulted, usually summarized as the following: hypersexuality, hyperorality, hypermetamorphosis (a forced attention to environmental stimuli), and tameness. As to this last item, the investigators noted that animals that previously had been fiercely averse to the experimenter's approach became placid and easy to interact with. The very observation of tameness is thus a social observation, requiring an understanding of the investigators' relation to the animal. Even more notable is that the original observations were made on caged laboratory animals. When Arthur

Kling (1972, 1986) performed the same operative procedure on monkeys that afterward were permitted to range freely in their natural habitat, the findings were quite different. The animals became social isolates, by no means approachable and not perspicuously described as tame. From this broader perspective on the Klüver and Bucy experiment, we can see that temporal lobe resection did not remove a "center for aggression"; rather the lesion disrupted a distributed network that, in its normal state, subserved social behavior, aggressive and otherwise.

The very concept of *centers* in the brain is both seductive and misleading: it is a concept that is useful heuristically and clinically but dangerous theoretically when overextended or taken too literally. As John Hughlings-Jackson pointed out over a hundred years ago, the location in which a lesion disrupts a function is not necessarily the location of that function in the normal state (Kennard and Swash, 1989). To put the point more methodologically, work with ablative lesions, whether in animal models or human disease, does not yield a flow chart of brain function with a single function deleted. Rather, the injured brain continues to solve the problems posed to it, but in a degraded fashion.

The notion of levels of organization within the brain, however, has proved more robust. Hierarchical organization was propounded by Hughlings-Jackson, who proposed that "higher centers" inhibit the function of "lower centers" and provide the structural basis for more "voluntary" and less "automatic" behavior. Today we must modify this scheme to acknowledge that each level of organization may contain networks that either inhibit or facilitate lower levels. Further elaborations can be proposed, but in what follows we will schematize aggressive behavior as organized by a network at the levels of hypothalamus, limbic system, and prefrontal cortex. This schema has been used by others (Bear, 1989; Weiger and Bear, 1988).

Forms of Aggression: Anatomic Paradigms

The fundamental discoveries about the brain mechanisms that organize aggressive behavior date from the late 1920s. Kevin Hess, and later Bard, working with cats, recognized the role of hypothalamic structures as crucial to the display of organized *rage* reactions (Moyer, 1987; Panksepp, 1982). It is now well accepted that there are sites within the hypothalamus whose ablation—and others whose stimulation—produces an integrated display of *affective attack*. The display was at first termed *sham rage*, the emotional content of the behavior being considered uncertain. The argument that the rage is not sham—that the behavior is well integrated with the animal's environment and not empty of content—rests in part on repeated observations that elicited aggression is organized in accord with preexisting social hierarchies of dominance and submission. What is more, Jaak Panksepp (1982) argues that the likelihood of producing aggression by brain stimulation depends not only on the site of stimulation but also on the preexisting temperament of the animal.

In the analysis of aggressive displays, it is important to recognize that there are several types of behavior under consideration. Kenneth Moyer (1987) distinguishes multiple forms of aggressive behavior: predatory, intermale, fear-induced, maternal, irritable, sex-related, and instrumental. The two most extensively investigated from neurobiological points of view, primarily in work with cats, are *quiet biting attack* and affective attack. These behaviors are distinguishable both by elements of the behavior observed and by the hypothalamic regions whose stimulation produces them.

Quiet biting attack—marked by stalking, pouncing, and biting without prominent autonomic activation—is elicited by stimulation in the lateral hypothalamus. The behavior is distinct from feeding behavior, and stimulation of the appropriate sites in the lateral hypothalamus even causes the interruption of feeding by quiet attack. Though many behaviors crucial to survival are organized within a very small area in the hypothalamus, the neural networks underlying these behaviors can be distinguished.

These attack behaviors are modulated by influences from higher centers. Allan Siegel and Henry Edinger (1981, 1983) have summarized an extensive series of studies on the effects of lesions or stimulation at a variety of sites within the limbic system. Basomedial amygdala seems particularly potent in the suppression of hypothalamically organized attack behavior, but dorsal hippocampus, lateral septal nucleus, lateral substantia innominata, and anterior cingulate gyrus each plays a role. The effects of these structures on hypothalamic neurons is balanced by a facilitatory effect of lateral amygdala, ventral hippocampus, and medial substantia innominata. Prefrontal cortex, which may be conceptualized as the next higher level of functional organization, exerts a powerful suppression of hypothalamically organized attack behavior. This pathway from cortex to hypothalamus is not direct but synapses in the medial-dorsal nucleus of the thalamus.

Affective attack is marked by a profound display of autonomic excitation, including piloerection and mydriasis, along with spitting and vocalization. This response, most commonly elicited by stimuli that threaten the organism's survival, is the behavior that evokes the term rage. Whether the forms of aggression that Moyer considers separately, such as territorial aggression, are subserved by the same neural networks as are implicated in other forms of defense remains uncertain. Affective attack is produced by stimulation of the medial hypothalamus. Here too the role of amygdala is clearly crucial: stimulation of the medial amygdala can provoke displays of rage, presumably by driving hypothalamic centers by way of the direct amygdalofugal pathway.

The inverse relationship between quiet biting attack and affective attack calls for comment. The medial amygdala inhibits predation and facilitates rageful attack; the ventral hippocampus facilitates predation and inhibits affective attack. By implication, the two forms of behavior are in inverse relation, that of aggression for defense when the environment threatens and of attack for predation when the environment permits.

Kindling: The Physiological Paradigm

Robert Adamec and his co-workers, in important and much-cited work using the kindling paradigm, have clarified the physiology of aggression and of the inverse relationship just discussed (Adamec, 1975). *Kindling* refers to the phenomenon of progressive reduction of the threshold for the production of an electrically stimulated seizure by the continued application of subthreshold electrical stimuli. Along with seizures, progressive behavior change results from the kindling process, which has been considered an important model of change through experience, that is, learning. In one experiment, Adamec stimulated the amygdala and simultaneously recorded discharge patterns from neurons in the hypothalamus. Stimulation produced an after-discharge, which is an evoked discharge short of seizure. Adamec studied cats, which were rated according to aggressiveness and fearfulness by observation of their behavior in an environment containing objects that normally elicit aggressive or fearful responses. Cats vary by temperament in their tendency to show these reactions, and not surprisingly, fearfulness and aggressiveness varied inversely in Adamec's study. Moreover, Adamec showed that cats varied as well in their threshold for showing an after-discharge; and that the higher the after-discharge threshold, the more aggressive and the less fearful the cat. This correlation of physiology and temperament is important in itself, but its robustness and implications are expanded by the kindling paradigm: following repeated stimulation, the after-discharge threshold decreased, and with this decrease, the cats' aggressiveness diminished. Thus, activity in the amygdala-hypothalamic pathway is clearly shown to be crucial in the mechanism of aggressive behavior, and individual variations in the susceptibility of this pathway to activation are shown to correlate with individual variations in temperament.

Additional investigations expanded these observations (Adamec, 1990, Adamec and Stark-Adamec, 1986). The extent of fearfulness in the cat temperament is fixed early in development, by about two months of life, and is thereafter relatively insensitive to environmental influences. The more defensive cats—those more fearful of novel stimuli or of other environmental stimuli, and conversely less apt to display predatory aggression—have definable physiological correlates of this temperament. The evidence shows that transmission between the basal amygdala and the hypothalamus is enhanced, so that sensory messages are preferentially routed along this pathway. In contrast, in cats more apt to display predation, messages are preferentially routed to the ventral hippocampus.

Neuroendocrine and Neuropharmacological Paradigms

In addition to the anatomic and physiologic approaches so far discussed, neuroendocrine and neurotransmitter perspectives offer information about the cerebral basis of aggressive behavior. The most robust finding in regard to hormones is the role of testosterone, which has consistently been shown to increase aggressive behavior by modulating activity in the pathways discussed above. Although the mechanism of this modulation has not been fully clarified, it may relate to an effect on the membranes of hypothalamic neurons (Panksepp, 1985).

If only because of clinical pharmacological implications, an understanding of the neurotransmitter specificities of circuits organizing aggression is important to achieve (Sheard, 1984, 1988). The neurotransmitter serotonin appears to be involved in the regulation of aggressive (and other impulsive) behavior. In many experimental models, a reduction of serotonin activity leads to an increase in aggressive behavior, and an increase in serotonin to a reduction in aggressive behavior. Serotonergic drugs such as trazodone, fluoxetine, and buspirone have been reported to reduce aggression. Lithium has also been shown to produce a reduction in aggression, perhaps by this mechanism. The benefit of lithium does not appear to depend on the presence of a manic syndrome, though surely when the other features of a manic disorder are present together with irritable aggressive activity, the clinician will think first of lithium.

Carbamazepine has become a widely used agent in bipolar disorder and has proved itself in aggressive states as well. Like lithium, its use is not limited to aggression related to mania. Its utility always raises the question of whether an unrecognized epileptic disorder is at the root of the aggressive behavior. The proven benefit of carbamazepine in bipolar disorder without demonstrable (for example, by electroencephalogram [EEG]) organic abnormalities suggests that epilepsy need not be present for carbamazepine to be effective; it is an agent with multiple actions and can be considered for clinical use regardless of the evidence for cerebral dysfunction of an epileptic type. Still, the fact that there is a benefit raises the question of *episodic dyscontrol*, a postulated limbic dysfunction with epileptic characteristics (Monroe, 1970). The nosologic status of this entity is uncertain (Fenwick, 1986). Russell Monroe proposed that certain individuals show unpremeditated behavior, often aggressive, uncharacteristic, and abrupt in onset; the acts lie on a continuum from those related more to "faulty equipment" to those related more to "faulty learning." The faulty equipment in question is, in Monroe's view, a limbic system predisposed to epileptoid dysfunction, often not detectable by scalp recording. To our knowledge, no studies address the utility of carbamazepine or other antiepileptic drugs in terms that do justice to Monroe's psychodynamically sophisticated intertwining of learning and equipment.

The transmitter gamma-amino-butyric acid (GABA) also appears to inhibit aggressive behavior. Benzodiazepines are GABA agonists, and in animal models these agents are effective as antiaggressive drugs. In states of aggression related to high anxiety levels, antianxiety agents such as benzodiazepines (and perhaps buspirone) are potentially beneficial, but for the most part clinicians have found these drugs less effective than one might hope.

Elevated norepinephrine levels are associated with increases in aggressive behavior, and the success of β-adrenergic blockade (for example, by propranolol [Yudofsky, Williams, and Gorman, 1981; Yudofsky et al., 1986]) in managing violence is a clinically important as well as theoretically telling discovery of the last few years. The blockade of dopamine is the key pharmacological intervention in aggressive states associated with psychosis, but the immediate resort to antipsychotic drugs to control aggression in patients whose aggression stems from other etiologies is a common clinical error.

Cholinergic agonists applied to the appropriate hypothalamic sites elicit aggressive behavior, and cholinergic antagonists inhibit it. Unfortunately, manipulation of the cholinergic system is not generally useful clinically. Important new information is now coming to light about the involvement of opiate systems in postictal events, including postictal aggressive behavior, but this research is not yet sufficiently advanced to be of clinical use (Caldecott-Hazard and Engel, 1987).

Clinical Illustrations: Lessons from Psychopathology

Hypothalamic Disease

Mrs. A, a woman of forty-two, presented to an endocrinologist with hypothyroidism and galactorrhea. Over the ensuing months she developed panhypopituitarism, diabetes insipidus, impaired vision, and obesity. Her cognitive function declined and she became emotionally labile. Magnetic resonance imaging showed a mass lesion at the base of the brain. Open biopsy of the mass revealed an infiltrative process involving the optic chiasm and hypothalamus; pathological examination showed granulomatous inflammation, believed to be sarcoidosis.

On neuropsychiatric examination, there were no elementary sensorimotor signs, but she was profoundly demented. For example, she was usually unable to remember the name of the hospital she was in for more than a few seconds after being told; in addition, she was perseverative and disorganized. When first seen, she was extraordinarily hyperphagic; she continually asked for food and made a beeline for any food in the environment, then ate voraciously. This behavior subsided when treatment of the sarcoidosis with high-dose steroids was discontinued. Although for the most part quiet and apathetic, she evinced episodes of profound agitation and combativeness that were not amenable to calming by any verbal or behavioral intervention. Generally, her aggressive behavior did not appear to be in response to any environmental provocation. The ideational content of the agitation was not accessible, but certainly when she attacked nurses she appeared angry. On two occasions nurses were significantly injured. Treatment with neuroleptics, carbamazepine, propranolol, and clonazepam was ineffective in mitigating her aggressiveness.

Clinical cases of hypothalamic disease with aggressive behavior are uncommon but well described. Alexander Reeves and Fred Plum (1969) described the case of a young woman with a medial hypothalamic hamartoma. She showed hyperphagia and dementia along with being intermittently aggressive, biting or hitting the people around her. Fred Killefer and Eugene Stern (1970) described a girl who suffered hypothalamic injury with the resection of a craniopharyngioma. In its aftermath, she showed hyperphagia and "episodic savage behavior," which, the authors say, was "accompanied by appropriate emotional manifestations." Unfortunately, the authors do not spell out what these manifestations were. Robert Haugh and William Markesbery (1983) reported a case of hypothalamic astrocytoma with clinical manifestations similar to the already-mentioned cases. The description of the abnormal behavior is limited to the comment that she "had episodes of combative, aggressive behavior" considered "unprovoked." All three patients also had endocrine derangements.

In our case, at times Mrs. A appeared upset, usually about missing her children, or frustrated, for example by restraint, but it was impossible to link confidently any particular ideational or emotional mental content to her outbursts of aggression. It seems highly likely that her hypothalamic lesion contributed, along with her cognitive impairment and her emotional distress, to the lowering of the threshold for aggressive behavior. Unfortunately, pharmacological treatment failed.

Limbic System Disease

Mrs. B, a woman of forty, had seizures in childhood, which remitted only to recur in adolescence. Through adolescence and early adulthood her epilepsy was well controlled pharmacologically, but in her late thirties the seizures, both partial complex and generalized tonic-clonic, were not well controlled despite appropriate pharmacotherapy. During this period of her life she was said to be hostile and stubborn and was unhappily married to an abusive man. She gave ample evidence of a personality disturbance, for example, by her tendency to lose jobs because of conflicts with supervisors. Some eighteen months prior to admission she suffered an episode of status epilepticus, after which she had a transient right hemiparesis. She recovered over several days, but the hospital stay was cut short when she angrily demanded discharge.

The family noted a pronounced behavior change after this episode. She was more angry and less aware of her own difficulties, thus less well able to care for herself and her teenaged daughter. Though there had always been tension in the family, her expressions of anger became more primitive, for example, biting her father's arm and uttering death wishes toward him. Concurrently, the family noted that her memory was impaired. The incident that led to her admission took place after she had had several complex partial seizures in the space of a day. She followed her mother around the house with a "cold mean stare"; she threatened to kill her daughter and in fact grabbed her and threw her against a wall. Paramedics were called and she cursed at and attacked them.

On neuropsychiatric examination she showed no abnormal elementary sensory or motor signs. There was a mild degree of difficulty with attention; this difficulty seemed to fade over several days. She was evasive, lacked insight, and occasionally showed a suspiciousness bordering on the paranoid. After prolonged observation, a trial of an antipsychotic drug modestly reduced her suspiciousness and anxiety. Once she grew angry at a nurse and threw a cup of water at her. Otherwise, her aggressiveness under observation was limited to a hostile tone congruent with her suspicious ideation. Interestingly, she had but one observed seizure during her three-month hospital stay; during the next day or two she was notably more suspicious and irritable.

Neuropsychometric examination showed a Wechsler Full Scale IQ of 89 with no psychometric evidence to suggest that this represented a decline from premorbid levels. There was a profound memory disorder for both verbal and nonverbal material and difficulty with cognitive flexibility and problem solving. Neuroimaging with CT and MR revealed only a (presumably incidental) small meningioma at the left frontal pole.

Despite modest success with pharmacological control of her persecutory ideation and irritability and good success with pharmacological control of her epilepsy, the prognosis remained guarded because of her denial of illness and of the need for help. She remained hostile but showed no further overt aggression.

The controversy over whether there is a specific link between violence and epilepsy has not been settled. The controversy concerns, in large part, whether the undisputed excess of aggressive behavior among epileptic patients arises from the epilepsy itself or from the underlying brain damage. In either case, the locus of dysfunction primarily involves the limbic system. Almost all authorities agree that disease of the limbic system can contribute to aggressive behavior disorders (Fenwick, 1989).

It is clinically useful to divide aggression in epilepsy into three types: aggression as part of the epileptic ictus itself, or ictal aggression; aggression during the confusional period immediately following a seizure, or postictal aggression; and aggression not proximate in time to the occurrence of clinical seizure activity, or interictal aggression. Ictal aggression provides the clearest evidence for specific neurophysiological mechanisms. Despite a good deal of disagreement about the incidence of such attacks, it seems clear that ictal aggressive episodes do occur. For example, Hans-Georg Wieser (1983) has documented "rage attacks" with "troubled higher cortical functions," during which the surface electroencephalogram was normal, but direct recordings from deep structures showed clonic discharges from the periamygdalar regions that lasted several minutes. Peter Fenwick (1989) has argued that it would be hard to document such electrical disturbances precisely because there is an interaction between the environment and the triggering of the patient's fits, such that aggressive fits are less likely to occur in the sterile environment of the laboratory. When to suspect and how to evaluate a patient for ictal rages are beyond the scope of discussion here. Suffice it to say that the occurrence of such episodes lends vivid clinical reality to the animal stimulation experiments discussed earlier: such patients have a spontaneously occurring limbic generator driving the hypothalamic areas that organize rageful behavior.

Postictal aggression shares the key characteristic of another postictal psychological disturbance, namely confusion. The "twilight state" that can last some hours to a few days after a seizure or series of seizures may include psychotic features, such as hallucinations or persecutory fears. The defining feature is a disturbance of consciousness, with less than fully coherent thinking and disorientation. In this setting, aggressive behavior may arise and is especially apt to occur when the patient is restrained or otherwise frustrated. There is no strong reason to think that its occurrence always bears a relationship to the patient's premorbid personality, but it does often arise in a more or less understandable relationship to the patient's current environment.

> An elderly man, Mr. C, was admitted to the hospital after a series of convulsions. Upon awakening gradually over the next few days, he shouted, cursed, spat, clawed, and struck at the medical and nursing staff caring for him. During this time he displayed confusion and disorientation as well as a remarkable tendency to give a running account of the features of his surroundings, reminiscent of the hypermetamorphosis of Klüver-Bucy animals: "There's a picture on the wall, you're wearing a tie," and so on. The electroencephalogram showed bitemporal discharges. When he awoke fully, the behavior disturbance disappeared; he proved to be a cultivated man with two master's degrees, retired from his job as a school principal. He was terribly regretful about his behavior and also troubled that his hoarseness—from screaming for days—temporarily prevented him from participating in his church choir.

It would require a considerable commitment to the prepotency of personality to believe that Mr. C's confusional state released a powerfully repressed aggressive tendency; rather the pathophysiology of limbic disease appears to be the primary determinant in this case.

With Mrs. B, however, the situation was more complex. She evinced a disorder in which aggression was only the most dangerous and dramatic element. Plainly, she had incurred a brain injury at the time of the status epilepticus, an injury that involved at least limbic structures. That this is so is shown by the prominent memory disorder: amnestic syndromes indicate dysfunction in the limbic system. In addition, a more generalized brain injury seems to have been likely, with the loss of insight being a reflection, in part, of an organic affective change. A life-long personality disorder also continued to have clinical significance, though the role in the formation of that disorder played by the presence of brain disease in childhood and of epilepsy in particular was difficult to specify. All this was present, but as in Mr. C, overt violence was limited to the postictal period.

The issue of interictal violence is controversial. If there is an excess of aggressiveness in epileptics outside of the periictal period—and the epidemiology of this is far from secure (Stevens and Hermann, 1981)—then is it due to epilepsy itself or to the underlying brain damage? The answer is as important for theory as it is for social stigma. David Bear and his colleagues (Bear, 1989; Devinsky and Bear, 1984; Weiger and Bear, 1988) have argued that, as a part of the deepening emotionality of the temporal-lobe epileptic, temper becomes more difficult to control, and planful, organized aggression can be the result. Plainly, this is a very different matter from the abrupt, often confused aggressive outbursts discussed above. Bear's argument is based on the physiological notion that the limbic system is involved in attributing meaning to sensory stimuli. In the *hyperconnection* syndrome postulated to result from limbic seizure discharges, sensory stimuli are attached to "too much" meaning or to an inappropriate meaning. But all workers in the field agree that the full-blown syndrome of interictal personality change is uncommon (Bear, Hermann, and Fogel, 1989), and it has been shown that violent epileptics differ from their nonviolent peers in regard to many variables—demographic, psychiatric, and organic (Herzberg and Fenwick, 1988).

Still, that there may be a specific connection between temporal lobe epilepsy and interictal violence is suggested by an occasional compelling clinical example and by some experimental evidence. In a rat model, John Pinel and his colleagues (1977) have shown that rats with a kindled focus in the limbic system are more aggressive than control rats with similar operative interventions but without the kindling; this implies that the epileptic nature of the lesion is crucial. They are also more aggressive than control rats with kindled foci in the basal ganglia; this implies that the limbic location is crucial. These findings thus support the idea that the limbic epileptic process itself is associated with a behavioral predilection toward aggression. Martin Brutus and co-workers (1986) have shown that the induction of seizures in limbic areas alters thresholds for the elicitation of aggressive responses by hypothalamic stimulation. Interestingly, the direction of alteration in the threshold was dependent on whether the seizure was elicited from areas that facilitate or areas that inhibit aggressive behavior. Neil Griffith and his colleagues (1987) have investigated emotionality in cats in which a temporal-lobe epileptogenic lesion had been produced experimentally. Cats that had elements of rage behavior as part of their persisting seizures also showed heightened irritability interictally; any trivial provocation, such as pinching the skin, elicited rage attacks. This interesting finding indicates that specific ictal features, presumably mediated by specific anatomic and physiologic characteristics of the seizures, may be related to the individual's mode of relationship to the environment, including his propensity to respond with violence. It is irresistible to relate this finding to the clinical report by Bruce Hermann and others (1982) that patients with fear as a feature of their complex partial (psychomotor) seizures have a greater tendency to interictal psychopathology.

Unfortunately, greater pharmacological and physiological specificity about the nature of epileptic alterations is for the most part not available, certainly not for the individual clinical case. Such microanalysis of lesions and disease processes in their relationship to abnormal behavior is one of the research tasks of the future. Despite the value of studies such as these for increasing our understanding of the physiological mechanisms of disturbed behavior in human epilepsy, it is obvious that no animal experiment can answer the disputed epidemiological questions nor gainsay the importance of the other variables relevant in human beings.

Frontal-lobe Disease

Before his traumatic brain injury Mr. D, aged sixty-two, had worked productively as a carpenter and independent builder on small projects and had maintained close and positive relationships with a large extended family.

While he was inflating a tire on his truck, a defective wheel rim "exploded," and he sustained a severe injury from the impact of the tire and rim on his forehead. He remained in coma for three weeks after the injury. EEG and CT-scan findings were consistent with extensive, bilateral structural damage to the prefrontal cortex. Upon emerging from coma, the patient was disoriented, agitated, and episodically violent. Over the next fourteen months, he was rageful and combative four to ten times a day, with aggressive events accompanied by rageful affect lasting from several seconds to a half-hour. Between episodes, the patient was usually calm and compliant, though his cognitive impairment precluded full insight into his disorder. After a rage attack, he appeared bewildered rather than guilty. The slightest frustration, such as being given warm rather than cold orange juice by a nurse, could precipitate a violent outburst with dramatic alacrity. During the episodes, he would punch angrily and dangerously at whoever was nearby. On one occasion he swatted the medication tray from a nurse's hand and, in almost the same motion, knocked off her glasses and injured her eye. Moments before, he had been conversing calmly with the nurse.

This patient had an extensive lesion in the frontal neocortex. This area of the brain connects intimately with both the hypothalamus and the amygdala and is the neocortical representation of the limbic system. It has been shown in animals to influence lower centers that affect aggression (Siegel and Edinger,

1981, 1983). In man, lesions of the dorsolateral convexities of the frontal lobes are associated with apathy, decreased levels of activity, and reduced initiative. Lesions in the frontal neocortex involving orbital regions are associated with impulsivity, difficulties in modulating behavior on the basis of social cues, and problems understanding and evaluating the way one is perceived by others (Damasio, 1985; Eslinger and Damasio, 1985; Luria, 1980). The most famous clinical example is Phineas Gage, who in the nineteenth century was the victim of a penetrating wound in the orbitomedial region of his left frontal lobe. The result was that an orderly and ambitious young man became impulsive, used profanity, and did not have the ability to delay the gratifications of the present to achieve future objectives (Macmillan, 1986).

Also associated with lesions of the orbitofrontal cortex are sudden explosive outbursts of rage and aggressive behaviors in response to modest or even trivial provocations. Interestingly, when the rage and violence pass, some of these patients are puzzled, upset, and embarrassed by their outbursts. This behavior is in marked contrast to violence with predominantly characterologic underpinnings (such as that seen in individuals with antisocial or borderline personalities). In these latter cases, the blame for the violence is usually externalized: "I wouldn't have hit the man if he hadn't lied to me." This broad clinical generalization, useful as a rule of thumb, does not address the interesting question of what brain dysfunction, if any, mediates or leads to these characterologic abnormalities. Some have argued that frontal dysfunction, often subtle, is characteristic of aggression in antisocial personality disorder (Miller, 1987). The evidence is not compelling, but it does fit with the clinical impression of many who work with these difficult patients that some fundamental abnormality of information processing is often present.

Wendy Wieger and David Bear (1988) believe that individuals with orbitofrontal lesions are deficient in the ability to gauge the appropriate time, place, and strategy of response to environmentally elicited anger. They contrast the clinical picture of aggression resulting from orbitofrontal lesions with the interictal aggressive behavior of people with temporal-lobe epilepsy as follows: (1) people with temporal-lobe epilepsy are aggressive in response to what they perceive as a strong, even moral, provocation; whereas patients with orbitofrontal lesions respond to minor provocation; (2) patients with temporal-lobe epilepsy experience intense and sustained anger for which they may contrive elaborate complex responses extending over long periods of time, whereas patients with orbitofrontal lesions have brief bursts of anger at which times they take impulsive action; (3) individuals with temporal-lobe foci or lesions may express remorse subsequent to an aggressive act, whereas patients with orbitofrontal lesions are usually indifferent to their violent actions. This latter point is inconsistent with the clinical experience of the authors, who have seen patients with frontal lesions whose aggressive acts were profoundly ego-dystonic. We also believe that the ideational and contextual elements of orbitofrontal aggression are not always the key variables to the behavior. We and other investigators believe that the orbitofrontal regions of the brain may have a generalized modulating activity on deeper brain centers associated with rage and aggression. In man as well as in animal models, both diffuse lesions involving widespread neurons in the cerebral cortex and more focused lesions in the orbitofrontal area can impair this modulation and result in an abrupt and violent response to mild provocations. Common illnesses that may result in such diffuse damage to the frontal cortical area are traumatic brain injury, Alzheimer's disease, and stroke (Yudofsky, Silver, and Yudofsky, 1989). The rapidity with which the violent response follows the stimulus as well as the apparent replication of the condition in several animal models has led us to believe that the condition is not solely the result of impaired cognitions (for example, the absence of the ability to be self-critical).

In part, psychoanalysis arose from Freud's abandonment of physiology, with his movement from the *Project for a Scientific Psychology* to *The Interpretation of Dreams*. Ever since then, many in our field have been checking their watches to see if it is time for a rapprochement—some nervously, as if their own work would be threatened; some eagerly, as if a grand unification (a Theory Of Everything, as the physicists say) were at hand. Some workers, more bravely and more modestly, have attempted to sound out the possibility of a practical combination of psychoanalytic and neurobiological insight (Cooper, 1989, Levin, 1990).

We believe that a great deal of additional empirical work is necessary before definitive principles of the biological foundations of psychoanalysis can be enunciated. After all, these are not theoretical matters, to be decided on the basis of careful *thought;* they are empirical matters, to be decided on the basis of careful *observation.* Certainly, theoretical clarity is necessary, but as Jean-Martin Charcot said in much the same context, "La théorie, c'est bon, mais ça n'empèche pas d'exister" (Theory is fine, but it doesn't keep things from existing) (Freud, 1893). We believe that the observations cited in this chapter demonstrate that there are neuronal systems that organize aggressive behavior, systems that differ quantitatively among individuals but that are qualitatively similar among species. Such data place constraints on psychoanalytic theorizing about aggressive *drive,* for example. The inborn neuronal wiring to organize and display aggression *exists,* just as such hardware exists for feeding. To argue that there is no aggressive drive because frustration is required to elicit it, makes no more sense than to argue that there is no feeding drive because hunger is required to elicit it. Integrating this information into a comprehensive psychoanalytic formulation of instinct theory is a task beyond our scope in this chapter, and, we believe, beyond the scope of present science. Nonetheless, the theorist who ignores the neurobiologic data does so at his or her own peril.

In the case material and discussions presented here, we have emphasized cerebral dysfunction as a crucial determinant of clinical disorder. We stress again that we do not mean that patients with brain disease lack the human characteristics of reacting to their environments and of doing so in a way influenced by their personal histories. Indeed, insofar as cerebral disease means a regression from the more voluntary to the more automatic (in Hughlings-Jackson's phrase), history and the environment are the more potent and reflection is the less so.

We believe the material offers lessons to the neuropsychiatrist and the psychoanalyst alike. A simple one is the need for carefully described clinical material. Precise description of the neuroanatomy as seen by high-technology imaging is too often coupled with vague, incomplete, ambiguous, or stereotyped descriptions of the clinical phenomena and especially of patients' experiences. The result is that attempts to determine how the anatomy and physiology manifest themselves in the clinical phenomena founder. Psychoanalysts have much to teach their neuropsychiatric colleagues in this regard.

The neurobiological data concur with the findings of infant observation in demonstrating that temperamental factors—inborn constitutional proclivities and aversions—are important determinants of most behavior and of aggressive behavior in particular. Psychoanalysts who postulate a heightened inborn tendency to aggression as a factor in certain forms of psychopathology may find support in these biologic data (Kernberg, 1975). But a postulate is not a proof, and much more thought needs to be devoted to the devising of methods other than clinical observation for assessing temperament—assessing biologic proclivity short of the overt brain lesions we have discussed. Jerome Kagan (1989) has shown how autonomic measures, such as heart-rate variability, reflect stable temperamental characteristics that are associated with behavioral tendencies, for example, inhibitedness. It will be a major challenge of the next epoch of research to discover indicators of brain function that are inborn and stable with respect to experience, and to learn how these predispositions interact with experience in the course of development to determine behavior in adulthood. Practicality demands that we find measures that can be obtained noninvasively in adults. Although the measures to which Adamec, for example, has access in laboratory animals are many steps away from clinical utility, it is well within imagination that simple variables measured by neuroimaging or by electrophysiology will prove informative. If we can discover such indices, we will turn the "complemental series" that Freud (1916–17) postulated from a slogan into a scientific tool.

In "Instincts and Their Vicissitudes," Freud (1915) expressed his doubt that "any decisive pointers for the differentiation and classification of the instincts can be arrived at on the basis of working over the psychological material." Rather, "it would be a desirable thing if those assumptions could be taken from some other branch of knowledge." The clinical neurosciences are readying themselves to assist in such a process.

REFERENCES

Adamec, R. 1975. Behavioral and epileptic determinants of predatory attack behavior in the cat. *Can. J. Neurol. Sci.* 2:457–466.

———. 1990. Does the kindling model reveal anything clinically relevant? *Biol. Psychiat.* 27:249–279.

Adamec, R. E., and Stark-Adamec, Cannie. 1986. Partial kindling and behavioural change: Some rules governing behavioural outcome of repeated limbic seizures, in *Kindling*, vol. 3, ed. J. A. Wada, 195–211. New York: Raven Press.

Bear, David. 1989. Hierarchical neural regulation of aggression: Some predictable patterns of violence, in *Current approaches to the prediction of violence*, ed. D. A. Brizer and M. Crowner, 85–99. Washington, D.C.: American Psychiatric Press.

Bear, D., Hermann, Bruce, and Fogel, Barry. 1989. Interictal behavior syndrome in temporal lobe epilepsy: The views of three experts. *J. Neuropsychiatry Clin. Neurosci.* 1(3): 308–318.

Brutus, Martin, Shaikh, Majid B., Edinger, Henry, and Siegel, Allan. 1986. Effects of experimental temporal lobe seizures on hypothalamically elicited aggressive behavior in the cat. *Brain Res.* 366:53–63.

Caldecott-Hazard, Sally, and Engel, Jerome, Jr. 1987. Limbic postictal events: Anatomical substrates and opioid receptor involvement. *Prog. Neuro-Psychopharmacol. Biol. Psychiat.* 11:389–418.

Cooper, Arnold M. 1989. *Will neurobiology influence psychoanalysis?* in *Psychoanalysis: Toward the second century*, ed. A. M. Cooper, O. F. Kernberg, and E. S. Person. New Haven: Yale University Press.

Damasio, Antonio R. 1985. The frontal lobes, in *Clinical neuropsychology*, ed. K. M. Heilman and E. Valenstein, 339–375. New York: Oxford University Press.

Devinsky, Orrin, and Bear, David. 1984. Varieties of aggressive behavior in temporal lobe epilepsy. *Am. J. Psychiat.* 141(5): 651–656.

Dietz, Park Elliott. 1987. Patterns in human violence, in *American Psychiatric Association Annual Review*, ed. R. E. Hales and A. J. Frances, 465–490. Washington, D.C.: American Psychiatric Press.

Eslinger, Paul J., and Damasio, Antonio R. 1985. Severe disturbance of higher cognition after bilateral frontal lobe ablation: Patient EVR. *Neurol.* 35(12): 1731–1741.

Fenwick, Peter. 1986. *Is dyscontrol epilepsy?* in *What is epilepsy? The clinical and scientific basis of epilepsy*, ed. M. R. Trimble and E. H. Reynolds, 161–182. Edinburgh: Churchill Livingstone.

———. 1989. The nature and management of aggression in epilepsy. *J. Neuropsychiatry Clin. Neurosci.* 1(4): 418–425.

Freud, Sigmund. 1893. *Charcot*, in *S.E.* 3:7–23. London: Hogarth Press.

———. 1915. *Instincts and their vicissitudes*, in *S.E.* 14:109–14. London: Hogarth Press.

———. 1916–17. *Introductory lectures on psycho-analysis*, in *S.E.* 16. London: Hogarth Press.

Griffith, Neil, Engel, Jerome Jr., and Bandler, Richard. 1987. Ictal and enduring interictal disturbances in emotional behaviour in an animal model of temporal lobe epilepsy. *Brain Res.* 400:360–364.

Haugh, Robert M., and Markesbery, William R. 1983. Hypothalamic astrocytoma: Syndrome of hyperphagia, obesity, and disturbances of behavior and endocrine and autonomic function. *Arch. Neurol.* 40(9): 560–563.

Hermann, B. P., Dikman, S., Schwartz, M. S., and Karnes, W. E. 1982. Interictal psychopathology in patients with ictal fear: A quantitative investigation. *Neurol.* 32:7–11.

Herzberg, J. L., and Fenwick, P. B. C. 1988. The aetiology of aggression in temporal-lobe epilepsy. *Brit. J. Psychiat.* 153:50–55.

Kagan, Jerome. 1989. *Unstable ideas.* Cambridge: Harvard University Press.

Kennard, Christopher, and Swash, Michael. 1989. *Hierarchies in neurology: A reappraisal of a Jacksonian concept.* London: Springer-Verlag.

Kernberg, Otto F. 1975. *Borderline conditions and pathological narcissism.* New York: Jason Aronson.

Killeffer, Fred A., and Stern, W. Eugene. 1970. Chronic effects of hypothalamic injury. *Arch. Neurol.* 22(5): 419–429.

Kling, Arthur. 1972. Effects of amygdalectomy on social-affective behavior in non-human primates, in *The neurobiology of the amygdala,* ed. B. Eleftheriou, 511–536. New York: Plenum Press.

———. 1986. *The anatomy of aggression and affiliation,* in *Emotion: Theory, research, and experience,* ed. R. Plutchik and H. Kellerman, 237–264. Orlando: Academic Press.

Klüver, H., and Bucy, P. C. 1937. Psychic blindness and other symptoms following bilateral temporal lobectomy in rhesus monkeys. *Am. J. Physiol.* 119:352–353.

Levin, Fred M. 1990. Psychological development and the changing organization of the brain. *Annual of Psychoanalysis* 18:45–61.

Luria, Aleksander Romanovich. 1980. *Higher cortical functions in man,* rev. expanded ed. Trans. Basil Haigh. New York: Basic Books.

Macmillan, M. B. 1986. A wonderful journey through skull and brains: The travels of Mr. Gage's tamping iron. *Brain Cognition* 5:67–107.

Miller, Laurence. 1987. Neuropsychology of the aggressive psychopath: An integrative review. *Aggressive Behavior* 13:119–140.

Monroe, Russell R. 1970. *Episodic behavioral disorders: A psychodynamic and neurophysiologic analysis.* Cambridge: Harvard University Press.

Moyer, Kenneth E. 1987. *Violence and aggression: A physiological perspective.* New York: Paragon House.

Panksepp, Jaak. 1982. Toward a general psychobiological theory of emotions. *Behavioral Brain Sci.* 5:407–467.

———. 1985. Mood changes, in *Handbook of clinical neuropsychology,* vol. 45, ed. J. A. M. Frederiks, 271–285. Amsterdam: Elsevier.

Pinel, John P. J., Treit, Dallas, and Rovner, Louis I. 1977. Temporal lobe aggression in rats. *Sci.* 197:1088–1089.

Poeck, Klaus. 1985. *The Kluver-Bucy syndrome in man,* in *Clinical neuropsychology,* ed. J. A. M. Frederiks, 257–263. Amsterdam: Elsevier.

Reeves, Alexander G., and Plum, Fred. 1969. Hyperphagia, rage, and dementia accompanying a ventromedial hypothalamic neoplasm. *Arch. Neurol.* 20(6):616–624.

Sheard, Michael H. 1984. Clinical pharmacology of aggressive behavior. *Clin. Neuropharm.* 7(3): 173–183.

———. 1988. Clinical pharmacology of aggressive behavior. *Clin. Neuropharm.* 11(6): 483–492.

Siegel, Allan, and Edinger, Henry. 1981. *Neural control of aggression and rage behavior,* in *Behavioral studies of the hypothalamus,* ed. P. J. Morgane and J. Panksepp, 303–340. New York: Marcel Dekker.

———. 1983. Role of the limbic system in hypothalamically elicited attack behavior. *Neurosci. Biobehav. Rev.* 7(3): 395–407.

Stevens, Janice R., and Hermann, Bruce P. 1981. Temporal lobe epilepsy, psychopathology, and violence: The state of the evidence. *Neurol.* 31(9): 1127–1132.

Weiger, W. A., and Bear, D. M. 1988. An approach to the neurology of aggression. *J. Psychiat. Res.* 22(2): 85–98.

Wieser, H. G. 1983. Depth recorded limbic seizures and psychopathology. *Neurosci. Biobehav. Rev.* 7(3): 427–440.

Yudofsky, S., Williams, D., and Gorman, J. 1981. Propranolol in the treatment of rage and violent behavior. *Am. J. Psychiat.* 138:218–220.

Yudofsky, S. C., Silver, J., and Yudofsky, B. 1989. Organic personality disorder, explosive type, in *Treatment of psychiatric disorders*. Washington, D.C.: American Psychiatric Press.

Yudofsky, S. C., Silver, J. M., Jackson, M., Endicott, J., and Williams, D. 1986. The Overt Aggression Scale: An operationalized rating scale for verbal and physical aggression. *Am. J. Psychiat.* 143:35–39.

IV

Historical and
Political Expressions

Finally, we move to *Historical and Political Expressions* of rage, power, and aggression. Applying psychoanalytic understanding to areas of human experience beyond clinical process demands critical attention to levels of abstraction and meaningfulness of observations. Psychoanalysis has been a rich and productive interpretive frame for history, literature, and political science. Psychoanalysts tend to view prominent cultural themes as broad-stroke expressions of individual psychology, as projections on the big scene of the intrapsychic world of representations and conflicts. Our myths of the gods and understandings of politics reflect features of our omnipotent fantasies and fears. Deeply rooted in the human character, our concerns with power and dominance surround us.

Elaine Pagels, in "The Rage of Angels," traces the transformation of early divine and demonic expressions of rage into the righteous wrath and fears of evil that characterized religious myths. For the early pagans, Babylonian, Egyptian, and Greek, the gods were rageful and destructive for reasons of their own. If provoked, they struck. To the Hebrews and early Christians, moral righteous wrath emerged from amoral godly rage. The righteous god was good and the demonic devil evil. With such a split, humanity's relations to the gods and their role in the life of people and their history changed.

In "Power," Kenneth Thompson suggests that on the geopolitical scale, powerlessness and vulnerability parallel the individual wish for power. Safety is the measure of the success of the political power structure. Nations, like people, can be seen as anxious and fearful, threatened and dangerous. Nations pursue safety through the exercise of power in what Thompson calls the "security power dilemma." Here the pursuit of safety through power and dominance can create and perpetuate new fears and threats to safety. By humanizing political power relations, Thompson describes crucial historical events and the power processes that characterize the conflicts and aspirations of nations as well as people.

12

The Rage of Angels

ELAINE PAGELS

As a historian of religion, what I have to share consists of notes on cultural changes in the interpretation of rage, power, and aggression. For as I began to reflect on these themes, I noticed elements I had never seen before in some of the sources most familiar to me; and I saw, too, certain shifts in the shaping of these themes from pagan to Jewish tradition, and from Jewish to Christian tradition.

Since I was looking for ancient psychology, I decided to look for it, as Freud and many others did, in sources of mythology and theology. What I offer here is a brief sketch of what I found—which, in brief, is this: first, that while pagan stories—Babylonian, Egyptian, and Greek—tend to depict their gods expressing (among many other emotions) undifferentiated rage, Jewish sources tend instead to moralize anger, dividing it into *rage* (which is bad) and *righteous wrath* (which is good). Next, I found that Christian sources increase this tendency: they not only moralize anger but insist that Christians inhibit its expression, while simultaneously projecting it onto God, who they expect will avenge them in the future. Third, I saw that by these means they—Christians, that is, like Jews before them and Muslims after them—demonize whoever opposes them (a fact with enormous social and political consequences, to say nothing of psychological ones).

On the first point, let's take as an example the Babylonian creation account—a story well known to Jews living under Babylonian rule and one that deeply influenced the Genesis account of creation. In Babylonian, Egyptian, and Greek mythology, as I have said, the gods are assumed to express a full range of emotion, from erotic desire and parental protectiveness to terrifying rage. Because the gods are known to be capricious, these myths show little attempt to account for shifts in divine mood; the shifts are assumed to be as natural and spontaneous as thunderstorms. Thunderstorms, of course, were often taken as manifestations of divine rage, since what we call "natural forces" are precisely what these myths regard as divine forces. Greek story-tellers seemed to take for granted that Zeus's temper could change in an instant from the sunny skies of genial hospitality to raging storms, lightning, and thunder—even volcanic eruptions. As one anthropologist recently observed, such disasters, to those who suffer from them, often feel like punishment; and it is these catastrophes that often evoked stories of divine rage.

According to the Babylonian creation account, all things began when the mother of all, the oceanic waters, called Tiamat, mingled with the fresh waters, called Apsu, the father of all; and the union of these waters brought forth the race of the gods, including Marduk, the sun god. But Apsu, finding his sleep disturbed day and night by the shrieking of his children, the young gods, was aroused to violent rage against them; so that when he was advised to murder them all, "his face grew radiant with joyful relief" (Enuma elish, 89.1). But the children, warned by their grandfather, succeeded in murdering their father first; whereupon their mother turned against them in rage and, together with her chief adviser, now her lover, gathered a horrifying army of serpent-headed monsters and set out to fight the armies led by her son. Marduk finally locked with her in single combat, split her apart "like a shellfish" (ibid., 109), and created this world out of her dismembered body.

This, of course, is a rather straightforward account of what contemporary jargon might call a dysfunctional family. Similar accounts describe other forces and phenomena essential to human life—oceans, sun, rain, and winds—whose destructiveness matches and alternates with their benevolence, corresponding to the Babylonians' experience of nature).

Turning, then, to Jewish tradition, we can see how, by contrast, it moralized divine rage. Compare, for example, that raging and murderous Babylonian father god to the solicitous and paternal creator described in Genesis who manifests anger only when his children disobey his explicit (if inexplicable) rules. Yet other elements of Jewish tradition demonstrate the tensions involved as storytellers wrestled with concerns similar to those expressed in the Babylonian story: When natural disasters occur, are they not expressions of divine rage? What do they express, if not arbitrary and capricious outbursts? Jewish tradition had tried to banish the raging gods of the pagans—gods like Apsu or the Egyptian goddess Sekmet, who went on a rampage, slaughtering humans indiscriminately, until the other gods finally stopped her by getting her drunk. Jewish storytellers tended instead to rationalize and moralize God's anger, to insist that God's rage—let's call it his wrath—evinces neither irritability nor frustration, much less arbitrary violence, but only his righteous anger. Although they admitted that their God could be jealous, impetuous, and even violent, they usually insisted that he acted only to administer just punishment on those who deserved it.

Consider, for example, the well-known story in Genesis that tells how

Abraham argued with God when he heard God intended to destroy Sodom and Gomorrah by raining down hot lava on them in a volcanic eruption (the God of Israel began, after all, as a volcano god at Mount Sinai). The moralizing narrator insists that what moved God to act was his outrage at the men of those towns who committed homosexual rape on a party of defenseless Jewish travelers. Still, Abraham dared to challenge (and even, apparently, to try to shame) God: What about the innocent people who would be destroyed along with the guilty?

> Wilt thou, indeed, destroy the righteous along with the wicked? Suppose there are fifty righteous men in the city; wilt thou then destroy the place and not spare it for the sake of the fifty righteous who are in it? Far be it from thee to do such a thing—to kill the righteous along with the wicked, so that the righteous fare no better than the wicked. Far be that from thee! Shall not the judge of all the earth do right? (Gen. 18:23–25)

God began by conceding to Abraham that he would spare the towns if he found fifty righteous men among them (women and children did not figure into this equation). Abraham bargained with God and finally succeeded in getting the number reduced to ten, but apparently there were less than nine righteous men in these towns because volcanic eruptions did, in fact, annihilate both towns. Following the logic of moralism, the narrator insists that all the men of Sodom had participated collectively in the crime, "both young and old, all the people, down to the last man" (Gen. 19:4).

God, then, is supposed to express, even in his most aggressive acts, only righteous anger, even against his own people. The story of the Exodus indicates how often violent anger characterized the relationship between Moses, the God he claimed to represent, and the people he had led out of Egypt. Finding that the people had turned to the worship of local gods while Moses was away on Mount Sinai, the Lord's wrath "burned hot against them" (Ex. 32:10), and he told Moses that he intended to kill them all and start a new nation from Moses and his family alone. Moses persuaded the Lord to spare the people's lives, but when he himself descended and saw evidence of their idolatry, Moses' "anger burned hot, and he threw the tablets out of his hands and broke them at the foot of the mountain" (Ex. 32:19). Moses immediately ordered all the men of the Levite tribe to arm themselves with swords, "and every man kill his brother, his companion, and his neighbor" (Ex. 32:27); they obeyed him and massacred three thousand people on a single day. This accomplished, Moses returned to the Lord. First he acknowledged the people's fault, but then Moses threatened not only to quit his position as the Lord's spokesman should God destroy the present nation, but he refused God's offer to make him the father of a new nation. In a marvelously terse, unfinished sentence, Moses declares, "But now, if thou will forgive them—and if not, blot me out of the book which thou hast written" (Ex. 32:31).

Yet other episodes and passages in the Hebrew Bible betray apparently unmotivated, darker perceptions of God's use of power. According to Exodus, Moses himself was well aware of this, for his own story includes such an episode. After God ordered him to go to Pharaoh to demand the release of his people, Moses set off. On the way, the Lord "met [Moses] at an inn, and tried to kill him"; but Moses' quick-witted wife, Zipporah, took a flint and cut off their son's foreskin, and touched Moses' feet with it, saying, "Surely you are my bridegroom in blood!" (Ex. 4:24–26).[1] Because of this God spared Moses' life. The point of the story, apparently, is to show that circumcision protects Israelites from the kind of sudden death to which the Egyptians are subject. This puzzling story, however, depicts the Lord as the kind of god who might suddenly, for no reason, kill his most trusted emissary.

The poem of Job, too, sometimes describes God as a being as dangerous as any Apsu or Sekmet: "He has torn me in his rage, and hated me; he has gnashed his teeth at me; my adversary sharpens his eyes against me. He seized me by the neck and dashed me to pieces; he set me up as his target, his archers surround me. He slashes open my kidneys, and does not spare me; he pours out my blood on the ground" (Job 16:9–13). Such discrepancies in Jewish images of God led Freud to posit two separate traditions; we now realize that many traditions merged in what we now call the Hebrew Bible. Yet increasingly, as time passed, Jewish traditions tended to divide anger into two qualitatively distinct phenomena, differentiated by moral judgment. On the one hand, there is anger in the form of rage, perceived as malevolent, violent, destructive, and entirely evil—which typically characterizes the anger of others toward oneself (or, speaking collectively, anger directed toward Israel). Thus, the psalmist asks, "Why do the nations rage so furiously together, against the Lord, and against his messiah [the king of Israel]?" (Ps. 2:1).

On the other hand, and virtually at an opposite pole, is one's own anger toward one's enemies (or toward the enemies of Israel): For to the question just quoted, the same psalmist retorts, "He who sits in the heavens laughs at them; the Lord holds them in contempt. Then he will speak to them in his wrath, and terrify them in his fury" (Ps. 2:4–5). Recall, too, that the nostalgic psalm that begins, "by the rivers of Babylon we sat down and wept," concludes with violent threats against the Babylonian conquerors: "Happy shall be he who takes your infant children and dashes their heads against the rock!" (Ps. 137:1–9). This, of course, is not rage but righteous anger, which God presumably shares.

Turning to Christian tradition, we see that after the Babylonians devastated Jerusalem, killing and exiling many of its citizens, certain Jews asked, Can all this catastrophe be divinely inflicted punishment? Whence comes undeserved

---

1. The story and its meaning remain a puzzle: some scholars have suggested that Zipporah circumcised Moses and so protected him; some suggest that she smeared him with their son's blood, either to protect their firstborn son from the angel of death or to use his blood to protect Moses, since the blood of the Passover lamb was said to protect other Israelites from being slaughtered.

suffering? Although their tradition banished all other gods from the heavens and from the ranks of the divine, certain Jewish storytellers began to suspect that there must be, nevertheless, spiritual forces that are either ambivalent or malevolent—forces that act contrary to divine justice. Who are these, then? Whence comes God's opposition? Since Jews acknowledged only one God, commander in chief of all angels, and modeled these angels either on the ranks of the army or the imperial administration, they reasoned that these hostile spiritual powers must originally have been members of that angelic army, or even trusted members of God's royal court. From such speculation comes the incongruity inherent in the title of this chapter: The Rage of Angels. Angels are not supposed to rage, but obviously some do; and some, apparently attempting to gain power over human beings, maliciously inflict harm.

How, then, did the bad angels become hostile, aggressive, and destructive? Jewish sources developed two theories (with considerable variation) of the psychogenesis of angelic rage. The first involves sibling rivalry, a theory articulated by the devil himself in a popular second-century Jewish text, *The Life of Adam and Eve.* Here Adam challenges the devil, asking, "What have I done to you? Why do you pursue us, since you have received from us no harm or injury?" The devil replies, "Adam, what are you saying to me? It was because of you that I have been cast down from there. When you were made, I was cast out of God's presence and excluded." The devil goes on to relate that when God made Adam, he ordered the angels to bow down to this newest creation. Michael obeyed but Satan refused, and when pressured, he burst out, "Why do you press me? I will not worship one who is younger than I am, and inferior; I am older than he; he ought to worship me!" Satan replies that the Lord God "was angry with me, and banished me together with my angels because of you; and we were grievously distressed to see you enjoying your pleasures so much" (Anon., ca. 150 C.E., cited in Charlesworth, 1985). Islamic tradition epitomized the devil's defiance in his words "I am better than he" (than Adam, that is); and the devil goes on to say, "By God, truly if he has given preference to this thing over me, I surely will defy him. And if I am put in charge of Adam, then I will destroy him" (Awn, 1975). The second theory about Satan's fall involves insubordination in the form of a military coup by one of the angelic captains, who, jealous of his commander in chief, initiated a rebellion in heaven. Whichever version one chooses, our worst enemy is not, as we might expect, an outsider, a stranger, or an alien. It is rather one's closest associate, either a relative (or older brother) or trusted colleague—one whose loyalty and goodwill are essential to family and social life but who turns unexpectedly hostile, jealous, and dangerous.

At the time of Jesus, certain radical groups of Jews living under Roman occupation believed their afflictions to be evidence that Satan and his armies had gained control over the earth, oppressing and enslaving the human race while waging cosmic war against God (*The Dead Sea Scriptures,* ed. Vermes).

The followers of Jesus come from one such splinter group, and so (as they tell it), Jesus' activity began when God's power descended on him at his baptism (Mark 1:9; Luke 3:21–22). Jesus began to challenge Satan's power over humanity—power evinced in disease, paralysis, blindness, insanity, and similar afflictions—and so he incurred Satan's implacable wrath. The gospels say that before Jesus began his public activity, Satan had appeared to him and challenged him to single-handed combat in the desert. There Satan offered Jesus all the power and glory of the kingdoms of this world. Jesus resisted and defeated Satan; and, Luke says, the evil one "departed from him, until an opportune time" (Luke 4:13). After this, Satan apparently chose to work through human agents, or at any rate, that is how the gospel writers tried to account for the violent anger that Luke reports Jesus aroused the very first time he spoke out in his hometown synagogue at Nazareth. According to Luke, after Jesus had been invited by the synagogue leaders to read a passage from the prophet Isaiah, he commented on the passage briefly, but so effectively that "all those in the synagogue were filled with rage, and they rose up and threw him out of the city, and took him to the edge of the cliff on which their city had been built, to throw him down the precipice" (Luke 4:29).

But Jesus escaped and so survived the first attempt on his life. Soon afterward, however, he dared to heal a man in a synagogue on the Sabbath, and the synagogue leaders, beside themselves with fury, "discussed with one another what they might do to [kill] Jesus." Responding to those who would regard Jesus as an obvious undesirable (since Roman and Jewish leaders alike treated him as a potentially dangerous criminal), his followers adopted the theory of cosmic war to interpret the resistance he encountered, as well as the violent controversy his presence aroused among his contemporaries. Jesus himself recognized this, for, Luke says, he asked rhetorically, "Do you think I have come to bring peace on earth? No, I tell you, but rather division; for from now on in one house there will be five divided, three against two and two against three; father against son, and son against father; mother against daughter, and daughter against mother" (Luke 12:49). Meanwhile, the accounts of the New Testament, like the story of Abraham's argument with God, thoroughly moralize the anger that pervades them like a dark and constant presence. Jesus himself, according to the gospel of Matthew, actually forbids his followers to express (or, it may be, even experience) anger, treating it as tantamount to murder: "You have heard that it was said to the men of old, 'You shall not kill; and whoever kills shall be liable to judgment.' But I say to you that every one who is angry with his brother shall be liable to judgment; whoever verbally abuses his brother shall be liable to the council; and whoever says, 'you fool!' shall be liable to the hell of fire" (Matt. 5:21–22).

Jesus himself is never explicitly described as angry, although this certainly seems implied when he attacks his opponents with such vituperative words as these: "You serpents, you brood of vipers; how can you escape being sentenced to hell?" (Matt. 23:33). Such anger is also implied in the events that precipitated his arrest. On entering the temple at Jerusalem during Passover, Jesus took a whip made from cords and drove out those who were selling animals for sacrifice and the moneychangers, overturning tables and scattering their money on the ground (Mark 11:15–18; Luke 19:45–46; John 2:13–19). Jesus' followers described this, of course, as righteous anger; but they characterized the response of the outraged temple leaders as satanically inspired rage, which ended in Jesus' execution. Luke says that as the chief priests were "seeking how to put [Jesus] to death" (Luke 22:2–3), Satan himself initiated Jesus' arrest by entering into Jesus' disciple Judas Iscariot, inspiring him to betray Jesus (Matt. 26:24–25; 27:24–26). Yet Luke insists that Satan's participation did not exempt either Judas or the Jewish leaders from the blame they deserved. Jesus' followers took for granted that God shared their anger. Thirty years later, when the Romans besieged Jerusalem, massacred thousands of people, desecrated the temple, and reduced it to rubble, Christians attributed these catastrophes to God's anger over Jesus' execution (Matt. 27:24–26).[2] According to Matthew, Jesus himself foretold this in a parable comparing God to a great king who, after several of his servants were killed, "was angry, and he sent his troops and destroyed those murderers and burned their city" (Matt. 22:7).

These Christian sources, then, while explicitly enjoining Christians to eradicate anger, simultaneously encourage Christians who encounter hostile resistance to hope that God will soon annihilate their enemies. One final vision of Jesus in the New Testament, in fact, given in the book of Revelation, depicts him returning on horseback to judge the earth and to kill his enemies. His eyes flashing with fire, he comes dressed in a robe dipped in blood, leading the armies of heaven: "From his mouth issues a sharp sword, and he will tread the winepress of the fury and the wrath of God the all powerful" (Rev. 19:11–16). In this vision, after Jesus kills his enemies with the sword, an angel shouts an invitation to all the carrion birds to "come, gather for the great supper of God" to eat the corpses of the slaughtered men and their slain horses (Rev. 19:17–18).

It is no wonder, then, that the Christian movement in the ancient world appealed most to people who were socially and politically disadvantaged—to slaves and women—for whom Jesus' counsel to suppress anger was probably necessary and expedient (Pagels, 1988, chap. 2). Yet Christian tradition also promised that God would soon "rain down coals of fire" upon their enemies. (The apostle Paul advised Christians in Rome: "Never avenge yourselves, but leave it to the wrath of God; for, it is written, 'Vengeance is mine; I will repay, says the Lord.' No, 'if your enemy is hungry, feed him; if he is thirsty, give him drink; for by doing so you will heap burning coals upon his head' " [Rom.

2. Jesus followers read Matt. 27:24–26 as evidence that the people of Jerusalem had cursed themselves—and sealed their own fate—in advocating Jesus' execution. This gospel was written about twenty years after the destruction of Jerusalem in 66–70 C.E.

12:19–20].) Paul explains that sometimes such behavior will win over one's enemies. Conversely, when it fails to do so, it will add to the enemy's culpability on the coming day of judgment, that is, heap coals on his head.) Finally, the Christian movement (as noted, like Jewish tradition before it and Islamic tradition since) succeeded in demonizing the opposition. We can see the enormous consequences of this from medieval times, when Christians demonized Jews and Muslims, who in turn did the same to them and to one another.

Consider, for example, how Martin Luther, the founder of Protestant Christianity, denounced as "offspring of Satan" everyone who opposed him. First, Luther bitterly denounced "the Jews and their lies" in a railing pamphlet; he then attacked as Satan's henchmen all who protested the power of the landowning rulers by participating in the Peasants' War. Third, he denounced as agents of Satan not only the pope himself and all Christians who remained loyal to the Roman Catholic church, but virtually all other so-called protesting (Protestant) Christians who disagreed with Luther's version of reformation (Oberman, 1990).

What is important is that the persistent power of such imagery does not depend on actually believing in God or Satan. Whether one believes or not, images of cosmic war—that is, world events read in terms of a conflict between forces of good and forces of evil—have nurtured countless movements, political and social, religious and some that are explicitly antireligious.

Many sophisticated people tend to dismiss these images as mere rhetorical flourishes. On the contrary, I suggest that such apocalyptic imagery has deeply, and often unconsciously (and more powerfully *because* they are unconscious), shaped the way millions of people experience their own anger and aggression. Consequently, these images have determined how people respond—even today—to social and political events. Satan remains a pervasive, although subliminal figure, in the way we tend to characterize opposition. Not for nothing did Churchill call Hitler "the devil," or Ronald Reagan denounce the "evil empire," and receive in turn the Ayatollah's denunciation as the "Great Satan."

Finally, we may well ask ourselves why Christians turned to the devil and demons to interpret such phenomena as anger and aggression. Although this topic is much too large to discuss here, I propose three practical functions of demons.

First: by identifying whatever outsiders said as demonically inspired (whether overtly friendly or hostile), Christians reinforce their determination to resist any appeals or threats from family, friends, or government officials that try to pressure them into abandoning their profession of Christianity. Consider, for example, the case of Perpetua, an educated, aristocratic twenty-two-year-old married Roman woman with an infant son nursing at her breast, arrested in the African city of Carthage on charges of professing Christianity—a capital crime that involved the charge of treason against

Rome. Perpetua wrote a diary in prison in which she describes the fierce heat, crowding, and stench of the African prison, as well as the terrible threat of torture and impending execution. She includes in her diary various dreams, including one of "a golden ladder of marvelous height, reaching up to heaven . . . and on the sides of the ladder weapons attached . . . swords, lances, hooks and daggers, so that if anyone went up carelessly . . . he would be torn to pieces. . . . And underneath the ladder was crouching a dragon, monstrous in size, who lay in wait for those who ascended, and terrified them" (*Martyrdom*, 202 C.E., in Musurillo, ch. 4, 1972). But as Perpetua started up the ladder, she stepped on the dragon's (Satan's) head, and finally, as she reached the top, she met a kindly, white-haired old man who welcomed her as a daughter and fed her milk and honeycake. As soon as she awoke, she writes, she reported this dream to her brother, "and we understood that [our fate] was to be suffering, and we ceased from then on to have any hope in this world."

Perpetua tells how her own father, "worn out with anxiety," came to the prison repeatedly to plead with her as his favorite child ("I have loved you more than all of your brothers") to consider her brothers, her mother, her aunt, and her infant son: "Put aside your pride; you will kill all of us. For none of us will ever be able to speak freely again if you suffer." Perpetua says that "my father said these things in his affection, kissing my hands, throwing himself at my feet . . . and I grieved over him" (ibid., chap. 2). She also "realized," however, that the devil was speaking through her father, using their relationship to weaken her resolve. Thus, with considerable difficulty, she rejected his pleas, and accepted instead torture and execution in the city's sports arena, becoming part of the public entertainment provided to celebrate the emperor Geta's birthday in the year 202.

Second: Christians who saw their opponents as demon-inspired could nevertheless regard them not simply, or not necessarily, as enemies, but as people duped, deceived, and victimized by Satan. This perception enabled Christians to appeal to their persecutors, offering to convert and liberate them (much as American Communists in the earlier decades of this century addressed their opponents as people unwittingly duped by capitalist propaganda).

Third: besides social and political functions, demonology developed as a language to describe conflicting impulses (especially those urging one to anger, pride, lust, envy, hatred, or greed). Throughout the centuries, Christians and Muslims developed extensive collections of stories about the interaction of humans with demons—the literature of what they called "spiritual formation" (what might be called *psychodynamics*). Here, of course, another enormous topic suggests itself: how Christians and Muslims developed various perceptions of demons as their intimate—and to some extent interiorized—companions, with whom they contended as "sparring partners" in the internal warfare they called *asceticism*. Monastic literature describes ascesis as the struggle for mastery in a psychospiritual sport most often described in the language of wrestling. Such traditions articulated a vast and subtle range of psychological observations, for, as the Sufi Muslims say, every person has his (and in this case I'm sure they would be glad to add, and *her*) own *satan*, "and he is as near to us as our bloodstream" (ibid., chap. 2).

REFERENCES

Awn, P. 1975. *Iblīs: Satan's tragedy and redemption.* Leiden. An excellent discussion of Satan perceived as an intrapsychic phenomenon in Sufi literature.
Charlesworth, J. L., ed. 1985. *The Old Testament Pseudepigrapha,* vol. 2. New York.
Knibb, M. A. 1987. *The Qûmvan Community.* Cambridge University Press.
Musurillo, H. 1972. *The acts of the Christian martyrs.* Oxford University Press.
Oberman, H. A. 1990. *Luther: Between God and the devil.* New Haven: Yale University Press.
Pagels, E. 1988. *Adam, Eve, and the serpent.* New York: Random House.

13

Power

KENNETH W. THOMPSON

Attitudes toward Power

Current thinking about power, especially as an aspect of international politics, has been influenced by four historic attitudes in Western society. The first treats power as a human being's highest end in life and the noblest expression of human potential. It is a viewpoint that sanctifies and glorifies power, whether for the individual or the group. The individual's fulfillment and self-realization is dependent on the domination of other people; it is in a person's nature to seek domination. In this view, the best in human nature emerges when one person seeks dominion over others. History's most compelling lesson is the survival of the fittest.

The German romanticists and those philosophers who hold this view of power, however, assert that religion and culture stand in the way of the attainment of the deepest aspects of a person's nature. Religious and humanitarian creeds shelter and protect the weak and perpetuate the lives of the infirm and the disabled. Even the Good Samaritan does a disservice by sustaining those who lack the inner resources to maintain themselves. This version of power, which some have called the idolatry of the strong, reached its most powerful expression philosophically in Friedrich Nietzsche. The most blatant form of this view is extreme nationalism. Its ultimate corruption came with the doctrine of national socialism and Adolf Hitler's conception of a superior teutonic race. Der Führer went Darwinism one better not only by celebrating an existing superior race but by calling for artificial and coercive methods for breeding a new one. Hitler freed his followers from all the restraints of religion and culture and gave them incentives to rise to ever higher levels of self-realization. As for the state, the great German philosopher Georg Hegel had argued that "the root kernel of the doctrine" was "the idea of a state, which ought to form one nation . . . [and] should be brought to realization by . . . all the methods necessary for that purpose" (Meinecke, 1984, 358).

A second attitude toward power has been particularly popular at times in the United States. In effect, it represents a denial or outlawry of power and power politics. It sees political power as an archaism or a transient condition of politics. Modern reformist and rationalist thought looks on power politics as a product of the European state system, which is a condition of nations crowded together in a conflict-ridden continent. The drama now is one between two main sets of actors, Europeans and Americans. An attack on the practice and reality of power politics comes naturally to Americans, who escaped the Old World to seek freedom in the New. They have shaken the dust of Europe from their feet and begun a new life. They see themselves as a chosen people arriving on the shores of a promised land, which for them is a new Jerusalem. Early on, their leaders had warned of becoming embroiled in Europe's ancient struggles and conflicts. The first president (and others) had spoken out against "entangling alliances." Europe's affairs were not our affairs and its historic rivalries were not our concern. We were shielded from danger by a vast ocean and by the protection of the British navy.

A century and a half later, Secretary of State Cordell Hull, returning from the Moscow Conference, heralded the United Nations as a new international institution that would do away with alliances, and balance-of-power and traditional power politics. He explained that he had studied the history of international relations and it was power politics that had brought about conflict and war. In a new and better world, ancient forms of international relationships would be eradicated by a system of law and world order.

A more subtle and less direct approach to the denial of power and power politics occurred with the rise of the middle class in modern industrial societies. Representatives of the middle class were proclaimed to be the carriers of democracy and freedom. They had triumphed over aristocracy; it seemed plausible to suggest that power politics belonged to the aristocracy and to aristocratic government. The greatest practitioners of diplomacy and power politics had, after all, been members of the aristocracy. With the supplanting of the aristocracy by democracy, power politics would come to an end.

A third attitude is one that sees power as wholly a result of economics. Marxists have argued that power politics are the result of the underlying means of production. In the feudal era, lords and rulers exercised dominion over their vassals; the bourgeoisie, in the name of capitalism dominated, the working class. As the historical process unfolds, the proletariat will replace the means of production. In the feudal era, lords and rulers exercised dominion over their vassals; the bourgeoisie, in the name of capitalism, dominated the state will wither away" and a classless society be ushered in. In Marx's oft-quoted phrase: the domination of man by man will yield to the administration of things. Power in our day is therefore a product of capitalism.

A fourth attitude views power as essentially an ongoing psychological relationship. Power is universal in the political relations of human beings and nations. Whatever a person's ultimate ends, he or she will use power in organized society to seek that end. Power can be channeled within a constitutional framework where it can be held in check by the separation of powers and countervailing power. Power, itself, however, does not disappear. It is present at every level of society and in all the communities of humankind except in remote primitive societies and constitutes a perennial factor in politics. No one has found a way to translate this nondiscriminating, generalized power into the world of the modern nation-state system. Power manifests itself in the relation of mind to mind or will to will. It has a lasting and universal relationship among people and nations.

Manifestations of Power

Thus power is said to be universal in modern societies. Scholars write of the ubiquity of power. It takes on at least four manifestations that analysts and statespeople have identified and evaluated. First, power is but one dimension of the human condition. The quest for dominion is deeply rooted in human striving; it is associated with creativity and dynamism, strength of character, and personality. It is a product of the spirit and creatureliness of man. It comes into play when soaring dreams and vaulting ambitions confront practical realities, for power is the mediator between dreams and realities.

"Pride and ambition," Winston Churchill explained, "are the prod of every worthy deed." The quest for dominion is the pathway to realizing values and goals and to controlling one's environment. In the simplest language, power involves taking charge. When the violinist Isaac Stern was asked the secret of being a great creative performing artist, he responded, "He must dominate his audience." He went on to say that from the moment the artist appears on stage, he or she must help the audience to know that the artist is in command of himself (or herself), of the music, and of them. If they have any doubt of the competence or the confidence of the artist, his or her presence must reassure them.

In politics, we speak of the charismatic leader; he or she, too, is in command. Wherever such a person is found, all eyes turn to him (her). Whenever present, he or she takes a place at the center of the discussion. Conversation flows to her (or him). (One criticism of the outstanding Democratic candidate for president in the 1950s, Gov. Adlai Stevenson of Illinois, was that as a member of various groups he was most often on the periphery in discussions rather than at the head of the table.)

For commanding leaders, an element of mystery persists about their power. As speakers, they may not employ the best grammar. For example, President Dwight D. Eisenhower's press conference answers often appeared garbled and confused, and he may not have been the most experienced executive or best-educated person as measured by formal education. Friends marveled at the warm and admiring relationship between the largely self-educated Harry S. Truman and his Groton-educated secretary of state, Dean Acheson. Yet those present when the president recounted the story of his political career to a group of some of the most powerful people in America at the New York Council of Foreign Relations were introduced to the sources of his strength. At first the audience of diplomats, bankers, and scholars sat back in their chairs slightly embarrassed by his simple, unabashed story of a first visit to Europe following his presidency. When he began describing his great foreign policy decisions of a fifteen-week period in 1946, everyone leaned forward in their chairs. They discovered then why Acheson and his colleagues had such respect for the little man from Missouri who knew where the buck stopped.

Yet viewed more broadly, the mystery remains. Some of America's greatest leaders, including George Washington, have resisted the ascent to power or cast it aside after briefly exercising it. Others, such as Richard Daley, Chicago's longtime mayor, have tried to avoid tests of power and are remembered for homey phrases like, "Don't make no waves, don't rock no boats." Some presidents, including Jimmy Carter, have come from small states without much national experience or power; others, such as Ronald Reagan, have had unusual backgrounds in preparation for political power. Apparently, neither youth, represented by John F. Kennedy, nor old age, represented by Ronald Reagan, qualify or disqualify men and women from the exercise of power. Culture and circumstances, however, may shape the environment within which power holders are chosen, as in China, where ancestor worship and respect for ancestors influence the public's response to aging leaders. Leadership and success in acquiring power sometimes move in cycles. It seems that for everything there is a time and a season. Kennedy's call for a new generation of leaders to take the torch of power followed the era of an aging hero-president, Eisenhower.

A second manifestation of power is in its link with anxiety and insecurity. We seek power in part to overcome fear and anxiety. Power is a function of a person's response to powerlessness. Human beings and nations are anxious about their insecurity and secretly fearful of their limitations and vulnerability. The macho image and the cultivation of feminine charms are especially visible responses to anxiety. Men and women search for security through power, hoping to enhance self-esteem and individual autonomy, but the search is unending and the dilemma insoluble at every point in life. Children seek security by reaching out for greater independence and power hoping to find an answer to the timeless question, "Who am I?" Parents respond with efforts to preserve their authority and maintain family values and controls. A child's personal growth is almost always in some kind of tension with family stability and the status quo.

To overcome social anxiety and achieve self-realization, persons seek power over others, endeavoring in a multitude of ways to subdue them lest they come to dominate. The struggle for political power between the holders of political authority and between them and the people is but one example, but a particularly poignant one, of the rivalry that goes on at every level of human life. The struggle for power manifests itself in relations between husband and wife, parents and children, spouses and in-laws (the classic rivalry between mothers-in-law and new spouses), children and remarried parents, and children and step-children. In the United States, contests for political power occur between ethnic groups, advocates of states' rights and national governments, and the three branches of government. The struggle is a constant feature of international politics involving a long succession of countries, each moving to the center of the international stage at different times: France versus Germany, the Soviet Union versus the United States, and China versus the Soviet Union. In the cold war, the Soviet Union sought control of Eastern Europe while the United States extended its sphere in Europe to the rimland of Asia. Far from disappearing, power rivalries have persisted with greater intensity in the postwar era, that era for which Secretary Hull had prophesied their demise.

A third manifestation of power in the postwar world is expressed in the truth that the struggle has been raised to the level of spirit where contests become limitless and the appetite for power insatiable. Being more than natural creatures, human beings are not interested merely in physical survival. They also seek prestige and social approval. To be sure, they share with animals natural appetites and desires, not least of which is the impulse for survival. Possessing the intelligence to anticipate the perils in which they stand, people seek security against those perils by enhancing their power. Thus, people—individually and collectively—place in jeopardy the security of their fellows. The quest for power is couched in the language of spirit and in ideologies so all embracing and controlling that people cannot retreat from them.

Domestically, minority groups that have been abused and persecuted for generations raise the struggle for autonomy and well-being to the level of spirit, thus threatening those who earlier were their sponsors. The intensification of the conflict may take the form of a holy war between two largely spiritual versions of politics, each seeking supremacy without compromise. The surge of one spiritual vision is met by effects of the backlash of another: blacks versus white ethnics, women versus the opponents of the Equal Rights Amendment (ERA), and a host of other struggles. Whoever the participants, the struggle manifests itself in appeals to the hearts of humankind. It is a struggle that is beyond resolution at the level of spirit and, with the suspension of the political process, is no longer susceptible to compromise.

A fourth manifestation of the problem of power is the security-power dilemma. Humankind is caught in a terrible predicament. The security-power dilemma is the most fateful and tragic expression of international politics. Nation-states find themselves in deadlock with their neighbors; the process repeats itself and is ever-recurrent. Weak men and weak nations assume that if they had more power they would be more secure. Yet the more power an individual or nation possesses, whether in arms, missiles, territory, bases, or allies, the more its individual or collective life threatens or impinges upon other lives and the more wisdom is required to bring about harmony or equilibrium.

The source of the security-power problem can be defined. Social movements and political parties are motivated, as are individuals, to seek (half-consciously at times) dominion over others. Labor seeks dominion over management as management does over labor. Every collective or corporate body competes for security and power in the manner of the individuals who constitute them. The intensity of group conflicts grows out of the tendency of collectivities—whether families or tribes, ethnic groups or nations, or corporations or unions—to express both the virtue and selfishness of their members. It is said that contempt for another group, whether family or nation, is the pathetic form that respect for one's own frequently takes. For families, the tender emotions that bind their members are sometimes expressed in indifference and distrust for others. The more one loves and protects one's own children, the more tempted to overlook the needs of others. The quest for the strengthening of ethnic groups at a subnational level may produce national disunity. Not "my country first," but "my family or ethnic group first," becomes the rallying cry. Prof. O. D. Corpuz of the University of the Philippines tells the story of a president of the Philippine republic. When President García was charged with having diverted funds from the public treasury to members of his extended family, he responded that he lived under two laws of morality: responsibility to his family and responsibility to the state. When the two conflicted, he said, family responsibility came first. Corpuz described these two laws as the two faces of Philippine morality. Not only family interests but special interest groups seek priority over national interest.

Contemporary nationalism is by far the most serious manifestation of the security-power dilemma. Nations seek power and threaten other nations, which increases *their* power and thus threatens others. One nation builds up its armory of weapons to ensure its security, generating a response in kind from its principal rival. The full force of the security-power dilemma stems from a mixture of psychological factors. Nationalism merges self-sacrificial loyalty to the state and the frustrated aggression of the masses, who seek through the nation to achieve the supremacy denied them as individuals. In an increasingly mechanized world, individuals may be deprived of the rewards that personal growth and fulfillment can bring. Historically, the example of the displaced middle class in Hitler's Germany is the most fateful and dramatic. Driven down into the lower class by the ravages of inflation, the so-called *lumpfen proletariat* helped to fuel the sinister campaigns of Der Führer. Because they had lost pride and a sense of fulfillment in their own unhappy lives, they sought them in the conquests of national socialism. They rallied to the harsh cries of Hitler because he promised what they imagined was their rightful dominion over others. The full fury of the German pursuit of security and the quest for power at the expense of almost every humane value found justification in the psychology of the German people.

Complexities of Power

In trying to understand the reality of power, it is important to consider not only prevailing attitudes toward power and some significant manifestations of power but also its root causes and its more important components, whether of individuals or nations. Writers on power alternately seek to condemn and deny power or to glorify and defend it. At some point, the student of power is driven back to consider such fundamental questions as the nature of man and of the international system. Yet the problem for the political scientist in addressing a discussion of root causes is profound and may be insoluble.

For almost two decades I worked overseas alongside agricultural and medical scientists, scientists for whom I came to feel growing admiration intermingled with awe and a little envy. As a group, they held to an overwhelming conviction that what they were doing mattered. They were single-minded in their concentration on what they called "the core problem." They united with fellow scientists, whatever their nationality or politics, with a wartime kind of camaraderie. As one of them put it, they had confidence they could "turn around" the agricultural or health delivery system of any country. They believed they could transform such systems. Their approach and dedication, I hoped, might be transferable to educational assistance in the developing countries, which was my responsibility. Two lessons or guidelines from their approach to science emerged. They were, first: identify the most urgent problem in any society; second, look for its root cause, not merely the symptoms.

These precepts of the natural sciences face a kind of inescapable resistance in the human sciences. Human and psychological obstacles stand in the way. Each of us constructs our own little escape mechanisms when asked to face *our* urgent problems. *Denial* is an ever-present reality in life. Infants react in rage when sources of comfort or gratification are absent or removed. Implicitly, they blame parents or an unfriendly world, or both. Child psychologists and counselors explain that they must begin their first counseling sessions with the words: "Excuses, excuses, excuses."

Why won't men face their problems? One response, from philosophy and religion, is the mixture of mortality and immortality of the spirit in man. The perplexities and contradictions of life are part of the human condition. We are children of nature subject to all the limitations of every living thing seeking to survive. An aspect of the human problem is that we are mortal. For men as for animals, life has a beginning, a middle, and an end; the essence of life is its finiteness. Yet as men and women, we are also unique among all living beings in the extent of our possibilities and potential. We are finite yet also infinite in our views of ourselves, of society, and of our destiny. Every religion and philosophy worth its salt acknowledges the dualism in man's nature. Reinhold Niebuhr began the Gifford Lectures by saying: "Man has always been his own most vexing problem. How is he to think of himself?" (Niebuhr, 1945, 1). First of all, we are creatures hedged in by circumstances and limits. We are caught up in the search for security and the lust for power. Our biological and intellectual limits are determined by our brute nature. The call for rationality in any classical and objective sense is denied us by the passions and vitalities of our lives.

At the same time, a human being is also creator and spirit, a creature who dreams of the infinite and pushes himself toward unending progress while imagining himself God or seeking to make himself Godlike. A human being is both rational and irrational, good and evil, capable of the most demonic acts but also of a sympathy that knows no bounds. Yet a person's dual nature poses myriad questions and contradictions. If we say that a human being by nature is essentially good and attribute all evil to his or her environment or to historical or social causes, we beg the question because it follows that such causes must be the result of human forces. Traced back, we conclude they are the product of humankind in history and therefore of human nature. But if we attribute all evil to human nature, how are we to explain how such a frail and fallible human being, bereft of all virtue, is capable of judging between good and evil? How can we recognize evil without knowing the good? If we can recognize the good, can we not be said to possess some good? Neither nihilism nor neutrality between good and evil can provide answers to this dilemma. Yet, how much simpler our discourse would be if each of us were unequivocally good or evil.

Having accepted, then, the dualism of a human being's nature in preference to any other explanation, the problem of relating a person's possibilities and his or her limits remains. The deeper paradox of human life results from the fact that we are suspended perilously between freedom and finiteness or between spirit and nature. Through spirit and human freedom we are able to soar in our imagination, to transcend our limits, and to survey the heights as no other living being—forgetting thereby the limits of our creatureliness. Yet because reason is finite and spirit infinite, we cannot know our limits, and not knowing them, we become anxious, troubled, and insecure. Animals whose lives are under the sway of self-regulating mechanisms are not cursed by the consequences of a human's genius. It is people alone who are endlessly tempted to deny the limits that offend the human spirit and to shy away from the implications of painful human problems. Because of anxiety, people excuse themselves and accuse others to justify their shortcomings and to keep alive the hope of progress. It is because one has a vision of the whole that one is often troubled by fragmentary strivings. Dreaming of perpetual health, we shrink from incurable illness. Hoping for long life, we pull back from the sense of our own mortality, the sickroom, and the lives of the aged and the infirm. Believing in perfect harmony, we prefer eternal peace to continuing rivalry and conflict. Yearning for tranquillity, we reject all force and violence.

Another factor in modern life has sharpened the conflict between what is finite and the spirit. The tempo of human existence has shortened the time frame of life. With the lessening of the public's faith in life after death, human consciousness has been compressed into a frantic pursuit for instant gratification and immediate utopias. We resist living with uncertainty. All our towering dreams are reduced to solving immediate problems and ending insecurity. Yet true security requires expressions of the spirit that narrow problem solving is unlikely to bring.

It is one thing for the plant pathologist, free from the public spotlight, to work five long years in the laboratory searching for new varieties of basic food crops to feed the world. It is another thing for the hard-pressed diplomat or statesperson to be given time to discover the root cause of conflict in Lebanon or of East-West tension or of building new universities or educational programs in East Africa. Compounding the pressures of time, intense nationalism, and competing goals, the diplomat or policymaker grappling with social and political questions is also part of the problem. For the scientist in the laboratory, his or her own personal or social attitude toward high-yielding varieties of rice, wheat, or corn is essentially as irrelevant to the research at hand as it is for the biologist searching for answers to the eradication of cancer. The same is not true for social scientists, whose social and political philosophy and attitudes are inseparable from their "scientific" findings. Thus, Marxist economists, whatever their scientific pretensions, are fundamentally committed to demonstrating the deficiencies of capitalism. Monetarists or free-enterprise economists, however rigorous their methods, are equally committed to the preservation of capitalism and freedom. The architects of grand designs for global peace look at the world through different lenses than the theorists of the protracted East-West conflict. Intellectual and moral allegiances affect the science of the social scientist.

Solutions in the social sciences, then, reflect the scientist's personal preferences and goals in a way that is not normally the case in the natural sciences. For these reasons and more, the search for the root causes of war or depression, social misunderstandings, and tensions by the social and humane scientist is encumbered by ideological presuppositions and social pressures from which the natural scientist is more nearly free.

Four Perspectives

To be more specific, the root cause of power, and especially of power in international politics, is determined in large part by which of four viewpoints or perspectives the social scientist adopts: the geographic, the economic, the military, or the political. Each deserves attention and analysis.

The geographic viewpoint defends the importance of power, first, in terms of the international system. In the words of Nicholas Spykman: "International society is . . . a society without central authority. . . . The result is that individual states must make the preservation and improvement of their power position a primary objective of their foreign policy" (Spykman, 1942, 7). Writing at the time of World War II, Spykman found that the interventionists and isolationists represented two distinct geopolitical schools of thought. In World War II, the interventionists saw the first line of defense for the United States in a balance of power in Europe and Asia and a second line of defense in the Western Hemisphere. The isolationists, who had been dominant before World War I, proceeded from the principle that only the Western Hemisphere mattered. The size of the geographic area making up the hemisphere, however, expanded from the United States to the Caribbean littoral to the whole of the hemisphere. Spykman described this expanded view as a streamlined version of the old isolationist position. The defense of the hemisphere through hemispheric isolation was the American strategy at the time of the Monroe Doctrine. By World War II, however, interventionism (or internationalism) had won out.

What is power viewed from a geographic or geopolitical perspective? Spykman's definition is: "Power means survival, the ability to impose one's will on others, the capacity to dictate to those who are without power, and the possibility of forcing concessions from those with less power" (ibid., 18). The basic objective of any foreign policy in the modern state system is the preservation of the territorial integrity and political independence of the state. Some observers suggest that power depends solely on military forces, but the geopolitical thinkers disagree. Rather, the relative power of a state is largely determined by "size of territory, nature of frontiers, size of population, absence or presence of raw materials, economic and technological development, financial strength, ethnic homogeneity, effective social integration, political stability, and national spirit" (ibid., 19). While geostrategic approaches often view power as broadly as suggested in Professor Spykman's list, going well beyond geographic factors, he elsewhere has narrowed his list to a handful of factors such as size and breadth of territory, location, topography, and the oceans.

Thus, power according to geopolitics is a function of geography. The entire earth's surface is a circle, and every nation is encircled by other groups of nations. The Western Hemisphere is encircled by Eurasia, which constitutes the primary security problem in American foreign policy. Hatford Mackinder had asserted that "whoever controls the Heartland controls the world" with the heartland extending along a large plain from Siberia through Germany to the North Sea and bounded on the south by the Alps, the Balkans, and the Himalayas. Spykman modified Mackinder's axiom to read, "He who controls the Rimland controls the Heartland and thereby controls the world," with the rimland extending from France to the Middle East and to South Asia and China. The rimland also controlled the oceans and gave access to all parts of the world. Britain, with twenty thousand ships, held strategic entrances to the Mediterranean at Gibraltar and Suez and through islands such as Malta in World War II. When it lost these key points, it lost the geographic locations on which its power was based, despite its navy remaining intact. Spykman concludes that Britain's power was even more geographic than it was naval before World War II.

If one sentence can summarize the major concept that underlies the geographic conception of power, it was a phrase Spykman composed in 1941 at the height of the Era of Good Feelings with the Soviets: "A Russian state from the Urals to the North Sea can be no great improvement over a German state from the North Sea to the Urals" (ibid., 460). Nothing ran more counter to popular thinking at the time, yet Spykman as a geostrategic thinker recognized that Russia was destined to emerge as the strongest power in Europe, with China and Russia also threatening to achieve dominance in Asia. The balance of power, therefore, required the active participation of the United States, Britain, and France joined not only with Germany in Europe but with Japan in Asia to throw the weight into the balance. He saw this as a clear geostrategic imperative. No one can be oblivious to the reality of power in the postwar world.

The economic viewpoint substitutes economics for geography as the main determinant of power. In the nineteenth century and the opening decades of the twentieth century, the dominant philosophies that shaped thinking about power were liberalism and Marxism. For liberalism, the individual rather than the group was more important. Education and reform held out the promise of an escape from the toils and burdens of power. Indeed, the middle class, which had taken the place of the aristocracy, was the carrier of a worldview offering in place of the struggles of rivalry and power the peaceful milieu of economics and commerce. It was the aristocracy that had perpetuated contests for power, and with its having yielded to the middle class, power had disappeared. The lessons of history confirm what economic theory postulates. The struggle of power lost its purpose with the rise of the middle class.

It is the commercial and trading class that strives to preserve peace and harmony when conflict and war threaten. Trade and commerce depend on a predictable environment, and war and the struggle for power substitute chance and indeterminacy for order. Obscured is the fact that the middle class owes its dominance to a victory over the feudal class that had earlier triumphed over the universal religious community whose sacerdotal authority had earlier gone unchallenged. A business viewpoint that prevails in certain segments of society even in the 1990s and that draws strength from its claim to be apolitical and opposed to all but the most minimal functions of government is but a contemporary expression of liberalism in economic theory.

Marxism has provided a similar ideological facade by which it hides and conceals contests for power. The paradox of Marxism's view of power is classic. On the one side is the Marxist prophecy that with the withering away of the state the dialectic of history will bring about the administration of things in the place of the domination of people by people. On the other side, the former Communist regimes, particularly of the Soviet Union and China, testify to the illusion that was Marxist utopianism. Far from witnessing the disappearance of power, the Soviet and Chinese experience with communism reveals some of the more grotesque consequences of the merging of economic and political power. Power that had been held in check through balances of power in some non-Communist regimes burst the bounds of civilized usage in Stalinism as it had in nazism. Thus, two philosophies that once offered hope for a respite from power had themselves become ideological rationalizations for the excesses of power.

Hans J. Morgenthau wrote of "the military displacement of power." He chose as an example the contrast between military and political thinking in Britain and the United States at the end of World War II. Winston Churchill argued unsuccessfully for the political significance of military action. Neglecting Karl von Clausewitz's dictum that war is a continuation of policy by other means, American military thinkers chose as their objectives goals such as unconditional surrender rather than political and territorial ends. In April of 1945 the issue came to a head. Leaders, such as Churchill, urged that military strategy be linked with military advance that would bring political advantage. The goal was to be the liberation of Czechoslovakia and in particular Prague by Gen. George Patton's army. Gen. George C. Marshall transmitted Churchill's proposal to General Eisenhower saying, "Personally, and aside from all logistic, tactical, or strategical implications, I would be loath to hazard American lives for purely political reasons" (Morgenthau, 1958a, 257). The following day, Eisenhower replied to General Marshall: "I shall not attempt any move I deem militarily unwise merely to gain a political advantage unless I receive specific orders from the combined Chiefs of Staff" (ibid.). In his memoirs, Gen. Omar Bradley challenged another of Churchill's proposals by urging the Americans to continue their advance to Berlin before the Russians reached that city: "As soldiers we looked naively on this British inclination to *complicate* [my italics] the war with political foresight and non-military objectives" (ibid., 258).

Professor Morgenthau asked what lessons might be drawn from these differences and observed: "To win a war without regard for the political consequences of the victory may create political problems as serious as, or worse than, those that the victory was intended to settle" (ibid.). A successful policy must always involve the right admixture of power and suasion. Americans have allowed themselves to gravitate from one to the other at the expense of a sound foreign policy. Having relied on suasion alone in relation with Stalin in the wartime and postwar period, we came to rely exclusively on force as a deterrent. We forgot that force is a means to the end of accommodation with other powers. In the 1920s and 1930s, the United States underestimated the use of force in international relations. By the late 1940s and after, we turned, at least in certain conflicts, to play the role of the international constabulary. In Professor Morgenthau's words, "Having realized the error [in the 1930s] of fighting for nobody but one's self, we are now willing to fight for anybody threatened by the common enemy" (ibid., 261). Collective security was the new version of foreign policy that based intervention on global rather than national interests.

Was there ever an alternative? Is the criticism of the kind of apolitical thinking Morgenthau singles out merely negative thinking, or can he and others point to a better way of thinking? Having denounced the military displacement of politics, what should the analyst put in its place? Morgenthau concludes: "For Sir Winston, the war was a military means to a political end, and the influence of the political end upon the military means was to increase with the speed with which the Armies of the Allies were approaching military victory. For the United States, the war was essentially a self-sufficient technical operation to be performed as quickly, as cheaply, and as thoroughly as the technical rules of warfare would allow" (ibid., 267–68). The American view of warfare was apocalyptic, "a thunderstorm darkening a peaceful scene," and an interruption of the normal state of peaceful international relations. For Churchill, the causes and manifestations of war were part of the natural environment of nations, and its consequences flowed from strategies followed during the war. Churchill's thought was both political and military, and he viewed the objectives of the war in this light. Even on the eve of the Potsdam conference, he questioned the American decision to withdraw troops to the zonal boundaries accepted at Quebec and Yalta. Thus, he assigned primacy to foreign policy objectives, whereas most Americans believed that bringing the war to a prompt conclusion would assure peace in the world and harmony with the Russians.

Churchill, therefore, is the foremost contemporary exemplar of the political view of power. All political action represents an attempt to influence human behavior. Individuals or groups seek to exercise dominion over others, who seek to exert influence in return. Neither can be oblivious to the role of power; both must determine the right quantity and quality of power to serve their ends. The process of gaining and preserving power and maintaining at least a rough equilibrium with a potential aggressor goes on increasingly. Geographic, economic, and military factors are part of the equation but not the most fundamental element on the world scene. The political factor is all important in the statesperson's and the public's calculations of the behavior of nations.

Power as Relationship

In the end, power involves relationships. Recognition of this fact brings us to the core of the problem and perhaps to its cause. Although power cannot be studied in the same way that biologists study cancer—seeking to control, if not eliminate it—students of power can endeavor to understand it. In doing so, they recognize that whatever the ultimate goal of a political act, attaining some worthy end in politics requires the use of power. At base, acquiring and maintaining power involve the imposing of a person's or a nation's will on another. Whatever the ultimate aim being sought, the quest for power is the process through which that aim is pursued.

Abraham Lincoln in a speech on 14 April 1864 at the Sanitary Fair in Baltimore spoke of freedom and power, explaining: "With some the word liberty may mean for each man to do as he pleases with himself, and the product of his labor; while with others the same word may mean for some men to do as they please with other men and the product of other men's labor." We perceive power relationships and praise or condemn them depending on the perspective from which they are viewed. In Lincoln's words, "The shepherd drives the wolf from the sheep's throat, for which the sheep thanks the shepherd as a *liberator,* while the wolf denounces him . . . as the destroyer of liberty, especially as the sheep was a black one." Lincoln found precisely this same difference among the citizenry, all professing to love liberty. As thousands escaped slavery, some hailed their being freed as "the advance of liberty" while others called it "the destruction of all liberty." Perspectives on freedom, as on other goals and values, are shaped by whether we are the holders or the objects of political power.

Morgenthau wrote of another interrelationship, widely misunderstood in the modern world, that between power and love. Morgenthau saw the two as organically interconnected, both having roots in loneliness, but modern thought, with its exclusive emphasis on only certain aspects of the relationship, such as sex and gregariousness, holds love and power primarily at surface levels. Attempting to understand their cause, Morgenthau observed that, "Of all creatures, only man is capable of loneliness because only he is in need of being alone, without being able in the end to escape being alone. It is that striving to escape his loneliness which gives the impetus to both the lust for power and the longing for love, and it is the inability to escape that loneliness, either at all or for more than a moment, that creates the tension between longing and lack of achievement, which is the tragedy of both power and love" (Morgenthau, 1958b, 8). Awareness of insufficiency drives people to achieve with others what they cannot realize individually. In a memorable phrase, Morgenthau explains that a mortal being seeks the extension of himself or herself "in offspring—the work of his body; in the manufacture of material things—the work of his hands; in philosophy and scholarship—the work of his mind; in art and literature—the work of his imagination; in religion—the work of his pure longing toward transcendence" (ibid.).

What, then, are the similarities and differences between love and power? For Morgenthau, one similarity is the effort through the duplication or, for nations, the multiplication, of individuality. The differences, between the two are recorded in poetry and prose. Love is a relation of spontaneous mutuality, power a union through "unilateral imposition." Ideally, love comes to a person as a gift of nature, a union that makes man (or woman) whole. Power is the result of an individual imposing his or her will on another so that the other mirrors the self. What is common to love and power, however, is that an element of the one is always found in the other. In common experience, love is power and power is love. "Power points toward love [or some other ultimate moral purpose] as its fulfillment, as love starts from power and . . . is corrupted by an irreducible residue of power" (ibid. 9). Herein resides the tragedy of love and power. Love in its purest form is symbolized by complete and spontaneous mutuality. Yet because of the inevitable transience of love corrupted by power, "the lover behaves as the master and the beloved as the object of the master's power." Thus love as the reunion of two persons tends to be short-lived. It is the paradox of love that in seeking the reunion of two persons, it attempts to preserve their individuality, only to lose it to the workings of power. Lovers in the end turn to power to do what love cannot do; power becomes a substitute for love. What mortal beings cannot accomplish for a sustained period through love, they seek to accomplish through power. "Power tries to break down the barrier of individuality which love, because it is love, must leave intact. Yet in the measure that power tries to do the work love cannot do, it puts love in jeopardy. An irreducible element of power is required to make a stable relationship of love . . . [and] without power love cannot persist, but through power it is corrupted and threatened with destruction" (ibid., 10).

In politics, the same ambiguous relationship between power and love manifests itself. Political stability depends in part on the submissiveness of the ruled to the ruler, but a political order based only on threats and promises will always be precarious. Therefore, political rulers seek legitimacy through the consent of the governed and approach it through appeals to the love of the subject for the ruler. Love of a monarch is invoked. By ritual and ceremony, nazism and Stalinism sought to depict the leader as beloved. Failing to earn the love of their subjects and aware that love was beyond their reach, rulers from Alexander and Napoleon to Hitler and Joseph Stalin sought compensation in the accumulation of more and more power. "From the subjection of ever more men to their will, they seem to expect the achievement of that communion which the lack of love withholds from them. Yet the acquisition of power only begets the desire for more; for the more men the master holds bound to his will, the more he is aware of his loneliness. His success in terms of power only serves to illuminate his failure in terms of love" (ibid., 12–13). The ruler ends by experiencing frustrated love that breeds hate and distrust of all men.

Morgenthau concludes: "The loneliness of men is, then, imperious to both love and power. Power can only unite through . . . subjection. . . . Love can unite only in the fleeting moments . . . [of] spontaneous mutuality. . . . Thus in the end, his wings seared, his heart-blood spent, his projects come to nought—despairing of power and thirsting for, and forsaken by, love—man peoples the heavens with gods and mothers and virgins and saints who love him and whom he can love and to whose power he can subject himself spontaneously because their power is the power of love. Yet whatever he expects of the other world, he must leave this world as he entered it: alone" (ibid., 14).

REFERENCES

Meinecke, Friedrich. 1984. *Machiavellism: The doctrine of raison d'état and its place in modern history,* trans. Douglas Scott. Boulder, Colo.: Westview Press.

Morgenthau, Hans J. 1958a. *Dilemmas of politics.* Chicago: University of Chicago Press.

———. 1958b. *Politics in the twentieth century.* Vol. 3, *The restoration of American politics.* Chicago: University of Chicago Press.

Niebuhr, Reinhold. 1945. *The nature and destiny of man.* Vol. 1, *Human nature.* New York: Charles Scribner's.

Spykman, Nicholas J. 1942. *America's strategy in world politics: The United States and the balance of power.* New York: Harcourt, Brace and Company.

Contributors and Editors

ROBERT A. GLICK, M.D. Admitting psychoanalyst and training and supervising psychoanalyst, Columbia University Center for Psychoanalytic Training and Research; clinical professor of psychiatry, Columbia University College of Physicians and Surgeons

OTTO F. KERNBERG, M.D. Training and supervising psychoanalyst, Columbia University Center for Psychoanalytic Training and Research; professor of psychiatry, Cornell University Medical College; associate chair and medical director, New York Hospital, Cornell Medical Center, Westchester Division

MELVIN J. KONNER, M.D., PH.D. Samuel Candler Dobbs Professor of Anthropology, Emory University; associate professor of psychiatry, Emory University School of Medicine, Atlanta, Georgia

LUCY LAFARGE, M.D. Assistant clinical professor of psychiatry, Columbia University College of Physicians and Surgeons; faculty, Columbia University Center for Psychoanalytic Training and Research

MICHAEL LEWIS, PH.D. Director, Institute for the Study of Child Development, Department of Pediatrics; professor of pediatrics, psychiatry, and psychology in the Department of Pediatrics, University of Medicine and Dentistry of New Jersey; Robert Wood Johnson Medical School

HELEN C. MEYERS, M.D. Training and supervising analyst and chair of the Training Analysts Committee at the Columbia University Center for Psychoanalytic Training and Research; clinical professor of psychiatry, Columbia University College of Physicians and Surgeons

ANNA ORNSTEIN, M.D. Professor of child psychiatry, University of Cincinnati College of Medicine; co-director, International Center for the Study of Psychoanalytic Self Psychology

PAUL H. ORNSTEIN, M.D. Training and supervising psychoanalyst, Cincinnati Psychoanalytic Institute; professor of psychiatry, University of Cincinnati College of Medicine; co-director, International Center for the Study of Psychoanalytic Self Psychology

FRED OVSIEW, M.D. Assistant professor of clinical psychiatry, University of Chicago School of Medicine

ELAINE PAGELS, PH.D. Harrington Spear Paine Foundation Professor of Religion, Princeton University

HENRI PARENS, M.D. Training and supervising analyst, Philadelphia Psychoanalytic Institute; professor of psychiatry, Jefferson Medical College

ETHEL SPECTOR PERSON, M.D. Training and supervising psychoanalyst, Columbia University Center for Psychoanalytic Training and Research; professor of clinical psychiatry, Columbia University College of Physicians and Surgeons

STEVEN P. ROOSE, M.D. Associate professor of clinical psychiatry, Columbia University College of Physicians and Surgeons; faculty, Columbia University Center for Psychoanalytic Training and Research

LEONARD A. ROSENBLUM, PH.D. Professor of psychiatry, State University of New York-Health Science Center at Brooklyn; director, Primate Behavior Laboratory

ROY SCHAFER, PH.D. Training and supervising psychoanalyst, Columbia University Center for Psychoanalytic Training and Research; adjunct professor of psychology and psychiatry, Cornell University Medical College

KENNETH W. THOMPSON J. Wilson Professor in Governance, University of Virginia; director, Miller Center of Public Affairs

STUART YUDOFSKY, M.D. Chair, Department of Psychiatry and Behavioral Sciences, Baylor University College of Medicine

Index